AF784077

SEXUALITY, WAR, AND SCHIZOPHRENIA

History of Ideas Series
Paul Roazen, Series Editor

Brother Animal, Paul Roazen,
with a new introduction by the author.

Character and Opinion in the United States, George Santayana,
with a new introduction by John W. Yolton.

Cultural Theory and Psychoanalytic Tradition, David James Fisher.

Doctors and Their Patients, Edward Shorter,
with a new introduction by the author.

Encountering Freud, Paul Roazen.

Female Psychology, the Self, and the Therapeutic Process,
Helene Deutsch, edited and with an introduction by Paul Roazen.

Free Associations, Ernest Jones,
with an introduction by Mervyn Jones.

Helene Deutsch, Paul Roazen,
with a new introduction by the author.

House of the Prophet, Louis Auchincloss,
with a new introduction by the author.

The Necessity of Choice, Louis Hartz, edited, compiled and
prepared by Paul Roazen, with a preface by Benjamin Barber.

The Public Philosophy, Walter Lippmann,
with a new introduction by Paul Roazen.

Sexuality, War, and Schizophrenia, Victor Tausk,
edited and with an introduction by Paul Roazen.

Sigmund Freud as a Consultant, Edoardo Weiss,
with a new foreword by Emilio Weiss and
a new introduction by Paul Roazen.

Women's Bodies, Edward Shorter,
with a new preface by the author.

SEXUALITY, WAR, AND SCHIZOPHRENIA

Collected Psychoanalytic Papers

Victor Tausk

Edited and with an introduction by
Paul Roazen

Translations by
Eric Mosbacher & others

Transaction Publishers
New Brunswick (U.S.A.) & London (U.K.)

Copyright © 1991 by Transaction Publishers,
New Brunswick, New Jersey 08903

All rights reserved under International and Pan-American Copyright Conventions. No part of this book may be reproduced or transmitted in any form or by any means, electronic or mechanical, including photocopy, recording, or any information storage and retrieval system, without prior permission in writing from the publisher. All inquiries should be addressed to Transaction Publishers, Rutgers—The State University, New Brunswick, New Jersey 08903.

Library of Congress Catalog Number: 90-11135
ISBN: 0-88738-365-3
Printed in the United States of America

Library of Congress Cataloging-in-Publication Data
Tausk, Victor, 1879–1919.
Sexuality, war, and schizophrenia : collected psychoanalytic papers / edited and with an introduction by Paul Roazen ; translations by Eric Mosbacher & others.
p. cm.
Essays translated from German.
Includes bibliographical references.
ISBN 0-88738-365-3 (paper)
1. Psychoanalysis. I. Roazen, Paul, 1936– II. Title.
RC509.T383 1990
616.89'17—dc20

90-11135
CIP

In Memory of
Robert Green McCloskey

Contents

Introduction

Paul Roazen

Psychoanalysis, almost a hundred years old, has sometimes been said to have now entered on an enlightened phase of pluralism. According to this recently advanced point of view, supported by the conservative powers-that-be in the profession, the old sectarian squabbles that once were so prominent in the field would be impossible to happen again; tolerance of divergent schools of psychotherapeutic thought is now supposed to be the order of the day. In an effort to welcome outsiders to the discipline, and to reassure the self-image of practitioners of analysis, ideological fanaticism is looked upon as an aspect of the distant past.

It is, though, not the case that those thinkers whom Freud excluded as "heretics," such as Carl G. Jung or Alfred Adler and others as well, have had their ideas taken seriously by the so-called mainstream within psychoanalysis. But we do find that at international meetings of analysts, supporters of North American ego psychology mix with adherents of Melanie Klein and advocates of Jacques Lacan, to name only three of the central streams of thinking in today's psychoanalysis. Still, a fourth ideological tendency, the self-psychology initiated by Heinz Kohut, has acquired a fashionability all its own. Sigmund Freud's own ideas continue to constitute the dominant paradigm, but almost everyone in the field would agree that more than fifty years after his death at least some changes have to be introduced into the framework he bequeathed.

There is a good deal of merit to the idea that contemporary psychoanalysis is broader and less doctrinaire than would have been true in the past. The early analysts, from the perspective of our own time, look unusually well-educated in the literature and philosophy of Western culture; ideas mattered to them, and they came to psychoanalysis at a time when Freud could approach his work in the embattled spirit of someone at odds with conventional wisdom. The general high cultural quality of the early analysts was also associated with some of the worst forms of sectarianism, for these pioneering analysts were attracted by quasi-religious motives to "the cause" that Freud fervently promoted, and precisely because of the spirituality of their objectives (which makes them especially attractive) they were willing to stigmatize "deviants" within the movement Freud had founded. Anyone Freud declared to have betrayed his calling could be combatted with more ferocity than what would be reserved for outsiders in general. And the intellectuality of the people involved meant that they had the capacity to express their opinions, including their personal preferences and dislikes, within objective-sounding terminology.

Today's analysts are more secure in their position. Freud's heirs no longer have the same sorts of struggles that the early analysts experienced. It is true that psychoanalysis does not now enjoy, at least in America, the medical popularity that it did in the 1950s and 1960s; a good deal of disillusionment has followed the earlier high expectations about analysis's capacities as a therapeutic agent. And rival treatment procedures, especially aided by advances in the biochemical field, have succeeded in attracting the interest of some of the most promising qualified young therapists. Within the general culture at large, on the other hand, psychoanalytic ideas are still accorded broad respect; and analytic practitioners retain solid standing.

Recently, the story of psychoanalysis has become more a legitimate part of the academic study of intellectual history, and students of the history of ideas have increasingly accepted the responsibility for understanding the past associated with Freud's school of thought. It is my firm belief that it is going to be impossible to make sense of what happened in those early days of analysis without taking seriously the various criticisms advanced by thinkers like Jung and Adler, among others, who presciently saw some of the key weak points in Freud's own approach.[1] Historians are going to have to break through various taboos that still constrain practicing analysts when they ritualistically cite the history of their discipline. Those of us in university life have nothing to fear, especially unconsciously, in terms of protecting livelihoods stemming from a clinical practice. And it should therefore be possible to examine all past controversies fearlessly and without the blinders that stem from the self-protectiveness of professional trade unionism.

It would be a mistake to underestimate how potentially explosive the study of history can be, which is why I remain skeptical about just how genuinely pluralistic organized psychoanalysis is now capable of being. All groups live by myths, and every historical search opens up the possibility of threatening some of the key sources of group cohesion. Freud was the first, in the course of a 1914 polemic against Jung and Adler, titled "On the History of the Psychoanalytic Movement,"[2] to present his side of things; but even years earlier he had had considerable historical consciousness, as he always chose to spell out the steps by which he arrived at his latest formulations. Freud knew the power of legend, and within the field psychoanalytic articles still today spend a good amount of preliminary time on the supposed historical sequence of preceding contributions.

But Freud's conception of what had taken place represented only what he chose to put into print; his account of things cannot be taken as any kind of impartial narrative. He was propagandizing in behalf of his new profession, and saw events in terms of what was helpful in forwarding his chosen doctrine. We now know a good deal about what lay behind what he picked to highlight, and we are partly aware of what he preferred to slide over—for he could not only present events tendentiously, but he would typically omit that which was inconvenient for the political purposes of establishing his "movement."

In the popular accounts of the various battles with those who became his opponents Freud has done comparatively well partly by virtue of default. For his key "defecting" former pupils usually decided to remain, if not silent, at least less than publicly forthcoming about the sources of their difficulties with the creator of psychoanalysis. Quarreling with Freud was not apt to be good for their therapeutic business, even if it might have attracted a certain temporary kind of notoriety.

Freud's capacities as a great writer were one of his most important assets in popularizing his psychology because he not only convinced people by what he wrote about that which he considered his "discoveries," but the subtleties of his written words were responsible for attracting a host of admirers. Those who came to him from outside of the therapeutic professions and were interested in his contributions because of a combination of personal motives and purely intellectual interest were apt to be more naive and contentious than the followers who actually knew about psychoanalysis firsthand. And, therefore, some of the most dogmatic on psychoanalytic issues have not necessarily been analysts but rather observers from the outside world. Literary critics in particular, but philosophers and social scientists as well, have done much to ensure Freud's standing within the history of Western thought. All too often, however, they have merely echoed Freud's own stated view of the origin of his ideas without being fully aware of the degree of their sharing in his partisanship.

If I am dubious about how truly tolerant psychoanalysis is capable of being nowadays, it is partly because of my own longstanding research interests in this area of historical inquiry. At a time when, in the Soviet Union, for example, all kinds of remarkable changes have been taking place so that history is being rewritten there more in accord with what we know actually took place over the last century, analysts have remained relatively frozen about their own past. I believe that the odds are there is more chance of Trotsky getting rehabilitated in Gorbachev's Soviet Union than that it would be possible to cite respectfully among analysts the ideas of, say, Jung. Psychoanalytic bureaucrats seem able to swallow almost any new suggestion coming from a newcomer in the field, as long as it is unencumbered by being associated with any past heresies in the field. It would seem that there are institutional resistances that have been set up against reconsidering any of the profession's early difficulties. If one asks any young analyst whether he or she realizes that Jung was the first to propose the idea of a personal training analysis for analysts, I am almost certain that there will be an uncomprehending blank reception of the news; and yet, despite how appallingly history is taught at our analytic training institutes, Freud himself credited Jung with that particular contribution.[3]

Part of the problem stems simply from the demands of different professional hierarchies for training. For a Freudian to acknowledge indebtedness to a Jungian concept would be to question the whole basis of the different educational centers. If one gets trained at a particular psychoanalytic institute, presumably that organization has a reason for being independent—apart from historical accident and lethargy. Each training bureaucracy justifies itself in terms of its own founding leaders, and for all of them it pays off to distinguish one such organization from another. Intellectual toleration, then, is potentially damaging to the life of each of the units that have been set up to perpetuate psychoanalysis for the future.

The story of Victor Tausk's life and conflicts is an example, I think, which serves to illustrate some of the remaining obstacles to the true emancipation of the history of psychoanalysis. Because of the tragic circumstances surrounding his untimely death in 1919, Tausk's contributions still have not been accorded their proper place in the history of analysis. I first wrote about him at length in my *Brother Animal: the Story of Freud and Tausk* (1969)[4] (that book has come out in 1990 in a second edition[5]). Even before *Brother Animal* first appeared I had tried unsuccessfully to get a publisher to bring out a collection of his psychoanalytic papers. The first appearance of *Brother Animal* set off a controversy that aroused the fiercest sorts of ideological passions.[6] A gratifying scholarly after-effect of *Brother Animal* was the publication of volumes consisting of Tausk's hitherto uncollected psychoanalytic essays—but all of them were published abroad. In 1975, Tausk's psychoanalytic works appeared in French; by 1977 they came out in Spanish; and they were made available in Italian by 1979. Finally, a German edition of all Tausk's writings, including his literary efforts which appeared before he entered Freud's immediate circle in 1909, was published in 1983.[7] Despite the broad-mindedness that English-speaking analysts like to think they have been capable of, it is only now with this book that Tausk's analytic papers have succeeded in appearing in a collected edition. If one travels on the Continent and talks to analysts today, I think it will be the case that analysts there are convinced that they are more cosmopolitan than in the United States, and the fate of Tausk's papers would support their contention.

In fact, I think that most groups think of themselves as being more ideologically diverse than is in fact the case. The tale of Tausk's difficulties in remaining within psychoanalysis may have been harder to accept in North America if only because analysts here had rather more to defend than elsewhere. For although psychoanalytic ideas have been widely influential throughout the Western world, they have achieved a status and power in the United States that has remained so far unsurpassed elsewhere. Tausk's death by suicide might have been enough by itself to squelch interest in him, since psychoanalysis is supposed to be life-enhancing. In addition, there were dark rumors about his final troubles with Freud.

Tausk was in fact one of Freud's most brilliant early pupils. He was a man of great versatility—a poet and a writer, a lawyer as well as a physician and a psychoanalyst. Within philosophy he felt at ease, for example, with both Spinoza and Schopenhauer. When Lou Andreas-Salomé entered Freud's world in 1912, she had previously been on close terms with Nietzsche and Rilke, and she found Tausk to rank in those pre–World War I days in Vienna "the most prominently outstanding"[8] among Freud's students. Freud's own three-page obituary of Tausk was to be the lengthiest one Freud ever composed. "No one . . . could escape the impression that here was a man of importance. . . . He is sure of an honorable memory," Freud concluded, "in the history of psychoanalysis and its earliest struggles."[9]

Brother Animal contains the most extensive account of Tausk's background. He was born in Slovakia on 12 March 1879, and he was initially trained in law. After separating from his wife in 1905, he tried to earn his living as a journalist in Berlin. Then, in the fall of 1908, Tausk went to Vienna to study medicine, already planning to become a psychoanalyst. Freud helped him from the outset by sending him patients and lending him money. Unlike Freud, who was trained as a neurologist, and in contrast to most of the figures then within Freud's movement (not all of whom were even doctors), Tausk chose to become a psychiatrist. It is historically significant that Tausk became the first member of the Vienna Psychoanalytic Society to try to apply Freud's concepts to the understanding of the great mental illnesses known as the psychoses. Although Jung, himself a psychiatrist trained in Switzerland, had long argued that Freud had not been differentiating enough between neurosis and psychosis, it was not in fact until the 1920s that Freud drew a conceptual line between these different difficulties.

Tausk's paper on the "influencing machine" has become a classic in the psychological undertsanding of schizophrenia. It only appeared in print, however, at the same time as Freud's official obituary of him. Tausk's original concept of "ego boundaries" was to be developed in modern psychotherapy by Paul Federn and others.[10] Tausk was also responsible for introducing the term "identity" into the psychoanalytic literature.[11]

Each of these papers by Tausk must be read in historical context. So many years have passed since these essays were first written that the formulations of that era are bound to sound alien, and sometimes antiquated, to our ears. Nevertheless, Tausk was as talented in presenting clinical cases as he was adept in using Freud's abstract theories (his metapsychology), and each of these papers still has something to teach. In addition, for the purpose of understanding the development of Freud's own ideas it is always helpful to be familiar with the writings of the best in his circle.

In general, Tausk stood for broadening the scope of Freud's psychology, and Freud was sometimes irritated by what he considered Tausk's impetuousness. Lou Andreas-Salomé's diary records how difficult Freud could find dealing with someone of Tausk's capacities. Tausk was, as a therapist, unusual at the time for being interested in problems of technique; one of the last presentations he made at the Vienna Psychoanalytic Society, unfortunately unrecorded except for the title and date, was on "Problems Connected with Psychoanalytic Technique." Tausk was also concerned with the psychology of art, wrote about the philosophic implications of psychoanalysis, and even anticipated some of Freud's ideas on the death instinct.[12] For a full understanding of the scope of Tausk's ambitions, the reader should consult the *Minutes* of the Vienna Psychoanalytic Society.[13] Lou Andreas-Salomé's diary is also especially informative about the extent of Tausk's unusual capacities.

For Freud, Tausk's originality was a key part of the problem he posed. In contrast to the famous "dissidents," Tausk's loyalty to Freud was not in question. In these psychoanalytic papers one will find him, for example, going out of his way in distinguishing Freud's psychology from that of Adler. And at the Munich Congress in 1913, where Tausk's intimate friend Lou Andreas-Salomé sat "right by" Freud's side at the final public confrontation between Freud and Jung,[14] she reported: "Tausk consequently also sat very close by, despite the fact that Freud plainly held him off now, although he himself admitted that in this new situation Tausk was the right man ('clever and dangerous,' said Freud, 'he can bark and bite')."[15]

So far as Lou could tell, part of the problem between the two men was that Tausk was so devoted to the problems that particularly intrigued Freud at the time. It troubled Freud because of old anxieties he had had about priorities in his work; Freud felt uncomfortable at the idea that Tausk might anticipate his own evolving work. According to Lou in 1913,

> There is no doubt about it that Freud acts with complete conviction when he proceeds so sharply against Tausk. But along with this "psychoanalytic" fact (that is, bearing in mind Tausk's original neurotic disposition), it is also clear that any independence around Freud, especially when it is marked by aggression and display of temperament, worries him and wounds him quite automatically in his noble egoism as investigator, forcing him to premature discussion, and so forth. The value to analysis of an independent mind can only be established in the future, and that must result in probably unavoidable battles of the present. Certain it is that for Freud it is all an annoyance.[16]

From Tausk's own point of view, Lou remains a key witness in having seen him as exceptionally devoted to Freud. In late 1912, she had observed after a lecture of Tausk's (he was the first in Vienna to give a course on psychoanalysis for the lay public), that "an occasional malicious reference to Adler might do harm to Tausk himself. . . ."* She got "the impression" from listening to Tausk "not only of classical Freudian theory but also of an unusually loving and reverent approach to the essential discov-

*Tausk and Wilhelm Stekel were also "enemies" within the Vienna Psychoanalytic Society.

eries of Freud. . . ."[17] She thought that Tausk "carried the banner of leadership well. In many of his observations . . . I found him *too* precisely Freudian; in any case, he is never likely to be reproached with the contrary."[18] Yet she also spotted how irritated by Tausk Freud could be: "Freud's rejoinders were more severe than usual and yet no other person presents his papers to him with such evident reverence. I think that Tausk is of all the most unconditionally devoted to Freud and at the same time the most prominently outstanding."[19]

As early as 1913 Lou thought she understood "the whole tragedy of Tausk's relation to Freud":

> I realize now that he will always tackle the same problems, the same attempts at solution, that Freud is engaged in. This is no accident, but signifies his "making himself a son" as violently as he "hates the father for it." As if by a thought transference he will always be busy with the same thing as Freud, never taking one step aside to make room for himself.

Lou also thought that Tausk was deceiving himself about the possibilities he might have with her; he was too enmeshed, she thought, in the emotional involvements from his earliest years.

> In the long run no helpful relationship is possible; there can be none when reality is cluttered by the wraiths of unabreacted primal reminiscences. An impure tone resonates through everything, buzzing as it were with murmurings from within.
>
> Yet from the very beginning I realized it was this very struggle in Tausk that most deeply moved me—the struggle of the human creature. Brother-animal. You.[20]

World War I disrupted Tausk's life just as he was about to get securely established on his new professional feet as an analyst. Although he practiced while attending the University of Vienna, he only completed his medical studies in June 1914. The wartime hostilities complicated the possibilities of analysis; in August 1915 he was called up as an army psychiatrist. Throughout the war he continued his psychoanalytic investigations, returning to Vienna for occasional meetings of Freud's Society. Tausk's papers collected here record some of his specific wartime work: for example, his essay on "The War Deserter" and his inquiry into the symptomatology of the "War Psychoses."

At the conclusion of the war Tausk returned to Vienna and undertook to resume his psychoanalytic practice. He also then turned to Freud for a personal psychoanalysis. (He had just recently, along with Otto Rank, successfully opposed the idea that a training analysis be made mandatory for future analysts.[21]) Tausk knew he had unresolved problems, especially in establishing a stable relationship with a woman. Freud, however, refused Tausk's request for an analysis. Ludwig Jekels, one of the other analysts in Vienna, also asked Freud to analyze Tausk, but Freud reportedly had replied: "He is going to kill me!"[22]

Instead, Freud sent Tausk for an analysis to Helene Deutsch, then a young psychiatrist just starting out as an analyst and at the time already undergoing an analysis with Freud. In sending Tausk to her as a patient, Freud explained that Tausk made an "uncanny" impression on him; Freud thought Tausk could take some of Freud's ideas before Freud had finished with them, and then come to think they were Tausk's own. Freud refused Tausk an analysis because of discomfort in his presence. Tausk, though, grieved over Freud's standoffishness toward him, and thought he would never be able to assert his own independent thoughts in Freud's world, but that Freud would always put his own mark on anything Tausk succeeded in coming up with. After three months of Tausk's being in analysis with Helene Deutsch while she was herself with Freud, Freud called a halt to the arrangement. Tausk's obsession with Freud was being fed by being in treatment with an analyst then being analyzed by Freud. Freud told Helene Deutsch that her own analysis with him was being threatened by her fascination with Tausk, and that either she had to interrupt treating Tausk or break off her analysis with Freud. She immediately chose to terminate Tausk as a patient and stayed on with Freud herself.

From Tausk's standpoint, things were now worse than ever. He had alienated official psychiatry in behalf of his championing psychoanalysis, and now Freud was decisively through with him. Tausk had sought therapeutic help only to have his efforts aborted. According to a close friend of his, Paul Federn, writing the day he found out about Tausk's suicide a few months after his analysis was broken off, Tausk finally "at the end . . . drove his psychological patients away, apparently in order to demonstrate the uselessness of the method, out of rancor against Freud." Federn, living in Vienna himself, knew what a tough time it was for the practice of analysis. No matter how dedicated to psychoanalysis Federn was, he had retained his old practice in internal medicine and was not wholly dependent either on analysis or Freud's favor. To Federn the explanation for Tausk's suicide was straightforward:

> the motivation was Freud's turning away from him. . . . If Freud had shown him a human interest, not simply recognition and support, he might have continued to bear longer his martyr-like existence. Because for a man of his sensitivity of mind, this kind of looking for bread was martyrdom. . . . But *he* was not *kind* as little as Freud is kind, i.e. Freud possesses so much love for people that he can be kind, but in his old age he became increasingly harder—and this is understandable with Freud because he, too, had to live a life unworthy of his greatness.—That we could not keep Tausk is our shame.[23]

It was typical of Federn's reaction to Tausk's suicide to see it in terms of imputing the power of life and death to Freud. Helene Deutsch, too, put all the responsibility for what had happened on Freud—although she acknowledged some of her own guilt feelings for having ended Tausk's analysis with her, she saw the suicide as not her own therapeutic responsibility but that of Freud. Freud's coldness about Tausk's death came in several of his letters to followers, in which Freud blamed what happened on the upheaval of the war. And as Freud wrote to Lou Andreas-Salomé, in sharp contrast to his high public praise for Tausk's capacities: "I confess I do not really miss him; I had long taken him to be useless, indeed a threat to the future."[24]

The particular circumstances of Tausk's death were especially cruel. According to an obituary in a Viennese newspaper for which Tausk had once worked, he had fastened to a nail in his room a cord which he twisted into a noose, put his head in it and then fired a bullet from a Browning pistol through his right temple. As his body fell he strangled himself; he had placed the gun so carefully that a female servant sleeping in the apartment did not hear the shot. The savagery of Tausk's suicide was in sharp contrast to the serene benevolence of the suicide note that Tausk wrote to Freud.[25]

Freud suspected that other feelings lay behind what Tausk had written him. Freud saw the struggle within Tausk in terms of a father-son conflict; as Freud wrote Lou after Tausk's suicide: "So he fought out his day of life with the father ghost." Just a few months after Tausk's death Freud wrote in a paper:

> probably no one finds the mental energy required to kill himself unless, in the first place, in doing so he is at the same time killing an object with whom he has identified himself, and, in the second place, is turning against himself a death-wish which has been directed against someone else.[26]

In the same letter in which Freud reported to Lou about Tausk's suicide, he also wrote her about having come across a new feature to the "death theme," "an amazing idea hailing from the instincts." Freud was now to go on to formulate his concept of a death instinct.

Tausk had been coping with his own private difficulties for years. He had, for example, been singularly unsuccessful in establishing a stable tie with a woman. A frustrated love affair led in 1907 to a brief stay in a sanitorium. And just before committing suicide, he had found himself, as on several prior occasions, unable to go through with an intention once again to marry. Tausk's efforts to alleviate his problems through his involvement in psychoanalysis had not solved his emotional problems; the brief personal analysis with Helene Deutsch had probably made his difficulties worse, and the tortured bond to Freud remained more frustrating than ever. By the most rigorous standards of rational conduct, Tausk ought to have been able simply to dismiss his fascination with Freud, and leave for Berlin, for instance, or go back to Belgrade or Zagreb. But the tragedy of his life lay in his inability to detach himself from his worst dilemmas.

The story of Tausk's conflict with Freud remained a closely guarded secret among Freud's most intimate disciples, and they exaggerated Freud's role in Tausk's final undoing. It was characteristically true of Freud's followers that they came to attribute to him all possible power. Quarreling with the master meant to them all the worst possible eventuality; and therefore they obliterated from their memory Tausk's personal problems and saw his inner struggle solely in terms of what Freud had come to mean for him. In future years Freud's followers, when reflecting on the natural deaths of other of his disciples, such as Sandor Ferenczi, Karl Abraham, and Otto Rank, would suggest that each of these men in some sense chose death rather than face up to a conflict with Freud.[27]

Freud achieved a kind of standing in the lives of his students that may be hard to imagine today, except that it ought to be striking how prescient they all were in anticipating what Freud's stature would be in intellectual history. As Tausk had written Freud in his suicide note: "Your work is genuine and great, I shall take leave of this life knowing that I was one of those who witnessed the triumph of one of the greatest ideas of mankind."

In reflecting on the particulars of Tausk's contribution to psychoanalytic thinking, it should go almost without saying that all Tausk's work was bounded by the circumference of Freud's framework. Tausk always took pains to specify where Freud's own most characteristic points needed to be acknowledged; and yet Tausk also sought to express his own observations and reflections in the course of his theorizing. Freud himself, both in his writings and his obituary of Tausk, acknowledged the originality of his brilliant follower.

Tausk's Papers

1. Tausk's paper "On Masturbation" was occasioned by an extended 1912 discussion on the subject at the Vienna Psychoanalytic Society, which was collected together to appear as a book. Freud had started out in the 1890s distinguishing between an "actual neurosis," stemming from the physiological consequences of disturbed sexuality, as opposed to psychogenic neuroses. It was the latter which came to be the special province of psychoanalytic inquiry. In Tausk's view, however, and here he was at odds with other of Freud's pupils at the time, "a purely toxic neurosis on a masturbatory basis—termed by Freud *actual neurosis*—cannot, in my opinion, be found as such."

Within Freud's school, the 1912 exchange of views on masturbation was deemed important enough for it to be reconsidered twice, once in 1928 and then again in 1950. Although now-famous figures like Ferenczi, Rank, and Stekel were among the original contributors, Dr. Annie Reich (Wilhelm Reich's first wife), in reviewing the discussion for a volume of *The Psychoanalytic Study of The Child* in the light of views that were "present-day" as of 1950, observed of Tausk's essay that it "appears in many respects the most brilliant."[28]

One of the advantages of putting effort into trying to understand what any early psychoanalytic paper is trying to talk about is that it should force the reader to put aside all later theoretical developments. In 1912, for example, Freud's theory of narcissism had yet to be worked out; Tausk's own thinking was working in that direction, and Lou's diary records how significant the topic was to both her and Tausk. By 1912 Freud's notion of the superego had also not yet been introduced. As Dr. Annie Reich pointed out, Tausk was the "only one of the authors" who "connected the guilt feeling with the internalized figure of the father, thus anticipating Freud's concept of the super-ego."[29]

It is still now, as in Tausk's time, an open question, considered by therapists unanswerable even today: "Under what conditions does masturbation become harmful?" Analysts continue to feel unsure, when patients ask about masturbating, whether their task is to ally with the patient's conscience or to ease guilt feelings. Although Tausk had only been in the Vienna Psychoanalytic Society since 1909, and was some two years away from graduating from medical school, he was still enough of a practicing analyst to be able to generalize his conclusions on the basis of work with eighteen patients.

Tausk was approaching the problem of masturbation not just as a therapist but as part of the Freudian program of trying to create a science of sexuality. Tausk therefore was concerned with the earliest signs of masturbatory activity, including the role of fantasy as well as the part in seduction that servants then frequently played. He was concerning himself with masturbation, incidentally, almost entirely from the point of view of the male; it would not be until the 1920's that Freud and his followers directly addressed themselves to female sexuality. But he was hardly unaware of the role of the social environment and wound up his paper with a critique of hypocritical moralism and the excessive constraints of traditional patriarchal family life.

2. "Compensation As A Means of Discounting the Motive of Repression" (1913), an important paper, was discussed at a meeting of the Vienna Psychoanalytic Society—the minutes of which do not survive—and also succeeded in entering the later analytic literature. Tausk was addressing himself initially here to the logic of memory: why do we succeed in remembering certain forgotten ideas? According to Freud's thinking, we repress that which is in conflict with our self-esteem. Tausk was proposing also that "there occurs in very many cases, immediately before the reproduction of a forgotten idea, an association which is accompanied by a pleasurable affect." We are in such circumstances compensating ourselves before revealing something that lowers our sense of dignity. Tausk also said, "This compensation has the effect of discounting the motive for repression and weakening the resistance against the painful reproduction of the idea, so that he finally succumbs to the tendency to continue the train of thought without interruption." In 1924 Freud added a note to his *Psychopathology of Everyday Life*, in which he refers to this paper of Tausk's: "An excellent paper by Tausk gives good examples of how the forgotten name becomes accessible once more if one succeeds in connecting it with a pleasurably toned association, which can counterbalance the unpleasure to be expected from the reproduction of the name."[30]

The implications of Tausk's argument were far-reaching. For why should, according to psychoanalytic thinking, anyone ever give up a resistance to self-knowledge? In 1926 Sandor Ferenczi remarked on being "involuntarily reminded of a very fruitful work by Victor Tausk, an analyst whose too early death we all deplore. In his 'Compensation As a Means of Discounting the Motive of Repression' he adduced the weakening of the motives of repression by compensation as a condition of the cure."[31] Although the concept of transference was not as much discussed in those days as it would be later on, the patient's relationship with an analyst can function as a compensation. In the course of treatment a patient should learn to give up neurotic repetitions; the analytic situation then is compensatory. Transference can mobilize the hope of the realization of repressed fantasies. Treatment may look in one sense like a repetition of an unaccepted situation of frustration; but it is also a profoundly gratifying setup, in that the interest and sympathy of the analyst is a compensation.

In a training analysis, for example, a candidate has the promise of becoming a future analyst, which compensates for the difficulties of undergoing the treatment itself. Identifying with the analyst is one ultimate goal of the treatment. The concept of compensation can also help explain certain aspects of psychological development as well; one does not give up one phase of gratification without achieving the promise of the pleasure to be gained from another period. Development is not just a matter of biological frustrations, but contains a psychological factor in the possibility of new compensations. All such reasoning would be in line with a 1908 pronouncement of Freud's own: "whoever understands the human mind knows that hardly anything is harder for a man than to give up a pleasure which he has once experienced. Actually, we can never give anything up; we only exchange one thing for another. What appears to be a renunciation is really the formation of a substitute or a surrogate."[32]

Tausk did not spend enough time exploring the implications of his concept of compensation. His paper was burdened by competitiveness with Freud, which took away some of the flavor of Tausk's own individual thinking. He weakened the paper by going into too many details, as if he found it necessary to prove to himself that he was right. He seemed to think he had to say everything he knew, and in a hurry, before Freud said more about it. He undermined his argument by bringing in elements that were not quite relevant. Tausk even thought he had to put in a footnote polemicizing against Adler. Freud, in Tausk's obituary, alluded to this side of Tausk's character: "His passionate temperament found expression in sharp, and sometimes too sharp, criticisms, which however were combined with a brilliant gift for exposition. These personal qualities exercised a great attraction on many people, and some, too, may have been repelled by them."

3. "A Contribution to the Psychology of Child Sexuality" (1913) was part of the psychoanalytic concern with documenting early developmental phenomena. Freud cited the paper both in 1914 and 1916, in additions to his *Interpretation of Dreams*.[33] Perhaps the most enduring aspect of this paper, however, is that is has

been demonstrated that Tausk was here in fact giving an account of his own two sons.[34] Many of the early analysts, including Freud himself, subjected their own children to psychological investigation. Some analysts, like Helene Deutsch and Melanie Klein, used their children as the basis for psychoanalytic papers. Others, following Freud's own lead in personally analyzing his daughter over a period of several years,[35] went much farther in the direction of using psychological knowledge within an intimate family setting. Nowadays, any such intrusion into the privacy of a child looks like a clear violation of the autonomy and integrity of a relatively helpless creature. It is worth pointing out again, though, that even in the course of Tausk's giving an account of some dreams of his sons, he could not forbear also to include remarks that were "directed polemically against" a key hypothesis of Adler's.

4. "Psychoanalysis of Philosophy and Psychoanalytic Philosophy" (1914) has never appeared before in English. Tausk first presented his thoughts here again at a meeting of the Vienna Psychoanalytic Society. Lou Andreas-Salomé recorded in her diary that Tausk had worked at her "place on his critique of Putnam. . . ." At the session itself, whose minutes once again do not survive, she reported that Tausk's "critique of Putnam burst out with the sound of drums and trumpets. Freud took the floor from Tausk and that was a signal to the others that they did not miss. I liked Tausk's behavior."[36]

Doubtless Freud had proceeded "so sharply"[37] against Tausk for the sake of preserving the momentum of the psychoanalytic movement. Freud privately did not think at all well of Putnam's philosophizing, but Putnam was at the time the great hope Freud had for maintaining the psychoanalytic movement's future in America. In his publication here, Tausk dealt with other writers much more than just Putnam, whom he scarcely touched upon—even though still disapprovingly. The philosophical side of Tausk is one that barely succeeds in coming through to us, partly due to the destruction of all his papers after his death, which Tausk had requested in his will. We know that in 1907 Tausk had published a moving dialogue with Spinoza, which has recently been translated into French.[38]

Freud was himself of two minds about Tausk's interest in philosophy, since Freud sought to draw a sharp line between his own psychology and more traditional philosophical inquiries. Nevertheless, in Tausk's obituary Freud stressed this aspect of Tausk's contribution to psychoanalytic thinking:

> his numerous contributions . . . were distinguished by sharp observation, sound judgment and a particular clearness of expression. These writings exhibit plainly the philosophical training which the author was able so happily to combine with the exact methods of science. His strong need to establish things on a philosophical foundation and to achieve epistemological clarity compelled him to formulate, and seek as well to master, the whole profundity and comprehensive meaning of the very difficult problems involved. Perhaps he sometimes went too far in this direction, in his impetuous urge for investigation. Perhaps the time was not yet ripe for laying such general foundations as these for the young science of psychoanalysis. The psychoanalytic consideration of philosophical problems, for which Tausk showed special aptitude, promises to become more and more fruitful. One of his last works, on the psychoanalysis of the function of judgment, which was delivered at the Budapest Congress and has not yet been published, gives evidence of this direction taken by his interest.

Tausk's paper on "The Psychoanalysis of the Function of Judgment" remained unpublished; evidently it was among the rest of his works destroyed at his instructions after his death.

5. "On the Psychology of the Alcoholic Occupation Delirium" first appeared in 1915. The *Minutes* of the Vienna Psychoanalytic Society report Tausk's initial presentation of this paper (although the modern editors, Herman Nunberg and Ernst Federn, chose to ignore the 1969 English translation of Tausk's publication that had been prepared under my editorship.[39]) Tausk's great ambition, which Freud relatively minimized in his obituary, was to use psychoanalysis to understand the psychoses. This paper was written about a problem that was a very common psychiatric syndrome in Tausk's time, the alcoholic psychosis. (In the discussion at the Vienna Society, Freud called Tausk's attention to his own teacher, Theodor Meynert, having earlier worked on the alcoholic occupation delirium.) Before World War I an entire ward was set apart at Julius Wagner-Jauregg's clinic at the University of Vienna for cases of male alcoholic psychosis. Although in America today such cases would be seen much more rarely, and usually in specialized hospitals, in Viennese psychiatric practice of that time

they played a prominent role. (The alcoholic psychoses of that era antedated our current concern with the effects and characteristics of hallucinogenic drug psychoses.) As Otto Fenichel put it in 1945,

> Psychoses in addicts, especially alcoholic psychoses, have been but little studied by psychoanalysis. . . . In a very instructive article, Tausk interpreted alcoholic occupation delirium as the expression of sexual excitement in patients who are erotically stimulated and at the same time rendered impotent by alcohol, and who are, on deeper levels, homosexual and narcissistic.[40]

To study the psychoses clinically at all was remarkable for a psychoanalyst of Tausk's time. In addition, he was interested in the psychology of alcoholics as he wanted to extend the scope of psychoanalytic treatment. The contemporary reader will be struck by a World War I psychoanalyst's lack of interest in adolescence; that special phase of development had yet to be emphasized by people like Siegfried Bernfeld and Wilhelm Reich. Much of the clinical material in this paper concerns an extended interpretation of the dream of a twenty-three-year-old student. Tausk was writing at a time when many of these ideas were uncharted subjects. Although the occupational activities he describes are interpreted in terms of sexual excitement in patients rendered impotent, from today's point of view it is striking that Tausk does not see this delirium as an outlet of aggressiveness, or as a defense against primitive brutality. A delirium can in fact serve about as many different purposes as a dream.

In those days the psychoses were psychologically almost unknown, and Tausk was one of the pioneers in trying to understand them along psychoanalytic principles. Our own time has seen tremendous advances in the biochemical side of comprehending insanity, and yet psychosis still retains its mysterious character. Freud himself always maintained some distance from such clinical material. It was not until the later development of ego psychology (and here again Tausk was ahead of others) that the distinction between neurosis and psychosis, clinically as well as theoretically, assumed the form we know it now.

6. "Diagnostic Considerations Concerning the Symptomatology of the So-Called War Psychoses" first appeared in 1916. De-

spite Tausk's continuing renown for his work on schizophrenia, his essay on melancholia has been forgotten. Yet in fact this paper is noteworthy for having appeared before Freud's own "Mourning and Melancholia."[41] Tausk's citation of verbal comments by Freud indicates the degree to which Tausk, along with Karl Abraham, was working in the forefront of this area. According to Freud's biographer Ernest Jones, Freud had "expounded the view expressed [later in "Mourning and Melancholia"] . . . at the Vienna Society on Dec. 30, 1914, on the occasion of a paper Tausk read on melancholia."[42] When Freud's own paper finally came out in 1917, he cited Tausk—but not for this obvious essay of his. Freud instead footnoted "Compensation As A Means of Discounting the Motive of Repression," and therefore his school has ignored the existence of Tausk's war psychoses essay.

In Tausk's lecture on the war psychoses, delivered in January 1916 in Lublin, Tausk included a complete review of Freud's concept of melancholia. He repeatedly referred to "verbal remarks" of Freud's. At one point he mentioned "a still unpublished conjecture of Freud's (which I quote here with his special permission). . . ." We can understand why Freud had to be cautious with this man; in addition to his having ideas of his own, he would rush ahead to fill out some of Freud's raw concepts with his own clinical material.

Tausk had a great need to be creative; as he remarked at one point in this paper, "it would be easy to become famous by laying claim to the discovery of a new psychosis. . . ." Yet Tausk's paper, which is historically important since he was working on melancholia simultaneously with Freud, was damaged by his competitiveness. Tausk could not simply accept his own originality. He spoiled his discussion by going into too many details of Freud's views, and he burdened his argument with references to Freud's comments. At the very end of his paper Tausk inserted a footnote criticizing a psychiatrist for writing without mentioning Freud's name. (Could it have been partly in behalf of Freud's cause that, despite Freud's having mentioned Meynert as a predecessor on the alcoholic occupation delirium, Tausk left his name out of the published version of his paper?)

Despite how Freud's pupils have silently passed over Tausk's war psychoses paper, it was an early effort to deal with psychoses that fall between Emil Kraepelin's conceptual entities—paranoid states and manic depressive insanity. What does one do if the patient is both depressed and paranoid? There is hardly a melancholia without a paranoid element; melancholics are so eaten by guilt feelings that it is self-protective to put the blame on others. Tausk proposed to explain melancholia and paranoia in relation to each other, the working up of heterosexual libido in depression and of homosexual libido in projection. While this particular formula might well be contested, his paper is important for the rich clinical material presented in relation to the existing social milieu and for Tausk's early attempt to help psychiatry absorb the insights of psychoanalysis. For, in addition to trying to make an original contribution to psychoanalysis, Tausk was trying to demonstrate the limitations of the formalism of classical psychiatry.

The modern reader will be struck by the absence here of the later concepts of the ego ideal and of the superego. Perceiving the central role of loss in depression, Tausk attempted to cope with the problem of melancholia in terms of libido theory so important to Freud and his followers at this early time.

7. "On the Psychology of the War Deserter" first appeared in 1916. During World War I, Tausk served on the Austrian front as an army psychiatrist. He acted with genuine heroism in protecting deserters from the Imperial Austrian Army, which enlisted peasants who had never understood what conscription meant. Freud thought it was "greatly to his honor that during the war he threw himself wholeheartedly, and with complete disregard for the consequences, into exposing the numerous abuses which so many doctors unfortunately tolerated in silence or for which they even shared the responsibility."

Helpless and confused young men found themselves in danger of being shot for their simple primitive desire to creep back to the shelter of their homes. Unlike psychiatrists who behaved sadistically toward all "malingerers," Tausk went out of his way to save people, using psychiatric diagnoses for humane ends. He intervened, for example, in behalf of a young boy who was to be court-martialed for failing to help shoot a whole group of enemy prisoners. Tausk saved his life by testifying that such a boy, reared in the highest standards of civilized life, could not be expected to assist in such an execution.

This paper demonstrates Tausk's earlier legal experience, both as a lawyer and a judge, as well as his loyal exposition of Freud's theories at that time. It is one of the first efforts to relate psychoanalysis to law. (Freud himself ventured only warily into this subject.[43]) Tausk presents us with the social drama of conscription, relating the inner disposition of the peasantry to the external social realities of war.

From today's perspective, Tausk's lucid presentation of psychoanalytic ideas during World War I helps highlight some of the concepts missing in the early days of Freudian theory. For example, once again a contemporary reader will be struck by the way childhood feelings are contrasted with those of adulthood, without mention of the intervening developmental stage of adolescence. Moreover, the ego as a mechanism of control or as a means of adaptation had yet to be incorporated into the psychoanalytic framework.

8. "Some Remarks Concerning Abraham's Paper on 'Ejaculatio Praecox' " (1917) was a response to a paper by Karl Abraham in 1917.[44] Abraham was then Freud's leading disciple in Germany; he later came to play a key role both in establishing the Berlin Psychoanalytic Institute, and in personally conducting the training analyses of a number of leading analysts in the future. In the context of the time it was not considered inappropriate for Tausk to have considered himself on a comparable intellectual level with Abraham, although it would not be long before it was apparent that Tausk lacked Abraham's stability of character. Freud himself wrote to Abraham that he viewed this particular paper of Tausk's as "not exactly distinguished."[45] It is not clear whether Freud was partly flattering Abraham, with whom he was in regular correspondence, or possibly Freud was continuing to find Tausk's work foreign. In that vein Freud had in 1915 written to Lou Andreas-Salomé: "I know that you were brought into close touch with the subject of narcissism through your interest in Tausk's work. But his arguments were quite incomprehensible to me."[46] (Finding someone's work "foreign" to him was Freud's special way of distancing himself.)

Unlike later in the history of psychoanalysis, when patients could come for treatment because of relatively innocuous difficulties—vague feelings of dissatisfaction, or even an inability to complete a Ph.D. dissertation—in the early days of psychoanalysis patients often saw analysts for the sake of strictly sexual dysfunctions. For example, impotency was a common problem for the males that analysts treated. (Nowadays, physical sources of such a difficulty would medically first come to mind.) Freud taught that every symptom had a history in terms of infantile sexuality, a structure as well as a meaning. Therefore, the subject of premature ejaculation was one that attracted the interest of analysts.

Tausk's paper, like Abraham's own, is bound to seem like a museum piece of analytic reasoning. Today we are aware of the variety of behavioral ways in which sexual dysfunctions can be treated. It would be far less likely for a therapist now to react to such a problem the way Abraham and Tausk did—tracing it back to its presumed infantile origins—when we know that education and enlightenment in adulthood can often succeed in satisfactorily curing such a problem.

In the context of the time around World War I, we should acknowledge that it was culturally advanced for analysts to want to help understand that specific sexual difficulty. Unfortunately, both Abraham and Tausk were framing their discussion within a mechanistic approach of the then-current libido theory that did not, for example, in any way take into account the sexual partner or her role in producing, sustaining, or altering the phenomenon during foreplay. Neither Abraham nor Tausk saw premature ejaculation as enough of a relationship phenomenon; it is after all something that occurs in connection with a partner, and the etiology is clearly related to anxiety and concern about performance. Many elements, such as long abstinence, fever, and other factors come into play aside from the extravagances of the libido theory that was then psychoanalytically fashionable. At least Tausk suggested other issues, such as "fear of infection and extra-marital pregnancy," implying, even though he did not specifically state, the interpersonal elements involved.*

9. "On the Origin of the 'Influencing Machine' in Schizophrenia" (1919) is Tausk's most famous paper, the one for which he was apt to be remembered. As one of the later editors of the paper commented, it had "never ceased to inspire subsequent authors, and in rereading it one is again struck by the still-un-

*I am indebted here to the helpful commentary of Dr. Leon Salzman.

tapped wealth of ideas, touching upon so many of the analyst's daily clinical problems." In this editor's view, Tausk had "a mind perhaps exceeding most of his contemporaries in its capaciousness. The acuity of observations, and ingenuity of conception . . . remind one of Abraham's work." He continued:

> Yet the paper violates almost all pedestrian standards for publication. Much of the text is contained in footnotes, no section can be given an adequate heading, and the paper cannot be abstracted without being practically re-written. This is so because, while dealing with the interpretation of but a single symbolic element in a psychotic delusion, the author discourses at length, but with unvarying acument upon all manner of disparate subjects.[47]

As the original 1933 translator of the paper, Dr. Dorian Feigenbaum also wrote:

> This study is a classic in psychoanalytic—and psychiatric—literature, presenting a brilliant analysis of a delusionary formation, throwing out penetrating comments on such fundamental problems as projection, hallucination and narcissism, and anticipating Abraham's formulation of the libido development as well as later studies by others.[48]

Tausk read his influencing machine paper before the Vienna Psychoanalytic Society on 6 January 1918, and another evening of the Society was devoted to it on 30 January 1918. A year later it appeared in print. The issue that published it also contained Freud's obituary of Tausk, along with Helene Deutsch's "A Case That Throws Light on the Mechanism of Regression in Schizophrenia."[49] When Freud had sent Tausk to Helene Deutsch for his analysis, she was, compared to Tausk himself, a relative nobody in Freud's school, and the referral was considered an insult. In her 1919 paper, she was following Tausk's lead about the role of ego boundaries in schizophrenia and how inner feelings can be projected onto the outside world. Tausk cited her clinical material in a footnote to his "influencing machine" paper, since she had brought it up in a discussion at the Vienna Psychoanalytic Society.

Tausk was developing the concept of projection in a clinical psychiatric context. Freud had postulated that psychosis involved a regression of libido back to primary narcissism; the most primitive stage of child development involves concentrating on one's own body. Tausk showed how schizophrenic symptoms can represent the earliest stage of the ego's contact with reality. Feelings of inner strangeness get projected onto the external world. Changes in one's own personality are experienced as coming from the outside world.

Tausk interpreted the common schizophrenic delusion of being influenced by machines in a persecutory way as an externalized projection of the patient's own body. The influencing machine, then, is a projection of the patient's body as a defense against regressing to primary narcissism.

Here Freud conceded that Tausk was ahead of him. Freud used Tausk's case material (as Tausk duly noted) in a paper he wrote in the spring of 1915. Freud commented briefly: "Dr. Victor Tausk of Vienna has placed at my disposal some observations that he has made in the initial stages of schizophrenia, which are particularly valuable in that the patient was ready to explain her utterances herself."[50] In Tausk's own 1919 paper, he seems to fall all over himself making acknowledgements. At one point, Tausk mentions Freud's earlier work on schizophrenia, and twice he cites Freud's comments on the paper at the Vienna Society. In addition, Tausk had highlighted a constructive role for "innate narcissism": "we must definitely understand that throughout life the ego develops with constant shiftings in the narcissistic libido position, that man in his struggle for existence is constantly compelled to find and recognize himself anew, and that the acquisition of narcissism is immanent in culture and is conceivable only on the basis of intact inborn narcissism that serves as a source of nourishment and regeneration."

With this one paper on the "influencing machine," Tausk won a pioneering place in the psychological understanding of schizophrenic delusions and this work has been built upon by many others.[51]

10. Additional papers include "Ibsen the Druggist" (no date), "Short Contributions to the Interpretation of Dreams" (1914), and "Contributions to the Psychopathology of Everyday Life" (1917). Somehow Tausk's Ibsen paper escaped being destroyed with the rest of his literary remains, and it first appeared in print in 1934. Tausk was continuing his interest in the feelings of strangeness that people have and then project. In addition, Tausk had long been interested in the problem of inhibitions in artistic creativity; Lou mentioned his having lectured on the subject in 1912. Freud had at the time objected that it was too soon to entertain the topic: "That with the persistent calumny of our whole movement on the part of official science, we should not

dare to move so boldly into new territory leaving the rear so exposed, and confirmation of earlier discoveries needs to be made again and again."[52] She had also noticed an autobiographical aspect of Tausk's interest in this matter of inhibition, for she spotted in him that "a certain gap in creativity is filled by identification with the other (sonship) which constantly begets the illusion of having attained the anticipated position."[53]

Tausk never overcame his difficulties with Freud; although he discussed them with Lou long after she left Vienna in 1913, his relationship with Freud was such a sacred matter that he never allowed his sons or ex-wife to find out the problems he had had dealing with Freud. Had Tausk lived he might never have permitted his "Ibsen the Druggist" to appear. For at the very end of this paper, in a footnote, Tausk revealed one version of his struggle with Freud. It was all so unknown in 1934 that the publishers of this article had no idea what the footnote referred to. The article dealt with a man called "B" who experiences a block in relation to a revered master, Ibsen. Tausk explains the situation within the jargon of the psychoanalytic terminology current in his day. Yet it remains a succint summary of his own quarrel with Freud.

> B's relation to Ibsen, that of a creative individual to the master who represents his ideals, is patterned after the father complex. . . . In the life of rivals struggling with their masters, the hatred . . . is derived from the son-father relation. Hence the conflict between master and disciple striving for independence resembles very closely the severest type of conflict between father and son.

I have included both Tausk's "Short Contributions to the Interpretation of Dreams" and his "Contributions to the Psychopathology of Everyday Life" because Freud cited them each in a 1914 addition to his *Interpretation of Dreams* and in a 1919 addition to his *Psychopathology of Everyday Life.*[54] The section entitled by Tausk "The Faith of Our Fathers" was clearly an autobiographical vignette.

* * *

Tausk's writings ranged over so many different fields that he never fulfilled his great promise. He had defied Freud's advice to his pupils that one must concentrate on a single theme. In addition to his exploration of manic-depressive, alcoholic, and schizophrenic psychoses, Tausk had notably contributed to the understanding of ego psychology, artistic creativity, sexuality, the philosophical underpinnings of psychoanalysis, as well as the relationship between law and psychiatry.

But Tausk died so early that his work now seems scattered. The circumstances surrounding his suicide have helped keep his contribution obscure, since Freud's most loyal disciples preferred to blot out the story of Tausk's unhappy struggle with the founder of psychoanalysis. Personal involvement with Freud and his circle, besides its liberating qualities, was simultaneously apt to smother and stifle. Tausk's work was tragically cut short at just the point, with his "influencing machine" article, that his talents had finally shown themselves the equal of his ambitions.

The story of Tausk's rebellion and Freud's rejection of him, spelled out in *Brother Animal,* provide an avenue by which one can reevaluate the tale of Freud's other controversies with some of his most gifted pupils. To Helene Deutsch, for example, who was so intimately acquainted with the difficulties between Freud and Tausk, when she later heard Freud complain in the mid-1920s about his former favorite student, Otto Rank, she was reminded of Tausk: an erstwhile son had turned into a rival, had taken ideas from Freud without adequate acknowledgment of the sources, and now Freud was furious and through with him. As Freud once wrote about a childhood relation with a nephew of his:

> My emotional life has always insisted that I should have an intimate friend and a hated enemy. I have always been able to provide myself afresh with both, and it has not infrequently happened that the ideal situation of childhood has been so completely reproduced that friend and enemy have come together in a single individual. . . .[55]

The problem of priorities played a role throughout Freud's life, in relation to his teachers, contemporaries, and disciples.

The history of psychoanalysis needs to be taught as more than the textual exegesis of Freud's writings. Each of his books and papers has to be understood in the historical context in which they were composed, and that also means that it is necessary to understand who his opponents were at any given time. Freud was a powerful innovator, and his ideas should be seen in the light of the full human struggles he was engaged in. The life and work of

Victor Tausk can help fill in a unique dimension to the early days of psychoanalysis and the history of the development of Freud's school of thought.

The ideological fanaticism aroused by my initial publication of *Brother Animal,* and the difficulties that continue to arise in trying to get people to rethink the controversies between Freud, Adler, and Jung, make me think that the period of pluralism in psychoanalysis, and the toleration of different points of view within the profession, has not yet succeeded in being securely established. The glacier of orthodox psychoanalytic historiography has only begun to thaw, and partisan studies are still all too prevalent.[56] We continue to await the period when the history of psychoanalysis will be a securely established part of the university curriculum, at which time differences in fundamental points of view will be as securely legitimated as in all other aspects of the history of ideas.

Notes

1. Paul Roazen, *Freud and His Followers* (New York: Knopf, 1975; New York University Press, 1985), pts 5–6; see also Paul Roazen, "Book Review of Kiell, ed., *Freud Without Hindsight: Reviews of His Work (1893–1939),*" *Journal of the History of the Behavioral Sciences*, January 1990.
2. "On the History of the Psychoanalytic Movement," *The Standard Edition of the Complete Psychological Works of Sigmund Freud*, ed. James Strachey (London: The Hogarth Press, 1953–74), vol. 14. Hereafter this edition of Freud's works will be referred to simply as *Standard Edition*.
3. Paul Roazen, *Encountering Freud: The Politics and Histories of Psychoanalysis* (New Brunswick, N.J.: Transaction Publishers, 1990), 51–54; Roazen, *Freud and His Followers*, 272–73.
4. Paul Roazen, *Brother Animal: The Story of Freud and Tausk* (New York: Knopf, 1969).
5. Paul Roazen, *Brother Animal: The Story of Freud and Tausk*, 2d ed. with a new introduction (New Brunswick, N.J.: Transaction Publishers, 1990).
6. Roazen, *Encountering Freud*, Chap. 6; cf. also Paul Roazen, "Reading, Writing, and Memory: Dr. K. R. Eissler's Thinking," *Contemporary Psychoanalysis* 14, no. 2 (1978), 345–53; Paul Roazen, "On Errors Regarding Freud," *International Journal of Psychoanalysis* 63, part 2 (1982): 260–61.

7. Victor Tausk, *Œuvres Psychanalytiques* (Paris: Payot, 1975); Victor Tausk, *Trabajos Psicoanaliticos* (Barcelona: Granica Editor, 1977); Victor Tausk, *Scritti Psico-Analitici* (Rome: Astrolabio, 1979); Victor Tausk, *Gesammelte Psychoanalytische und Literarische Schriften* (Vienna-Berlin: Medusa, 1983).
8. *The Freud Journal of Lou Andreas-Salomé*, trans. Stanley A. Leavy (New York: Basic Books, 1964), 57.
9. "Victor Tausk," *Standard Edition* vol. 17:275.
10. Bertram Lewin, "Obituary of Paul Federn," *The Psychoanalytic Quarterly* 19 (1950): 296; see also Paul Federn, *Ego Psychology and the Psychoses*, ed. Edoardo Weiss (New York: Basic Books, 1952).
11. Edith Jacobson, *The Self and The Object World* (New York: International Universities Press, 1964), xi; Mark Kanzer, "An Autobiographical Legacy of Victor Tausk," *International Journal of Psychoanalysis* 52, part 4 (1971): 429.
12. John Kerr, "Beyond the Pleasure Principle And Back Again: Freud, Jung, and Sabina Spielrein," in *Freud: Appraisals and Reappraisals, Contributions to Freud Studies*, vol. 3, ed. Paul E. Stepansky (New York, The Analytic Press, 1988), 51.
13. *Minutes of the Vienna Psychoanalytic Society*, ed. Herman Nunberg and Ernst Federn, trans. M. Nunberg, vol. 2–4 (New York, International Universities Press, 1967–75).
14. In 1913, Jung published a reply to Tausk's criticism of a Swiss disciple of his. See Carl G. Jung, "A Comment on Tausk's Criticism of Nelken," trans. R. F. C. Hull (Spring 1973), 183–87.
15. *The Freud Journal* 169.
16. Ibid., 97.
17. Ibid., 51.
18. Ibid., 56.
19. Ibid., 57.
20. Ibid., 167–68.
21. Roazen, *Brother Animal*, 64–66.
22. Ludwig Jekels, "Early Psychoanalytic Meetings," (Library of Congress, Bernfeld Papers), 8. I remain grateful to Peter Swales for first bringing this passage to my attention.
23. Roazen, *Brother Animal*, 153. See also Paul Roazen, "Correspondence Arising from the Publication of 'Reflections on Ethos and Authenticity in Psychoanalysis,' " *The Human Context* (1973): 676.
24. Roazen, *Brother Animal*, 140.
25. Ibid. 127–28.
26. Ibid. 132.
27. *The Clinical Diary of Sandor Ferenczi*, ed. Judith Dupont, trans. Michael Balint and Nicola Zarday Jackson (Cambridge: Harvard University Press, 1988), xi, xxvi; Roazen, *Freud and His Followers*, 331.
28. Annie Reich, "The Discussion of 1912 on Masturbation and Our

Present-Day Views," *The Psychoanalytic Study of the Child*, 6 ed. Ruth Eissler (New York: International Universities Press, 1951): 85.
29. Ibid.
30. "The Psychopathology of Everyday Life," *Standard Edition* 6: 270.
31. Sandor Ferenczi, *Further Contributions to the Theory and Technique of Psychoanalysis*, comp. John Rickman, trans. Jane I. Suttie (London: The Hogarth Press, 1960), 369.
32. "Creative Writers and Day-Dreaming," *Standard Edition* 9: 145.
33. "The Interpretation of Dreams," *Standard Edition* 4: 131, 304.
34. Kanzer, "An Autobiographical Legacy of Victor Tausk."
35. Roazen, *Freud and His Followers*, 438–40.
36. *The Freud Journal*, 97.
37. Ibid.
38. Victor Tausk, *Gesammelte psychoanalytische*, 456–63; Viktor Tausk, "De La Vie et Du Savoir," *Psychanalyse a L'universite*, 2, no. 6 (March 1977): 201–12.
39. Paul Roazen, "Victor Tausk's Contribution to Psychoanalysis," *The Psychoanalytic Quarterly*, no. 3 (1969): pp. 349–53, and Three Papers by Victor Tausk, 354–431.
40. Otto Fenichel, *The Psychoanalytic Theory of Neurosis* (New York: Norton, 1945), 380.
41. "Mourning and Melancholia," *Standard Edition* 19: 243–58.
42. Ernest Jones, *The Life and Work of Sigmund Freud*, vol. 2 (New York: Basic Books, 1955), 328.
43. "The Expert Opinion in the Halsmann Case," *Standard Edition* 21: 251–253.
44. Karl Abraham, "Ejaculatio Praecox," in *Selected Papers on Psychoanalysis*, chapt. 6, trans. Douglas Bryan and Alix Strachey, ed. Ernest Jones (London: The Hogarth Press, 1954), 280–98.
45. Hilda C. Abraham and Ernst L. Freud, ed., *A Psychoanalytic Dialogue: The Letters of Sigmund Freud and Karl Abraham*, trans. Bernard Marsh (pseud.) and Hilda C. Abraham (New York: Basic Books, 1965), 273.
46. Ernst Pfeiffer, ed., *Sigmund Freud and Lou Andreas-Salomé: Letters*, trans. William and Elaine Robson-Scott (London: The Hogarth Press, 1972), 27.
47. Robert Fliess, in *The Psychoanalytic Reader* (New York: International Universities Press, 1948), 31.
48. Dorian Feigenbaum, *The Psychoanalytic Quarterly* 2 (1933): 519.
49. Helene Deutsch, "A Case That Throws Light on the Mechanism of Regression in Schizophrenia," ed. Paul Roazen, trans. Eric Mosbacher, *The Psychoanalytic Review* 72, no. 1 (1985).
50. "The Unconscious," *Standard Edition* 14: 197.
51. Henry Brosin, "Contributions of Psychoanalysis to the Study of Psychoses," in *The Impact of Freudian Psychiatry*, ed. Franz Alexander and Helen Ross (University of Chicago Press, 1961), 178–

99; Gregory Zilboorg, *A History of Medical Psychology* (New York: Norton, 1941), 502; Bruno Bettelheim, *The Empty Fortress* (New York: The Free Press, 1967), 233–339; Rudolf Eckstein, "The Space Child's Time Machine," Chap. 16, in *Children of Time and Space* (New York: Appleton-Century-Crofts, 1966).

52. *The Freud Journal*, 57–58.
53. Ibid., 167.
54. "The Interpretation of Dreams," *Standard Edition* 5: 411–12; "The Psychopathology of Everyday Life," pp. 92–93, 226–27.
55. "The Interpretation of Dreams," 483.
56. See Paul Roazen, "Book Review of Young-Bruehl's *Anna Freud: A Biography*," *The Virginia Quarterly Review* (Autumn 1989): 749–55.

1

On Masturbation

The elements which are essential for a presentation of masturbation may be summarized in the following outline:

1. The subjects of masturbation
2. The origins of masturbation
3. Aim and effects of masturbation
   a. the significance of masturbation for the individual and society
   b. under which conditions does masturbation become harmful?

This outline might create the impression that masturbation could be clearly and unequivocally presented and explained as a well-defined phenomenon occurring in isolation. This is not possible, however. As a special phenomenon in man's sexual life, masturbation—which in every case is representative of the subject's entire sexual attitude—has as many relations to all manifestations of life as sexuality itself. It may be regarded, right from the start, as an illusory undertaking if anybody should venture to present the significance of sexuality in all its ramifications for life in general.

Victor Tausk's contribution in *Die Onanie: Vierzehn Beiträge zu einer Diskussion der Wiener Psychoanalytischen Vereinigung*. Wiesbaden: J. F. Bergman, 1912. pp. 48–68. Translated by William G. Niederland, M.D. (New York).

As a partial manifestation of sexual life, masturbation appears to the superficial observer as a special form of activity of the sexual instincts which results in a self-gratification and a discharge of sexual excitation without the use of any object other than one's own body. The conception of masturbation which is based on this popular definition proves to be inadequate, however, and does not sufficiently describe the real situation, not even from a purely empirical point of view. In the first place masturbation is practiced as often with the use of outside objects of all sort as without them. Inanimate as well as animate objects, animals as well as human beings of both sexes, are used in masturbatory activities, and particularly human beings are often used in such a way that no external criterion can be applied to determine whether a masturbatory act or a full-fledged sexual act, which unconditionally presupposes the participation of a partner, is practiced. Many a man will confess that he masturbates with his penis in the vagina of the woman. Although the act of genital union between individuals of different sex is the only type of true sexual intercourse in bisexual species, it is perceived as an onanistic activity. The criterion which determines whether a sexual act is either a masturbatory one or intercourse is not given in the external form of the sexual behavior but in the psychic superstructure of the physical process.

The concept of masturbation must be defined and delimited not only in relation to coitus as a full-fledged sexual act, but also in relation to human activities which apparently do not possess the character of sexuality at all. When women become sexually stimulated by playing with the nipples, or men induce ejaculation by frictions in the anus, such acts will be recognized as masturbatory ones without objection, although they do not involve manipulation of the genitals as such. But when a person sucks his thumb, picks his nose, incessantly licks his lips, or pulls his ear lobe, one must expect that the assertion that these are masturbatory acts will be disputed.

Furthermore, we must prove that the above-mentioned activities are truly sexual activities. Here we are confronted with the problem of the limitations of the concept of sexuality, and it becomes apparent that the problem of onanism, as far as can be seen from these acts, is only a special form of the sexual function.

The concept of sexuality on which my views are based, is Freud's concept of its scope and nature as stated by him in the various areas of the science of psychoanalysis. According to Freud, the human species possesses two basic instincts: the reproductive instinct and the instinct of self-preservation. The reproductive instinct is represented in each human being by the sexual instinct; the instinct of self-preservation, by all the other instincts, through the activity of which the individual secures his existence.[1]

The special organ which serves the reproductive function is the genital organ. However, sexuality is practiced not only for the purpose of reproduction, which is in fact only the least part of its objective. It is practiced mainly for sexual pleasure and in this respect, sexuality has at its disposal—in addition to the genitals—other organs which at the same time serve the instinct of self-preservation. Freud calls these organs the erogenous zones and the genitals are spoken of as the principal or genital zone. As to the erogenous zones, a distinction should be made between those which are directly utilized for the attainment of sexual pleasure by directly furnishing sexual stimulations, and those which via symbolization and secondary cathexis assume the role of sexual zones. In the first group belong the sense organs; in the second, all parts of the body. The essential importance of this distinction cannot be further explained here. A more thorough study of psychoanalysis is necessary for its understanding. At any rate, at this point, it can be stated that every organ which can furnish sexual pleasure lends itself to sexual activity and therefore also to masturbation.

As sexual activity, apart from the genital function, we understand that activity of an erogenous zone which is undertaken in the service of an idea or fantasy of sexual activity. The hand which touches another body accomplishes a sexual act only if its action is accompanied by the idea that the body to be touched is an object for the attainment of sexual pleasure. Without this fantasy the touching hand merely performs orientation work in the service of self-preservation. Psychoanalysis teaches that the fantasy which determines a certain action need not be conscious. It can be completely unconscious, i.e., it can be deduced from the action that it had been undertaken for the attainment of sexual pleasure, although the acting person cannot give any information about the purpose of his activity.

But quite apart from the question of consciousness, even in the case of an existing sexual aim which can be demonstrated psychoanalytically, not every activity is relevant for a definition of onanism. Sexuality also breaks through in neurotic symptoms and sublimated activities. There, however, sexual pleasure is symbolized as wish only and is not attained directly or specifically.

Accordingly, I define masturbation as that kind of sexual manipulation of the genitals or of an errogenous zone which has no partner as an indispensable prerequisite, and the aim of which consists in the direct discharge of sexual excitation. I do not include, therefore, the symbolic representation of the sexual pleasure (neurotic symptom, sublimation). Whether the masturbatory fantasy is conscious or unconscious is irrelevant to the concept of onanism.

Subjects of masturbation are individuals of both sexes in all age groups and in all social strata. However, the masturbation of children in the first year of life plays a different role. It is to be regarded in the same light as any other orientation activity of the infant on his own body, i.e., as a purely instinctual action. Only when certain manipulations, mainly on the genitals (later successively on the lips, navel, nipples, etc.) excite the specific sexual pleasure, and the activity of the child is directed toward the attainment of this specific pleasure which has already obtained psychic representation, can one speak of masturbation in the true sense of the word. The idea of the specific sexual pleasure must be immanent in the activity.

This situation certainly develops very soon. It can best be understood by the fact that children deliberately touch the genitals again and again, despite all objections on the part of the persons who take care of them. This obviously means that the child has already recognized the specific sensations of these organs and already seeks to attain sexual pleasure as such. The question whether sexual pleasure is known during the first period of childhood must be answered, in agreement with Freud, in the affirmative. Even theoretically it would be difficult to understand, indeed, why such a powerful innate instinct should not manifest its force from the beginning of human life—an instinct, whose purposeful function must be practiced both in the service of the preservation of the species and of the individualized highly differentiated means toward the attainment of pleasure, requiring a knowledge of all environmental objects. The degree to which children in the first years of life are capable of sexual tension and its discharge varies. Some authors have observed cases of orgasm-like excitation and subsequent increased sleepiness in one-year-old children. Ordinarily, however, masturbation at this age is rarely so intense. Rather it serves to bring about specifically toned pleasurable sensations and nothing else.

The origin of masturbation is plainly to be found in the sexual instinct. At first, onanism is nothing but that form of activity of the sexual instinct which corresponds to the infantile age.

The causes which lead to masturbatory activities vary according to age, environment, and the particular characteristics of the individual. The first causes are sexual stimulations induced by manipulations performed by the child on the various parts of his body for the purpose of orientation, through his sense of touch. To these stimulations, brought about by the individual himself, are added those which the persons who take care of the child habitually cause by touch and friction of the sexually excitable organs when they clean and dress the children. The manipulations of these persons are the first sexual seduction to which the child succumbs. In this way the child begins to know the source of pleasure which springs from the act of touching the sexual zones by other persons and he also learns to use this source of pleasure without arousing suspicion. These first seductions are of the greatest importance for the life of the individual. They give rise to the fact that the child makes his needs for pleasure dependent on other human beings and tries to satisfy these needs with the help of others; they plainly constitute the first and indispensable precondition for the development of affection toward human beings, i.e., for the rise of love.

Inasmuch as the secondary erogenous zones as sexually unsuspicious areas are left accessible to the child for the attainment of pleasure (and they fortunately are accessible because our antisexually oriented period does not attribute to the child any "sinful" desires) they effect the exchange of love and the discharge of sexual excitement by caressing and fondling in close contact with other human beings. However, the amount of sexual excitation discharged in this way is not enough to bring about a complete release. The child, therefore, resorts to the principal sexual zone which provides the greatest pleasure and the most complete discharge. By so doing, the child comes in conflict with his guardians who do not tolerate a manifest sexual activity of this kind and try to suppress it by the use of all available educational means. Then it will depend upon the strength of the instinctual drive whether the need for sexual pleasure or the educational measures are victorious. From this conflict results the largest part of the significance which masturbation can acquire in the life of an individual. This conflict, indeed, is not the conflict between a permitted and a non-permitted form of sexual activity. The conflict of sexuality *in nuce,* manifesting itself in masturbation, clashes with the social law which is conveyed through the prohibitions of the guardians, and later, when education is removed from the care of individuals and transferred to society, it awaits the child with reward and punishment as the old prohibition under the new name of "moral law."

The degree to which the sexual fantasies can be removed from consciousness determines the degree to which the liberated energies can be employed in the service of other functions. Part of these energies are utilized, in the form of cultural or spiritual interests, by "sublimating" them into activities of a "higher" order. But another part cathects the erogenous zones and becomes active as specific sexual pleasure without genital fantasies. In this way the erogenous zones are sensitized for corresponding libidinous objects, and the manner in which the child reacts to them determines his attitudes of sympathy and antipathy toward the persons of his environment. Objective observation shows that the child's likes and dislikes are expressed according to the same erotic reaction forms as we see them in adults. Body odor, hair color, organ contours, tenderness, etc., determine the attitude of the child toward other persons. However, inasmuch as one or several of these erogenous zones grow oversensitive for certain reasons (for instance, through a particular type of frequency or their use or through constitutional disposition) we notice in the child a spontaneous use of such a zone. The child then picks his nose, licks his lips, sucks his fingers, voluptuously touches various parts of his body, craves for strong smells, and so on. These infantile activities impress as "naughty," but they are in most cases true masturbatory acts connected with the erogenous zones, i.e., infantile precursors of perversions. Of particular significance as a precipitating factor in masturbatory activity is the sadistic-masochistic component of the sexual instinct. Through the fact that this component is related to punishment it gives rise to fantasies of inflicting or of suffering pain. The sexual nature of such fantasies does not remain concealed to the child for long. These fantasies, in fact are closely connected with definite genital excitations and their ideational content—if not already in existence—becomes the sexual fantasy *katexochen,* i.e., the genital fantasy. The child practices sadistic-masochistic masturbation by beating, biting, and scratching himself. A very common practice is that the child lies on his stomach and beats with his heels on his buttocks. Well known also is nail-biting or scratching legs and arms until blood comes.

As soon as imagination is sufficiently developed, conscious fantasies accompany the onanistic acts. They can also function as releasing agents by transferring the excitation obtained through reading, talking, or looking, to the principal genital or erogenous zone. The fantasies retain this significance also later on. Under certain conditions their use can become so independent that an interplay of such fantasies alone becomes sufficient to effect a complete discharge of the sexual excitation without any need for supporting physical manipulations. This is called *psychic onanism.* Just as the fantasied sexual aim of a masturbatory act can be unconscious, the specific fantasy which underlies the act can also be unconscious, such as a single fantasy or a combination of fantasies with a well-defined ideational content derived from the objective reality of pleasure-providing objects. The ideational content of an unconscious masturbatory fantasy can be elicited either by the individual himself—if the fantasy later becomes conscious—or by analysis of the special type of masturbatory activity.

The content of the first masturbatory fantasies centers around defecation, urination, fantasies of a masochistic and sadistic nature, as well as fantastic infantile ideas about sexual acts practiced by adults among themselves, by adults with children, and by children among themselves. It often is not easy to unmask these fantasies as sexual in nature because the fantasied pleasure objects are not always the genitals. Freud succeeded in establishing the true character of these often entirely bizarre and incomprehensible fantasies; he did so by means of the investigation of infantile sexual theories, the understanding of which frequently requires the application of Freud's method of symbolic interpretation. In this way one can invariably detect in the persons appearing in the first masturbatory fantasies—apart from the child himself—parents and nurses, as well as servants and siblings. Often enough there appear in these fantasies animals as well as inanimate objects (dolls, urinals, etc.) as objects of sexual pleasure. On the basis of my experience, I have enumerated the persons occurring in the masturbatory fantasy in the order of the frequency of their appearance. This sequence is determined by the intensity of affection which governs the child's relation to these persons. Siblings appear last in this sequence. This has its good reasons. Sibling love is a late product resulting from the habit of living together. Hate, envy, resentment, and jealousy precede sibling love. However, as soon as a child has reconciled himself to the fact that he has brothers and sisters, the siblings, in most cases, take first place in the incest fantasies. The reasons for this are obvious. Siblings are free from shame in front of each other, and provide each other with sexual notions which the child has no reason to reject since they are offered to him with the permission of the parents. If children are not intimidated, one can easily induce them to confess these fantasies at any time. If the person in charge suspects that the activities of the siblings are of a sexual nature and therefore prohibits them, the incestuous siblings fantasy nevertheless remains in force, because such fantasies are composed of real images, based on distinct sensory impressions, which are not easily erased from memory since they form part of the actual life experiences, repeated each day.

Under the impact of these more recent fantasies, the older and more remote fantasies involving the parents recede. The child's sense of the immediate present replaces in his fantasies the vague, long-past impressions connected with the parents' bedroom with the actual and well-defined ideas related to the nursery. (In neurotic regression, we notice the occurrence of the opposite process:

the present disturbing reality loses its significance for the creation of fantasies in comparison to the old childhood fantasies.)

However, in so far as children continue to derive direct and intense sexual pleasure from the parents also later on, the incestuous fantasy centering on the parents has a good chance to become fixated. This is especially the case with children who sleep with their parents. By touching, smelling, and looking, they form quite realistic ideas of the parents' importance as sources of sexual pleasure. Precisely because these ideas correspond to an actually existing reality, they prove to be as resistant to repression as the sexual fantasies about siblings. The role of servants in the sexual fantasies of children is of the utmost importance. There is little doubt that servants commit true acts of seduction much more frequently than is ordinarily supposed. On his part, however, the child uses servants to release his own sadism by identifying himself with the parents and physically attacking the servants in violent outbursts of anger. Observation teaches that on such occasions the child tries to touch preferably the buttocks, the genital region, and the stomach. On the other hand, the child takes refuge with the servants against parental severity, thus intuitively perceiving the servants' hostility toward the master and allying himself with them. Such children like to stay close to the servants, always hang around the kitchen, establish close friendships with the personnel, and gain many and highly pleasurable sexual experiences by such apparently innocent contacts.

The masturbatory fantasy not only discloses to us the incestuous sexuality of the child; it also reveals to us that the child turns his sexual cravings, without discrimination, to animate and inanimate objects, persons of his own or opposite sex. Toward the fifth to sixth year of life, however, the manifoldness of sexual reactions becomes limited in most children, and heterosexual fantasies begin to prevail. With the start of the latency period which lasts from the sixth year to prepuberty, we observe a noticeable decrease in the sexual excitability in all areas. Physical masturbation, in particular, is then less frequent and in some children ceases completely (Freud). Entering school life and the regular occupation with lessons contributes to this decline to a considerable degree. This is obviously a period of high biological importance is which final sexual maturation, concentration of the sexual desire on the genital functions, and object choice are prepared.

With the great impetus of the sexual libido in puberty, apart from a few exceptions, there occurs a resurgence of masturbation. But now it has thoroughly changed its character. It has become a conscious sexual act. As a rule, it is practiced as a temporary satisfaction of the sexual desire, as a sort of *provisorium* until a complementary sexual object is attained.

It is obvious that masturbation becomes a problem *sui generis* only at the moment when it is no longer an age-adequate sexual practice corresponding to the specific developmental stage. We must bear in mind that "age-adequate" from the viewpoint of society does not coincide with "age-adequate" from the viewpoint of the individual's development. Sexual abstinence after puberty is a cultural-pedagogical demand imposed on the normally developed individual. It is an artificial postulate which can be explained only in terms of cultural requirements but not in terms of the individual's biological development.

For the time being, during puberty and frequently even for several years longer, the phase of infantile sexuality—of masturbatory satisfaction—remains in existence simply because masturbation must continue to be the only available form of sexual activity. This is an artificial prolongation of childhood caused by social circumstances. At the same time, the gratification of sexuality through the various erogenous zones is now reduced to a minimum. All the many possibilities for discharging sexual excitation—such as kissing, fondling, caressing, and letting oneself be spoiled—which until now could be employed almost without objection, are liable to the most extreme inhibitions in puberty both by the adolescent himself and by the environment which suspects the sexual nature of his libidinous demands. The young adolescent is no longer able to ward off conscious sexual excitement resulting from what were formerly "innocent" affectionate activities, and he therefore suppresses any revealing actions under the pressure of the moral law with which he has meanwhile become acquainted.

The Effects of Masturbation

The effects of masturbation must be considered from various aspects, though it will not be possible to treat them separately. Our discussion will primarily focus on the following questions:

A. 1. The effects of the struggle to abstain from masturbation.
   2. The effects of the masturbatory activity.

B. 1. The somatic effects of masturbatory activity.
   2. The psychological and social effects of masturbation.

The Struggle to Abstain from Masturbation

This struggle occurs in two developmental phases, in the transition to the latency period and in puberty. In both phases two opposing principles are at work to achieve abstinence: a biological and a pedagogical one. The biological factor of the latency period seems to be a developmental necessity aimed at the partial elimination of sexuality for the purpose of the socialization of the individual. In fact, we observe that children who do not want to relinquish sexual pleasure during the latency period are difficult to educate, unmanageable, spiteful and moody. Their adjustment to the social environment fails to the extent to which they withdraw their libidinal component drives and affects from social regulation. It is possible that the latency period is not only a preparation for the individual's adjustment to the social order, but also for the utilization of sexuality for the attainment of a certain cultural level. Here education has actually taken over in effecting the achievement of an evolutional tendency. It is at this time that the child begins to make upon his environment the social demands which he himself has to fulfill. He also appraises sexual objects from the viewpoint of his own ego. It is as a result of this developmental phase that—with only a few exceptions—human beings subsequently attribute to the sexual object its final complementary value from a social standpoint.

The demand for abstinence from masturbation during puberty is determined by a biological factor—the necessity of object choice in the service of the preservation of the species. This factor is presented by the pedagogues in a somewhat modified way not entirely in accord with biological facts. For the cultural postulate demands abstinence from masturbation and postponement of object choice. The adolescent is to be a man by renouncing his infantile sexual activity, i.e., masturbation; at the same time, he is not to be a man because he is not supposed to choose a sexual object. The actual present situation for the adolescent is such that it offers no compensation for this renunciation. It offers only punishment for defiance of the prohibition, and strives to divert the adolescent's desires for sexual activity into "spiritual" channels.

However, the instinct is, of course, without such insight and does not respect any plans for the future. The individual is therefore bound to provide a reason for himself which, apart from the fear of either punishment or the evil consequences of masturbation, shall enable him to be abstinent, i.e., to wait. In this way the individual must "rationalize" the required abstinence, and must strive to make the objects of his desires artificially inaccessible. This is done by means of overvaluating the sexual object (Freud). The artificial overvaluation has its strongest motivating power in the qualities of the love objects themselves whom the adolescent, consciously or unconsciously would be inclined to choose at first. For these objects are distinguished by the incest taboo. The adolescent returns especially to these objects because he is prohibited from choosing other sexual objects. He obeys the command to remain a child, by reinstating the infantile love objects into their old position which they have retained in the unconscious in any event. Their effect can be curtailed only by replacing them with other objects and "transferring" the libido invested in them to other objects.

If at this time parents and siblings are not declared *sacrosanct*, they are not safe from the libidinous aggression of the adolescent. Then the quality of overevaluation and with it that of unattainability are transferred from the above-mentioned persons to other sexual objects. The adolescent has thus paralyzed his aggression in all directions. This is the birth of lyricism. Its content is longing and not gratification, as it corresponds fully to the true status of the lyricist's libido.

However, rationalized longing is still not sufficient to dispense with sexual activity by masturbation. In most people, there appear, sooner or later and to a greater or lesser degree, symptoms which indicate that masturbation is not well-tolerated. A certain sickly appearance, a distracted air, anxiety, inability to concentrate, and guilt feelings are popularly regarded as signs of masturbation.

It is certain that this syndrome remains conspicuous only for a few years and does not ordinarily carry over into adulthood. A permanent damage resulting from masturbation occurs only under certain conditions.

The Somatic Effects of Masturbation

As regards the somatic effects, apparently only the quantitative factor is important. Moderate masturbation, in the view of all authors, is harmless or even helpful. Excessive onanism adds toxic symptoms to the picture of the damaged masturbator. Moreover, it is likely that the frequent pollutions following excessive masturbation are caused by an organic weakening of the secretory and nervous systems, and that in this way so-called physical impotence results in extreme cases. In our civilization, however, a purely toxic neurosis on a masturbatory basis—termed by Freud *actual neurosis*—cannot, in my opinion, be found as such. In order to study this type fully, one would have to find an environment completely devoid of civilization, where masturbation is practiced excessively and where no psychogenic disturbances connected with the moral law are complicated by the purely toxic ones of masturbation. In this respect, there exist some observations from African countries which seem to indicate that extremely excessive masturbation, practiced over a period of many years, can lead to mental deterioration.

The Psychological Effects of Masturbation

From a psychological viewpoint the effects of masturbation must be ascribed partly to the masturbatory activity and partly to the struggle for abstinence. The most striking factor among the effects of masturbation, etiologically as well as symptomatologically, is anxiety.

Anxiety

Anxiety arises whenever abreaction of the sexual excitation is quantitatively incomplete or qualitatively inadequate (Freud). In each case there remains an undischarged amount of excitation which manifests itself as anxiety, is converted into anxiety, or produces anxiety. It cannot be determined here which of these formulations can be applied in the case of anxiety arising out of the damming-up of libido. The facts are that most people react with anxiety to incomplete sexual gratification or to abstinence in the case of an overly strong libidinal drive. The rise of anxiety as a result of abstinence from masturbation in childhood cannot be regarded as specific for onanism, since onanism is the form of sexual activity corresponding to that very age. Only at a period when adequate and masturbatory sexual activities should become differentiated, can we observe the specific anxiety produced by onanism.

Since we empirically postulate an excess amount of undischarged excitation for the development of anxiety, the question now arises in what way masturbation during puberty and at a later age can bring about full sexual satisfaction. The answer is this: it depends on the degree to which the libido has progressed toward object choice and also on the extent to which the perversions which have developed in a given case are gratified by masturbation.

If at the time of masturbation the discrepancy between the developmental-libidinal phase and the actually possible form of sexual gratification is so great that the individual demands with sufficient force another object for intercourse, yet has to resort to his own body, no full sexual satisfaction can be expected from masturbation, and anxiety is bound to develop as a natural reaction to it.

Whenever, during puberty, the libido is still at the infantile stage of development and the individual still is psychologically autoerotic at that time, masturbation is the adequate type of sexual activity. It will allow a complete discharge of the libidinous excitation and anxiety will not develop. This case, however, has two important exceptions: masturbation can fail as an adequate means of gratification after puberty, despite the persistence of psychic infantilism, whenever the organism is overstimulated by excessive abuse and a toxic actual neurosis has developed. Second, whenever the fantasy accompanying masturbation is connected with a perversion that cannot be replaced by the fantasy as such (for instance, olfactory perversion without the capacity for olfactory hallucination).

From the coincidence of masturbation with a certain stage of libidinal development result the following possibilities for a harmful effect of onanism:

Feelings of Guilt

Anxiety, first a free-floating feeling of insecurity and oppression, is rationalized, i.e., it is bound to an idea, the anxiety-producing significance of which has validity before the judging conscience. This idea is derived from the punishment complex, and is directly related to experiences of early childhood which were determined by the child's sadistic instinctual impulses. Anxiety bound in this way constitutes the feeling of guilt. The content of the guilty feeling can be separated, according to the analyses made by me, into a series of formulae in which the conscious parts could be successively replaced by unconscious ones (in parentheses) in the following way:

"I feel guilty because I have debased something very high (because I commit incest in my masturbatory fantasy, or debase the sanctity of the woman by my sexual fantasy)."

"I feel guilty because I am so weak and constantly give in to the stimulation (because later on I shall come to women in a weakened condition and women will despise me. They will ask me: Where is your virility for which we have been waiting?)."

"I feel guilty without knowing why. I am a sinner (I expect punishment for having defied the prohibition of incest)."

"I have always felt guilty, even as a child (but only when I had done something bad or had fantasied bad wishes against the parents. I always was afraid they could guess my thoughts and punish me)."

"I feel guilty before mother (I wanted to overcome father, to replace him vis-à-vis mother, and now he remains the victor, because I am no man; I am only a boy, and my mother only respects a real man)."

"I feel guilty before father (I have always wanted to be like father. Father indeed always expected this of me. I shall disappoint his hopes and I shall not be able to take his place in the family)."

The content of guilt feelings resulting from these formulae is derived from childhood, and has attached itself to masturbation, because masturbation, like those childhood "sins," represents a forbidden rebellion, a selfish abuse of higher values. The content of the feelings of guilt represent a real guilt vis-à-vis an unconscious demand. This demand was first made by the parents in earliest childhood; subsequently the child identified himself with the parents, whereby the demands of the parents became his own demands. But the child is not conscious of the fact that these are demands, he is aware merely of the wish to be the person whom the—by now already unconscious—demands of the parents required him to be. After the socialization of the ego has taken place, the requirements become the "idealized" demand, i.e., it is attributed to an idea which is nothing but the father acting in the unconscious, yet stripped of the personal quality. The mother acting in the unconscious is replaced by the "ideal love." The old punishment, too, reappears. It comes to the fore in the form of threatening harmful consequences if the forbidden pleasures are indulged in. But it must be emphasized that I have found guilt feelings only where masturbation does not give full satisfaction and where as a result anxiety developed. Conversely, I could see that there was no feeling of guilt in masturbation whenever it provided full satisfaction.

Damage to Object Choice

It is in the nature of masturbation that the masturbator derives the entire amount of pleasure from his own body, and that the latter is the object of his sexual desires. Masturbation is the autoerotic form of sexuality. As a manifestation of infantile sexuality it is a normal phenomenon corresponding to the developmental period in which it occurs, i.e., as long as the demand to socialize the sexual instincts does not exist. This demand confronts the individual from two sides, from within and from without. From within, it manifests itself as a postulate of an animal species which has individuals of two different sexes. The species requires, in the interest of its self-preservation, that individuals gratify their sexual needs not by using their own body but by intercourse with individuals of the opposite sex, with the aim of propagation. From without, the demand for socialization of the sexual instinct is fulfilled by the prohibition of autoerotic gratification. In this manner, the individual unconsciously becomes aware of the fact that other persons have a claim on him as regards his sexual activity, that he is responsible to others for this activity, and that he has no right to indulge in sexual pleasure for personal and selfish purposes only.

Object choice is delayed or completely put aside by masturbation. It is true that this delay first serves a cultural demand but only up to a certain point, which, though it varies considerably, usually coincides with the twentieth year of life. Beyond this age, the delay of object choice must be considered as an abnormal manifestation. The following factors, either acting together or separately, contribute to the delay of object choice:

Where onanism provides full satisfaction it perpetuates and fixates infantilism. The individual has no reason to compete with others for a sexual object since he finds all sources of pleasure easily within himself. *Omnis sua secum portat.*

When the individual is later faced with the demand to choose an object—a demand imposed by his own ego—the aggression necessary for the acquisition of an object has not been sufficiently put in to practice yet and may by that time be so damaged that it is inadequate to the task at hand.

If there is enough aggression present—and various supportive environmental factors—to win an object, the outcome may be that the libido remains invested in the individual's own body just the same; in this case the sexual object has not been able to divert the pleasure which the masturbator has gained from his own body. He then rightly likens masturbation to full-fledged coitus and coitus to masturbation.

The significance of masturbatory fantasies for the inhibition of object choice is great. First of all, any reality compared to the perfection of the fantasied images must necessarily appear as a poor and inadequate substitute for masturbation. The fantasy thus bars the masturbator from reality. When he approaches the object, he becomes intolerant of the unavoidable shortcomings of corporeity because he has "spoiled" his libido by the masturbatory fantasy. Moreover, the fantasy furnishes to the masturbator perverted ideas which activate the infantile affects of perversion. In this way a perversion which could well have been repressed through normal and timely sexual activity can be fixated by masturbation. Masturbation thus becomes the bridge which leads to neurosis.

Masturbation undoes the subordination of homosexuality to heterosexuality required by the species, and makes each of these sexual components independent by means of the fantasy. In this process, homosexuality unconsciously becomes hypertrophic, because it finds a real substratum for its activity in the individual's own genitals. The individual gradually develops an enormous interest in his own genital. In some cases I have observed, this interest went so far that the genitals were completely personified, i.e., they were treated like real persons. Some masturbators carry on conversations with their genitals, call them "the little one," or "the little son," or "the little friend," and thank them for their loyalty, generosity, etc. Some individuals are really in love with their genitals. It is not surprising that in so strong an infantile attitude the boastfulness concerning the genitals leads to exhibitionism. Moreover, it is easy to understand that such a braggart also wants to see other genitals of the same sex, partly to get satisfaction out of the fact that his genitals impress others, and partly to convince himself that his fear concerning the inadequacy of his genitals is without foundation. In these cases, masturbation causes the growth of narcissism to the highest degree by means of the exhibitionistic and voyeuristic components of the sexual instinct. When this late form of an infantile developmental phase is reached at a time when a full and unselfish appraisal of the objective world is required from the individual, the masturbator has also become inadequate in his relation to human society from the standpoint of his own ego. Narcissism liberates sadism; the narcissistic person becomes cruel because the suffering of others augments his self-confidence and flatters his vanity.

However, the narcissism which is produced by masturbation at puberty is not a pure product. We must not forget that we are dealing here with a pseudo infantilism and that the uncritical attitude to oneself has meanwhile been transformed, at least in part, to a critical one by the school, and by the example set by the environment. We thus find that the masturbating narcissist, after puberty, is permeated with self-distrust, regret, and self-reproaches deep down in his heart. The treatment of the damaged masturbator has to be approached from this angle.

Another circumstance which can become fatal for the future love life of the masturbator lies in the fact that in libidinous activities, masturbation directs the individual's exclusive attention to the genitals. I have often heard masturbators who thought of their form of sexual activity as a sort of evil *provisorium*, express the opinion that they could be cured by intercourse. Analysis showed that they thought only of female genitals. It became clear that the whole striving of these individuals was directed to the conquest of female genitals and not to that of a woman in her total personality. It further became clear that the central position held by the genitals in the minds of such individuals can determine the fate of the love life of the onanist. By virtue of making the genitals dominant, he loses his inner relation to the total personality of the woman. The perversions which were partly repressed and partly autoerotically or homosexually fixated by the fantasy are no longer available to the onanist in a heterosexual relationship. They cannot be brought into the foreplay, cannot fulfill their role as carriers of sexual forepleasure, and cannot add their own amount of excitation toward perfecting the sexual act. The onanist cannot wait. He is anxious for the immediate climax because to him the road to coitus is nothing but joyless avidity. Thus, the masturbatory coitus results in a disappointment of all illusions about the glorious nature of the female. The undischarged amount of sexual excitation produces anxiety, feelings of guilt and depression, the *tristitia post coitum*. More impoverished than ever, the onanist leaves the partner and, if he simultaneously gives up the hope for improvement, he returns again to masturbation. The desire to conquer a female genital and the simultaneous lack of inner relation to the woman as a person drives the onanist, at too early a stage, to prostitutes.

The rationalized disappointment in the woman may find its expression in cynicism. The onanist who uses a woman as an onanist does—i.e., who regards the whole woman as a female genital because he himself is only in love with his genital whose dominant position he has cultivated—is bound to consider love as a fraud. Since a partner cannot offer him more than he can offer himself, he proclaims that sexual intercourse is but individual pleasure devoid of any higher idea. With this, the social value of sexuality declines and the female becomes an object of lust to satisfy the sexual hunger in the same way that devouring satisfies the need for food. This withdrawal of personal feelings from the complexity of social and sublimated values is the essence of cynicism. The same man who has but contempt for love, because it serves him only as a means of self-satisfaction, shows by this that he only respects social values in the unconscious mind and that cynicism is but a symptom of his incapacity to perform a higher synthesis of the instinctual components with the partner. As a counterpart to this phenomenon one often hears masturbation referred to as "foolish" because "it doesn't give joy to anyone except the onanist himself, though another person could also derive pleasure from it."

As regards human society, masturbation produces three essentially destructive factors: By fixating autoerotism and damaging a man's self-respect, it diminishes his capacity for competition. By perpetuating psychic infantilism, it undermines the sovereign position of the man in public life and in the family. By damaging potency, which develops as a physiological result if masturbation is practiced too early and too often, and finally by damaging the perversion-synthesis, love life is impoverished, and enormous disappointments for women ensue. In all probability, the masturbation of men can be considered as a substantial factor in the rise of the feminist movement for emancipation.

We now come to the last question, namely, the conditions under which masturbation becomes permanently injurious. No doubt a relatively poor constitutional resistance is to be regarded as responsible for the onset and extent of the damage.

This constitutional factor has to be considered in the etiology of the masturbatory damage. Neither the specific nature nor the extent of its influence, however, can be fully determined in the development of the damage. There is no reason, furthermore, to deviate from the empirical principle that weakness or strength of a constitution is only a relative concept, measured by the magnitude of the demands which are made upon it. A constitution becomes inadequate for maintaining the individual euphoria only when the demands of the environment surpass the range of its capacity. The disease develops on the basis of this relative insufficiency whenever the individual tries to adapt himself to the excessive demand but fails in the struggle for adaptation. The disease is the symptom of a miscarried attempt at adaptation.

The conditions responsible for the development of damages through onanism may therefore be sought in the environmental circumstances of the individual. And it can hardly be regarded as a coincidence that all the eighteen cases on which the views presented here are based, show in certain respects the same environmental constellation. The children's upbringing in these families was characterized by a tendency to prevent the children from acquiring an honest understanding of the nature and importance of sexuality. The fathers in these families all had similar character traits: they were prudish and oversensitive to any expression of sexuality; they were domineering and much concerned with emphasizing their paternal position; they considered it a dogmatic necessity to appear to the children as unapproachable, perfect persons. Most of all, however, these families clearly aimed at deceiving the children concerning the sexuality of adults.

If we now return to our assertion that the growth of masturbatory damage is determined by the development of the ego at the time of masturbation, we can see that we have found in this particular milieu the factor which keeps sexuality artificially at an infantile level. At the onset of puberty, then, masturbation is coupled with the infantile incestuous fantasies.

In the meantime, however, the ego has progressed to that point of development which is sufficient for the regulation of social relations in accordance with the child's age. At the same time, the ego proves inadequate for the integration of sexuality into the social pattern because the sexuality available to the ego has remained socially useless and infantile. In order to bring this retarded sexuality to an adequate maturation, the ego would first have to legitimize it.

It is obvious that the ego cannot fulfill its regulating function vis-à-vis sexuality if the incestuous fantasies are unconscious. When the latter become conscious, the ego can normally reduce their significance, because the adolescent knows that the incest barrier cannot be overcome and that the incestuous fantasy cannot be realized. Since incest must be renounced and the libido cannot remain without an object, it is then transferred to other objects.

At this point, masturbation as well can be given up; for the adolescent now has a chance to attain a love object, though at some later date, and he preserves himself for real object love. It is a well-known fact that masturbation is given up in most cases when an individual falls in love. One could expect, therefore, that as soon as the incestuous fantasy becomes conscious and still more so, as soon as object choice occurs, masturbation is given up. Nevertheless, in pathological cases, onanism continues and produces the above-described damages by its perseverence.

I have found in these cases that masturbation is the expression of an unconscious rebellion against the father. It is a compromise between the ego and sexuality. This could be formulated in the following way: Father wants me to remain a child by preserving my infantile sexuality. But my father is wrong in forcing infantilism upon me. I masturbate to spite him, and it will be his fault if I should suffer any damage from it.

In confirmation of this view, I may point out that masturbation was given up as soon as the unconscious sadism against the father was uncovered and terminated. I saw onanism recur after intervals of many years when the individual was again thrown into an infantile passive role against an authoritative social milieu. Analysis showed that this passivity had all the characteristics of that helplessness in which the individual originally found himself vis-à-vis the father, and that the compelling situation contains the same tendency which the father wanted to enforce against the will of the boy.

An environment where the children are kept in fear and submission, where false ideas about sexuality and its importance are engendered, and where the naiveté of infantile sexual manifestations is combatted with an intensity which can no longer be excused by lack of understanding alone—it is this sort of environment that I have found in the eighteen cases on which these observations were made.

This type of milieu is thoroughly prone to breed artificial infantilism and to expose the child, helpless and without support, to the libidinous storms of puberty. It is in this semidarkness, artificially produced by education, that fantasy and the secret lust for forbidden pleasures flourish, and from which there is no escape. Communication with the correcting and regulating forces of the outer world is blocked "for reasons of morality."

The rebellion against this environmental pressure feeds the sadistic component which, however, the adolescent can turn only against himself. Devoid of any power, what else should he do but turn his libido toward his own body? And if this is not the proper thing, if he cannot liberate himself any more, if he does not find the ways which he has never come to know—what does it matter to those moralistic, faultless, disciplinarian asexual educators?

Notes

1. The instinct of self-preservation must be credited with the creation of consciousness which came into being as the organ of temporal distance perception. Orientation in time (i.e., contemporaneousness and succession) is identical with the perception of the sequence of images and affects—that is, with the perception of inner processes. Hence, consciousness is an organ for the perception of the individual's own psychic processes. In the service of self-preservation it creates the consciousness of the self, the consciousness of the individual's own unique existence, which has distinct boundaries in relation to all other individuals, and which is a unit of self-preservation in the species. The ego, therefore, is a representative concept for all those functions by which an individual endeavors to secure the preservation of his own unique existence. Inasmuch as this representative concept has been based on the reality of self-preservation, the ego becomes the regulating principle of all of the individual's relations to the external world. In this sense we are justified to speak of the group of ego instincts, in the case of the entire group of instincts which serve self-preservation, in contradistinction to the sexual instinct.

2

Compensation As a Means of Discounting the Motive of Repression

I

Freud's discovery that forgetting ideas is invariably motivated by some painful affect accompanying them suggests the correlated problem: how is it that repressed ideas re-enter consciousness at the end of a series of free associations? Is it possible that during the process of association a repressed idea loses its painful tone, or is it that the painful affect loses its quality as a motive for repression? Looked at from this angle, the problem is seen to be a general psychobiological one; and the answer in accordance with the teaching of Freud would run as follows: the subject accepts a lesser pain—namely, that which is involved in reproducing the repressed idea—in order to avoid the greater pain which would follow from frustration of the mental activity already undertaken. Where psychic parapraxes (blunders) are concerned, occurring in normal persons whose thinking processes are consciously directed to an end, we may certainly assume that the impulsion towards uninterrupted mental functioning is sufficiently strong to overcome the resistance to recollecting the repressed ideas that should make their appearance in the train of thought. The parallel with neurosis is self-evident. There it is the burden of the illness which acts as an incentive to recovery and therefore to the relaxation of the repression. In every case we see that the avoid-

Published in the *Internationale Zeitschrift für Psychoanalyse*, Bd. I. 1913.

ance of pain which is the aim of repression is relative; the overcoming of the resistance must be regarded as due to a relative discounting of the impulse to repression in consequence of a threat of greater pain resulting from frustration of a mental activity consciously directed towards an end. The pleasure which recompenses the overcoming of the resistance consists in the increase of mental power that accrues from having at one's disposal some idea indispensable to the particular train of thought. The "pain" which the resistance was designed to banish becomes a means of attaining pleasure and that which produces pleasure is in itself of the nature of pleasure, even though it may be accompanied by distress: there is even such a thing as painful pleasure.[1]

From a purely psychological point of view the problem lies in the fact that the reproduction of the repressed idea is preceded by a *definite number* of associations terminating when that idea emerges; so that we have before us a certain definite amount of material to be investigated, in which we may expect that both mechanisms—that of repression and that of the removal of the repression—will be represented and exposed. In other words: the question is why the forgotten idea makes its appearance just at that particular point rather than at another, i.e. at the end of a longer or shorter chain of associations. Since we have referred the forgetting of the idea to the influence of the affect it arouses, we must also bring its emergence into consciousness into relation with this particular affect.

There must be some *motive* for the admission of the affect into consciousness at that particular point in the series of associations, and, moreover, in a specifically psychic activity the motive must be a psychological one. During the process of association something quite definite must have happened to the affect to enable it to re-enter consciousness at a given point in the series of associations. In other words: we have to look for the psychological representative of that relative discounting of the motive for repression which has taken place. Obviously, biological assumptions of the existence of a mechanism designed to preserve a state of euphoria will not serve here. At this point the essential difference becomes clear between the two modes of thought in psychology—the biologizing and the psycho-analytic. The choice of psychic reactions which are admitted to consciousness—a choice which lies with the endopsychic censorship—does not in the first instance depend upon the value of these reactions for social intercourse or for orientation in regard to the outside world. The work of censorship is conducted on a principle for which the social capacities of the individual are only of a conditional value. Otherwise it would be inexplicable that ideas which are generally at our disposal automatically may suddenly be reft away from a train of thought directed towards a certain end; or that, often in spite of close concentration, the train of thought proposed is invaded by ideas which show that the notion that the individual is tending to the achievement of a state of euphoria is purely illusory. On the contrary, the principle which determines the capacity or incapacity of ideas to enter consciousness is the criterion of pleasure or pain, and this is altogether conditioned by the laws of the individual's psychic development, a correlative in the single individual of the evolution of human instincts. And so it may happen that the endopsychic censorship is guided in its choice of ideas by a prinicple which has no currency in the conscious, socially-determined economy of the mind.

II

These reflections followed on an observation made: namely, that in a series of associations there occurs in very many cases, immediately before the reproduction of a forgotten idea, an association which is accompanied by a pleasurable affect. This pleasurable idea is of such a kind as to restore in anticipation, so to speak, the self-esteem of the subject which must suffer a blow from the subsequent reproduction of the repressed idea. The subject *compensates* himself, so to speak, before he reveals the fact which lowers his self-esteem. It is as if he tried to brace himself against the distress he anticipates by emphasizing encouraging factors, and by a cheering contemplation of himself he robs of its sting the pain he is about to experience. This compensation has the effect of discounting the motive for repression and weakening the resistance against the painful reproduction of the idea, so that he finally succumbs to the tendency to continue the train of thought without interruption. Let me give some examples to illustrate my points.

A

I was discussing with H. the question of sexual life in present-day civilization. He began to tell me about the time when he first learnt the existence of a system of paid prostitution. "When I was sixteen years old," he said, " a schoolfellow told me that there were women of that sort in . . . I can't remember the name of the street my schoolfellow mentioned." Upon my encouraging him to arrive at the forgotten idea by means of free association, he produced the following series of associations:

1. "It was the name of a battle." Three names then occurred to him in the following order, none of them being the name he was trying to recall:
2. "Lissa, Custozza, Canossa."
3. "The name of the victor at Lissa was Tegetthoff; there is a monument to him in one of the municipal divisions of Vienna. In the same district there is also a street called the Custozzagasse."
4. "At Lissa and Custozza the Italians were defeated by the Austrians. It occurs to me that the professor who taught us history in the lower forms of the *Gymnasium* always represented the Italians as the embittered enemies of Austria."
5. "Not long ago I remarked to a woman fellow-student, who thought I was an anti-feminist, that in the matter of the emancipation of women I had long since gone to Canossa."
6. "The phrase 'to go to Canossa' means to ask pardon, to humble oneself. The historical incident at Canossa then occurs to me: the Pope standing on the balcony with the Duchess Mathilde and King Henry IV of Bourbon[2] down below barefoot in the snow."
7. "Tannhäuser had to go barefooted on a pilgrimage to Rome."
8. "The Venusberg in the opera *Tannhäuser*."
9. "The Ninth Symphony."
10. 'Seid umschlungen Millionen.' [Be folded in this embrace, ye millions.] The quotation is from Schiller—the phrase also has a voluptuous sound."
11. "Schiller's line 'Ein Schlachten war's, nicht eine Schlacht zu nennen.' [It was no battle but a butchery.]."
12. "I wrote this sentence to a fellow-student instead of giving her news of my examination. As a matter of fact I was very nearly ploughed in that examination."

At this point H.'s expression of concentration suddenly changed (I must explain that he had just stood for an examination in medicine) and the tension of his mental condition came to an end with the reproduction of the forgotten idea: the street was called Novaragasse; it is in the district I mentioned.

The forgotten name for which he had hunted had thus come to light. The first thing was to test its affective tone for H.

Questioned as to this he gave the following information:

"When my schoolfellow told me that there were prostitutes in the Novaragasse, I paid a visit to that street. An old prostitute in dirty clothing accosted me, calling me 'Bubi' [German: *Bube*, a boy]. I did not know that even grown-up men were addressed thus and so took the word to be a reflection on my youthful appearance. My manly pride was deeply wounded, the more so because I could not but admit the justice of the criticism. This feeling, combined with the shyness natural to my years and the consciousness of treading a forbidden path, turned my first sally on the battlefield of love into a complete rout. The effect was enhanced by the disgust with which the women inspired me. I did not answer her, but made off hastily. It was a very disagreeable experience. But I appeared to myself in a very interesting light afterwards, though I was not quite clear about what had happened."

When the forgotten idea was reproduced it turned out to be accompanied by a painful affect. The connection between the various associations was shown on analysis to be the following:

The name of an Italian town where a battle took place.

The names of three Italian towns, two of which have given their names to battles (Lissa, Custozza).

The victor at Lissa was called Tegetthoff.

The Tegetthoff monument in a certain district of Vienna.

The Custozzagasse in the same district.

Lissa and Custozza—Austrian victories over the Italians.

Enmity of the Italians towards the Austrians. This fact learnt at school.

Conversation with a woman fellow-student (school).

The subject of the emancipation of women.

Use of the phrase " to go to Canossa."

At Canossa a king (a leader of armies, a soldier) abased himself before the Pope (ecclesiastical over-lord) and before a (royal, emancipated) woman (who was a duchess and so fully emancipated that she carried on a love relation with the Pope).

The king's name was Henry IV of Bourbon.

The king stood barefooted before the Pope of Rome.

Tannhäuser went barefoot to the Pope of Rome.

Tannäuser visited the Venusberg. In the Venusberg there was sensual indulgence and this was forbidden—forbidden by the Pope. He who transgresses the prohibition—command—of the Pope—over-lord—is punished—humiliated—must ask forgiveness. Both Henry IV and Tannäuser rebelled against the command and therefore had to abase themselves barefoot before the Pope.

The story of Tannhäuser was set to music—the first act is called the Venusberg—the music is voluptuous.

The Ninth Symphony is voluptuous music.

The words of it are: "Be folded in this embrace, ye millions." To embrace means to take into one's arms, i.e. in a voluptuous, erotic sense.

The words are by Schiller, so too the line "It was no battle but a butchery." This line comes from the *Jungfrau von Orleans*. The Jungfrau was a war-like women who killed men—butchered them.

The line is of a voluptuous nature. To be butchered by a woman would afford a voluptuous gratification. (See below on the subject of masochism.)

This verse also states that the Maid butchered her foes. Men—Englishmen, soldiers—were defeated by a woman—an emancipated war-like woman.

I am a soldier, in my first year of service. I am a man who is always overthrown by women. This is because I have no aggressive tendencies, for I am a masochist and with every woman I assume the passive role. Women do not like this attitude; they despise it. I require a woman who does not despise it but seeks for it. In my circle a woman of this sort would most probably be an emancipated woman, possibly a student or a colleague.

It is on account of my lack of courage where women are concerned that I cannot win any woman's love. Other men all succeed in their wooing; I alone fail. This depresses me and takes away all my self-confidence. The lack of self-confidence manifests itself in other departments of my life as well. I am afraid of professors and examinations. At the last examination I was so much distracted by nervousness that I very nearly failed. Nevertheless I did pass. I was very glad about this. If a man has succeeded in the field of intellect he may succeed in pleasing an emancipated woman; so that possibly success of this sort might lead to my winning a wife.

I quoted Schiller's line to a fellow-student, instead of telling her how the examination went. As a matter of fact I did immediately use the first success which came my way to make myself seem desirable to a woman. The fact of passing the examination encouraged me in my relation towards women.

I hope that in future I shall not be so much inhibited by my masochistic tendencies as I was that time when I was still a young boy in the Novaragasse, treading forbidden paths, submissive to women, lacking self-confidence and the instinct of aggression.[3]

Association 12 brings the compensation, the consolation for confessing the need for consolation. Its content is a restoration of the self-esteem which had suffered a blow in the incident in the Novaragasse. It acts as an antidote to the motive for repression, and permits restitution of the memory by setting the greater strength of the present and better hope for the future against the weak and feeble past. The significance of the compensating association comes out even more clearly in the following supplementary remark: "That incident certainly did not affect my future at all decisively. I really was only a boy at the time, the woman couldn't take me seriously. Besides, I did not like her either."

B

Frau M. had put ten kronen into her purse one evening. The next morning the bank-note had vanished. At first she thought she had mislaid the money and instituted a search in every possible place, but without success. She then thought the servant might have taken it; but the rest of the family would not hear of such a suspicion and suggested that Frau M. might have spent the money and forgotten about it. Frau M. denied this possibility most emphatically. She described exactly when and how she had got the money, how afterwards she had only gone from the kitchen into the bedroom, and who had been in the room before she went to sleep—in short, it was out of the question that the money could have disappeared in any other way than by being stolen. She spent the day in a state of ill-humour and annoyance, constantly tormented by the thought that even in one's own house one has no security against thieves. In this mood she left the house towards evening to make some purchases. She returned home beaming with joy, though at the same time ashamed. Everything, she said, was explained; she knew all about it, she had done the maid an injustice. What had happened was this: she had met a Galician Rabbi whom she disliked so much on account of his unpleasant behaviour and his meanness that she was glad when he left her. What at last he had taken his leave she could not help saying to her companion: "I really am glad to get rid of that creature." The moment she gave vent to her ill-humour, a sudden disconnected thought occurred to her: she had given the ten-kronen-note the evening before to a Turkish teacher as his fee for the religious instruction he had given to her children.

The following facts came to light in analysis. Frau M.'s children had formerly received religious instruction from the religious instructor belonging to the official Jewish community. Frau M., however, was dissatisfied with his method of teaching. She bluntly called it "Galician," a word which she used to imply a whole complex of disagreeable qualities in her husband's relatives which she found intolerable. The only way to withdraw the children from this religious instruction was to transfer to the Turkish congregation.[4] There were, however, two reasons for hesitation. In the first place her husband must know nothing about it and in the second place she would have to pay the Turkish instructor a separate fee, whilst the official religious instructor was included in the school fees. The secrecy as well as the extra expenditure created very unpleasant situations for Frau M. As it was, she knew that her husband's relatives had often suspected her of disingenuousness and of extravagant tendencies. And now it seemed that their criticisms would be justified! There was nothing for it, however; in Frau M.'s opinion the worst thing of all was this religious instructor. And so she did what she felt herself compelled to do; she transferred the children without any authorization to the Turkish congregation and used the housekeeping money to pay for the religious instruction. But the situation she then found herself in was most uncomfortable and caused her self-reproach, for it could not be justified "perfectly simply." Here we have the motive for her forgetting that she had paid the Turkish teacher his fees. But when the following day Frau M. met another Galician Rabbi who was a most glaring illustration of the qualities she hated, which had caused her to leave the former teacher, her conflict came to an end: she had been right, perfectly right; anything was allowable in order to free oneself from such creatures. Her husband's relatives might say what they liked about her lack of straightforwardness and her extravagance. And no sooner did this compensating thought occur to her, constituting as it did a justification and a satisfaction, than the forgotten idea came back.

In some analyses the compensating thought does not form part of the chain of associations. In certain of these cases one can discover that it did come into consciousness, nevertheless, but was suppressed. It is then produced subsequently, when the patient is questioned or spontaneously in the form of an excuse. Nor is compensation lacking, moreover, in the analysis of the neuroses. Here it often appears just as plainly and at the same point as in the analyses of psychic parapraxes in normal persons. Often, however, it disguises itself in a peculiar form of resistance, namely, that in which the patient endeavours to get the better of the analyst, to prove that he has made a mistake or to make him feel the patient's superiority. When this happens it complicates the mechanism of compensation in the analysis of a neurosis, because in this way not only is the physician depreciated but the incentive to the patient to tell everything is weakened. Often it is only the pressure of the illness which succeeds in breaking down this resistance. At such decisive moments the compensating association is sometimes to be observed immediately before the one which is being looked for. This may explain the fact that repressions are so often suddenly removed when the patient has given the physician 'a bit of his mind.' Nevertheless it sometimes happens that the resistance is overcome at a single blow when the analyst suggests the compensating thought to the patient in an appropriate manner and at the right point.[5]

III

In therapeutic psycho-analysis we see clearly that the discounting of the motive in repression is often effected so radically that patients can give vent to the most distressing and dangerous ideas unaccompanied by any affect whatsoever, so that their uttering them remains quite without value for the purposes psycho-analysis has in view. Now in such cases there is one definite pathological type in which any sort of compensation is entirely lacking, whilst a second type is characterized by the megalomaniac nature of the compensating thoughts. The first type belongs to the schizophrenic (or according to Freud, the paraphrenic) syndrome, the second to the paranoiac. In my opinion it is possible from a certain point of view to discriminate two different kinds of discounting process in the specific mechanism of the symptoms in these two diseases. Freud once remarked[6] that in dementia præcox the discounting of the motive for repression proceeds from the patient's displacement of the painful affect from the idea of which he has to speak on to another idea, so that he can give associations entirely free from affect. This statement of Freud's is fully corroborated by the fact that patients suffering from dementia præcox at times exhaust their frenzy in symbolic actions and ideas accompanied by enormously violent affective disturbance, yet revealing the true meaning of this symbolism, however terrible it may be, with a stony calm. They have in fact attached the affect to the symbol. That part of their ego which conducts communications with the outside world remains free from guilt. The sufferer from paranoia, on the other hand, who has projected outwards the unconscious inner processes so that they encounter his 'social' ego in objective fashion, protects himself against the onslaught of the painful unconscious idea by opposing to it a compensating idea of a megalomaniac nature. All these considerations must here be included under the higher common principle of narcissism. In every instance it is narcissism which represents for the morbid psyche the element in it that still has a capacity for life; it is the patient's narcissism which is defended against the dissociated affects which threaten it from the unconscious and it is for that same narcissism that compensation is designed. The sufferer from dementia can do without the formal achievement of compensation because by the process of introversion he has drawn the whole world into the domain of his narcissism and finds his recompense in this identification.

Notes

1. The masochistic principle which is visible in this mechanism requires to be discussed separately as part of the psychology of masochism.
2. As a matter of fact it was Henry IV, the Salian, not of Bourbon, who went to Canossa. This mistake in history was explained in the course of analysis, but it need not be discussed here, as it is irrelevant to the subject.
3. In this example it is interesting to note that the forgotten idea 'Novaragasse' is related, as regards its content, to every link in the chain of association. Novara is the name of an Italian town, where a battle took place, in which the Italians were defeated by the Austrians. The street is in a certain district of Vienna, close to the monument of the victor of Lissa and to the Custozzagasse. Austria's enmity towards Italy is a fact recollected from schooldays and the recollection is affectively toned. (The significance of the idea 'school' as a line of association is further determined by the associations: schoolfellow, a woman colleague, emancipation of women and examination.) H. had had a love adventure in the Novaragasse, like Tannhäuser in the Venusberg, by forbidden paths. He suffered a defeat there, as the Italians did at the hands of the Austrians and the English at those of the Maid of Orleans, a humiliation like that of Tannhäuser in Rome and Henry IV at Canossa. He longed for sensual pleasures as described in the opera *Tannhäuser* and indicated by the words of the Ninth Symphony (and their sound). Love, defeat, humiliation and lack of courage come from H.'s masochistic tendencies and from the fact that to be slain by dominating women like the Duchess Mathilde and the Maid of Orleans would be quite in accordance with his phantasies. These phantasies were at their height at the time of the incident of the Novaragasse, and H. blames them for his lack of success in love-affairs. A schoolfellow told him about the Novaragasse, where prostitutes (i.e. women emancipated from the moral law) make a trade of sensual pleasures. The emancipated type of woman is the last possible refuge for the masochist. Again, he told a woman fellow-student, i.e. an emancipated woman, of his submission to the idea of the emancipation of women and also about his success in his examination which he hoped would act as a passport to her favour, as he possessed no other means of forwarding his suit. His weakness in the sphere of love found compensation in his self-esteem in the sphere of intellect, just as on the occasion of his adventure in the Novaragasse when he tried to make capital for his

self-regarding feelings out of an incident not calculated to enhance them and in his own eyes played the part of hero in an interesting affair.

4. The Turkish congregation is composed of Jews who have emigrated from Turkey and Bosnia.
5. I think this explanation brings the mechanism of defiance and of the masculine protest, described byAlfred Adler, into its true place: It is the *form* imposed by the ego in which the conflict of the instincts is fought out. Like everything else to do with logic its importance for character and neurosis is secondary.
6. When this paper was discussed at a meeting of the Vienna Psycho-Analytical Society.

3

A Contribution to the Psychology of Child Sexuality

When attempting to gather information on the subject of the sexuality of children, one should not overlook the fact that their communicativeness in these matters is a qualified one, even with the greatest possible confidence in their parents. In spite of the gentlest handling, the process of weaning them from their infantile sexual activities has as result a certain amount of taboo upon everything relating to sexuality. This is, moreover, reinforced by two factors; the first is that pointed silence about everything which has to do with sexuality, which is broken only on particular occasions; the second is the unequivocal exclusion from school of everything to do with sexuality. The results of most psycho-analytical attempts with children teach that even in the frankest children these resistances are still strong enough to lead to a toning-down and a falsification of their communications. Apart from this, there is the fact that in the family life of schoolchildren who have already learnt to be clean and to behave properly there is hardly ever occasion to institute an examination into their sexual phantasies without running the danger of isolating to a pronounced degree the child's attention upon sexual things. This risk is avoided when the children are enabled to reveal their sexual phantasies in the course of a personal account, which is different, apparently harmless, and at the same time interesting, as is possible during the analysis of dreams. The children are then com-

Published in the *Internationale Zeitschrift für Psychoanalyse*, 1 (1913).

pletely engrossed in the process of the analysis and the associations, and lead the analyst into their secrets by way of the least possible resistance. How successful this work can be will be shown by the two examples to follow.

Both are dreams of a boy of ten, attending the fourth class of a preparatory school. Dream analysis on the scale shown was only possible because the dreamer, a child of unusual intelligence, displayed a very ripe and shrewd interest in causal and associative connections, often quite spontaneously, and also because the near relationship of the analyst to the little dreamer and his accurate knowledge of the boy's daily life made control of the facts possible.

I
The Dream of the "Category"

The dream was related in three parts. Both the second and third parts had remained forgotten during the reproduction of the first part, and were successively remembered only after a part of the analysis had in each case offered an associative possibility for reproduction.

First part of the dream: *I had a funny dream. I had been in for the entrance examination to the Gymnasium* [grammar-school] *and that was called "category." To get to the examination-room one had to go up several stairs and through several passages; there were many doors and many boards. Upon a white notice-board was written in red letters "Category." I don't know any longer what it looked like in the room or who was my professor.*

Associations: Fritz, the dreamer whose dream of the 'category' thus led to the second analysis in his life—the first had taken place six months earlier—had understood right from the beginning how to associate freely and without tendency. The invitation, 'What occurs to you about that?' he took literally and expressed his astonishment that 'something really occurred to him, which sometimes had something to do with it and sometimes not.' He now looks at his own ideas like a second person and is greatly interested objectively in how they turn out and what they lead to. When an idea does not "fit in" he does not suppress it, but merely remarks "there's nothing in that" after he has related it. The analysis was taken sentence by sentence.

I had been in for the entrance examination to the Gymnasium. Fritz would very much like to attend the Gymnasium. To be admitted to the school an examination has to be passed. This entrance-examination he has already passed in his dream, and he has thus fulfilled his vivid desire to be a grammar-school boy.

That was called "category." In the paper among the advertisements I read: "Female Category, Situations Vacant." That is done so that one can find it more quickly. When the lady teacher in M. (with whom Fritz and his brother were lodging) wanted a servant she read these advertisements.

To get to the examination-room one had to go up several stairs and through several passages: there were many doors and many boards. That was exactly like the Town Hall. I have been there twice. Once with Aunt Ella to register our maid Anna. The second time with mother when my brother was to be sent to school. In the Town Hall was the school-doctor, by whom my brother had to be examined before being sent to school to see whether he was well.

Upon a white notice-board was written in red letters "Category." The door and the notice-board are those of the school-doctor. Only the word "category" doesn't fit in.

Question by analyst: What about this "category"? At one time it is "female category," and the next it is the notice on the door of the school-doctor?

Fritz: I have just remembered a continuation of the dream, and category occurs again in it.

Second part of the dream: *I was back again in the preparatory school. The boys asked each other: 'Have you already categorated?' I happened to be sitting on the first form from the front, not in my usual place, next to a chap who had been with us last year. The fellow's name is Kohn.*

Associations to the second part of the dream: *I happened to be sitting . . . name is Kohn.*

In reality Berg used to sit where I was sitting in the dream. During class Kohn always used to slide up to Berg and pinch him.

At last Berg reported him. The master said: 'Berg, choose your own punishment for Kohn'. Then Kohn was made to write five lines.

Analysis: It was surprising that Fritz produced no association to the remarkable use of the word 'category' in the form of a verb ('categorate'). The conjecture of the analyst that the queer distortion of the foreign word might have been due to an obscene motive seemed to find some confirmation in the reminiscence of the bad boy on the form. Analytical consideration led to the interpretation that the dream-situation in which Fritz is seated next to a bad boy, beside whom he does not sit as a rule, might mean that he was comparing himself with the bad boy. The fact that he was in the place of Berg, the tormented and compassionate boy who awarded his tormentor such a very mild punishment (five lines), found an analogy in the behaviour of the boy towards his own brother. The relation between Fritz and his brother is somewhat similar to that between Berg and Kohn; he is ill-treated and tormented by his violent and jealous brother, but for homosexual reasons which shall not be further discussed, he reacts very mildly and he is extremely sorry when his brother is punished on his account. He tries as much as he is able to extenuate his brother's guilt, and he would like it best of all if his brother were not punished at all. The dream-situation that Fritz is sitting next to Kohn on the form may therefore mean that he compares himself with Kohn, who is a bad boy: that is to say, he is also a bad boy. He wishes like Berg that Kohn should be only mildly punished; strictly speaking, he wishes that Kohn should receive only a mild punishment, because Kohn is no worse than Fritz. This is to say that Fritz pleads for a mild punishment for himself. The general idea that leniency towards the faults of others may be deduced from a sense of one's own guilt follows readily from the arguments of this particular case, and apart from the fact that it has been discovered not only psycho-analytically, but also by various philosophic minds, finds further special confirmation through the psycho-analysis of the relation between Fritz and his brother. Fritz is the elder of the two, and he did not view the arrival of the by two years younger brother with pleasure. Hostile demonstrations were expressed against the little newcomer, who for a long time completely claimed the mother's attention, and after a short time the boy distinctly turned away from his mother, by whom he felt himself neglected, towards the father who offered him unlimited tenderness and therewith a homosexual substitute for the unsatisfied love towards the mother. When two years later the father left home for a long period, Fritz assumed the role of the father towards his younger brother; he looked after him, felt himself a protector and treated his brother with great tenderness and love. By this means he compensated for the hostility which previously he had felt towards the younger brother as his rival.

The interpretation of the part of the dream about the form is therefore: Fritz pleads for a mild punishment, i.e. he has done or wished something that is forbidden, and which may be punishable. The connection of this dream-portion with the sentence: "Have you categorated?" brings the mutilation of the words into connection with Fritz' suspected culpability. We now remember that the word 'category' was brought into immediate connection with school matters in the first as well as in the second manifest dream-portions. "Category" is at one time "examination," and on the second occasion it is the superscription over a room which the dreamer recognizes as that of the school-doctor, where his brother was inspected, i.e. "examined." If it is permitted to equate "examine" and "inspect"—it will be seen that this is permissible—then we may expect to find in the relation of "inspect" and "category" the same element of guilt which we imagine we encounter in the sequence of "category" and a school-scene in the second dream-portion (category—examination before admission to the Gymnasium—inspection of the brother before admission to the preparatory school—school-doctor—school—recollection of bad school-boys). Moreover a third reference to the word "category" occurs in the first part of the dream. We recollect that the building in which the school-doctor functioned is the Town Hall, and that Fritz had been to another room of this building with his aunt in order to report the engagement of a new maid. The concept "maid" is associated with a recollection of the landlady in M., who intended to engage a maid, and for this purpose searched the advertisements under 'Female Category: Situations Vacant.'[1] The word "category" now becomes a bridge between two centres of association. One association-series proceeds in the direction of the concept 'maid,' the other in the direction of the concept "school." Common to both series of associations in the manifest content is the concept "engage—admit" (in service—to school). In the series "admission to school" the concept "examination" or "inspection" is interpolated, with the significance of a condition. This conditional concept was at first not associated in the series "maid." But in this respect the word "category" has received a determination by the definition that it applies to "Female category."

At this point in the interpretation the connection between the concepts "examination" and "inspection" and that of "female category" could be established from the analyst's personal knowledge of the life of the dreamer.

Anna, the maid, has played an important part to Fritz and his brother. The two boys, who had no sister, had thought that all human beings, women included, had male genitals. One day they voiced this opinion during the course of a conversation with the analyst who enlightened them as to the true state of affairs. The result of this disclosure was that from then onwards the brothers eagerly endeavoured to inform themselves of this difference of the sexes by inspection, and on a suitable occasion they acquainted the analyst with their desire.[2] Thereby it appeared that the boys were much interested to see how one could urinate with this "slit" or "hole," and they wished to examine this curious apparatus in the maid Anna. The series 'category—female—examine—forbidden action' receives a coherent structure in the light of facts known personally to the analyst, and not derived from the dream-analysis itself.

The survey of this series gained by interpretation prompted the analyst to the following deduction: In all probability "category" means "female genitals." Since Fritz had long been eager to see how these genitals function, being apparently so different from his own, it is possible that "to categorate" signifies the function of "category," namely that process which is performed by this organ, just as "to hammer" signifies the process performed with a hammer. Thus "to categorate" may mean "to urinate."

This interpretation was proposed to the dreamer, who answered surprised and pleased: "Yes, there is another bit of the dream which I had forgotten."

Third part of the dream: *When I left school again I passed through the S—— street towards the P—— street. About the middle of the S—— street there is a drain-grating, and several men stood there in the street and urinated into the grating in broad daylight. I was walking with Anna, and said: 'Look, they aren't a bit ashamed'. Then I heard someone else say, I don't know who it was: 'When one categorates one gets thirsty'. In the dream it seemed to me as if it meant that one had to go to the W.C.*

Associations to the third part of the dream: *The drain-grating in the S—— street*. This grating really exists. From it one can see the urinal at the corner of the S—— and P—— streets.

"When I was in Graz in the summer, I bathed in the swimming baths. My bathing drawers were torn, and we said they looked like a grating."

Two or three days before the dream, Emil, the dreamer's brother, had a bath in the kitchen. His bathing drawers were also torn, and he did not wish his Uncle Heinz to come into the kitchen because his uncle embarrassed him on account of the torn drawers. One could see everything through them. But after all the aunt let his uncle come into the kitchen. Emil was annnoyed about this, but his aunt told him: "Men are not embarrassed among one another."

After the recital of this association, which, moreover, in its last part also determines by association the scene of the men urinating in front of the drain-grating, it will be understood that the analyst felt himself justified in deciding to say to the boy:

"Therefore, because men are not embarrassed in the presence of men they were not ashamed to urinate together through the drain-grating. It seems to me you would wish that the people should not be embarrassed, so that you could see how men urinate."

FRITZ: Yes, that is true. As Uncle Heinz was once in the W.C. he left the door open and I wanted to see how he urinated.

ANALYST: Why do you want to see that?

FRITZ: I want to see how big it (penis) is in grown-ups.

ANALYST: Do you only wish to see how men urinate?

FRITZ: I should like to see women, too; Anna and Aunt Ella. But as I can't see it anyhow, I said to myself: "I don't care."

One can hardly imagine a more beautiful example of the process of repression *in statu nascendi* than this frank and simple confession by this child. At the same time one also gains an insight into the mechanism of the weakening of heterosexual interest, which clearly stands under a prohibition, and its transference to the homosexual erotic object. We cannot here discuss the pedagogical significance of this.

It now remains to prove unequivocally that "to categorate" in the dream really signifies "to urinate." Disregarding for the moment that the analyst's conjecture of the meaning of this word led to the reproduction of the third dream-portion and the associations following it, and not counting the dream-sentence: "In the dream it seemed to me as if it meant that one had to go to the W.C." as confirmation of that interpretation, another well-known dream-mechanism will assist our efforts to translate that peculiar word.

Then I heard some one else say, I don't know who it was . . . A person not seen in a dream is the dreamer himself. When Fritz therefore does not know who has spoken the words which follow, then he himself is probably the speaker, and the speech is his own spoken train of thought. The correctness of this consideration is immediately confirmed as follows.

ANALYST: What does that mean: "When one categorates one gets thirsty"?

FRITZ: Every time I drink water I want to urinate. (He adds laughing:) That is also a water-supply, there is a tap, and a pipe, too, and the water flows from above downwards.

ANALYST: Therefore the sentence ought to be reversed: When one is thirsty one "categorates."

FRITZ: Yes, I am a reversal fiend. I always speak the "reverse language."

The "reverse language" is a special chapter in Fritz' life. In his eighth year he spontaneously began to form a secret language, admittedly for the reason that his parents discussed certain matters in the presence of the children in a foreign language which they did not understand. As the parents had a secret language in the presence of the children, Fritz revenged himself by likewise inventing a secret language so that the parents should realize what it felt like not to be able to understand what people were talking about. This language Fritz taught his brother, under concentration of his whole teaching ability, and as soon as they became expert, the brothers discussed all their affairs in their invented language.

The technique of this language is of some significance for the psychology of the two brothers. It consisted in reading the words backwards (e.g. rehtaf = father) and the boys gained so much practice in this that they could speak backwards without halting and with the greatest facility. The sequence of the words was not altered (e.g. "father is not there" ran "rehtaf si ton ereht").

The significance of reversal in the performance of the unconscious has been demonstrated by psycho-analysis as indicating a homosexual tendency. This is also confirmed by the interpretation of the present dream, the latent dream-thoughts of which leave no doubt but the dreamer has chosen the homosexual path in giving up his wish to see the female genitals, and in henceforth directing his interest towards male organs. Other observations of Fritz' life also confirm this. The sentence "When one categorates one gets thirsty" is therefore to be interpreted as "to categorate" means to "urinate." As appears from its associative genesis the word itself represents the female genitals (Female Category). The reversal of the contents of the sentence signifies the reversal of the sexual inclination, so that the wish-fulfilment of seeing men urinate turns the infantile scoptophilia in this way into a means of gratifying a true sexual inversion. A hint of this inversion is also found in the first dream-portion, where after the idea of "Female Category" that word appears as a notice over the room of the school-doctor in which the brother, whose significance as a sexual object of Fritz is beyond doubt, is examined. Three further elements remain for the completion of the interpretation.

The first is the question why the word "category" was written in red letters. The interpretation of the red colour in this connection is given in the dream of the 'girls' closet (note 5). As will be seen, Fritz caught a glimpse of the gaping genitals of a little playmate in the summer preceding the dream. Owing to the unfavourable conditions he could not clearly make out the form; the red colour of the mucosa, however, remained firm in his memory. That this red colour, which, strictly speaking, belongs to the female genitals, stood above the school-doctor's room where the brother is examined may indicate that Fritz is still oscillating in his sexual choice, a fact which will become more apparent in the dream of the "girls' closet." The localization of the colour may, moreover, be attributed simply to the fact that the school-doctor examines both boys and girls.

The second element to be discussed further is supplied by a technical detail of dream-interpretation. In the first dream-portion we find the surroundings described in two ways with reference to the distinctness of the dream-vision. The stairs, passages, and doors leading to the examination-room are clearly seen by the dreamer, but he is unable to say what the examination-room itself looked like. Now the writer can state that in his analyses an indistinct representation of surroundings corresponds to a definite dream-technique. These indistinct places are a product of secondary dream-elaboration, belong to the external façade of the dream, and simply serve the purpose of rationalizing a process distorted by the dream-work by the addition of a place in which it could be arranged in the manifest representation. In the present case the following consideration arises; the manifest dream tells of an examination-room; the latent dream-thoughts, however, and their interpretation reveal the identity of examinations in school and examination of genitals. In the first dream-portion, the dream-incident itself ends by the dreamer's seeing the "category" in red. The continuation of the dream in the direction of showing the examination-room itself clearly, too, is merely an attempt to think that dream-part to a finish as a school episode. For the wish-fulfilment itself this final portion of the dream-performance is superfluous. This way of representing surroundings must be distinguished from the symbolic utilization of space-images in dreams. Space-images with a symbolic significance rarely—according to the author's experience, never—lose anything of their visual distinctness. Places which are only realized or mentioned, but not seen, are therefore of no importance in dream-interpretation. The passages and stairs clearly seen in this dream correspond in the form of reminiscential images to the actual prototype. Whether they should have been interpreted symbolically was not ascertained in this analysis.

The third element, of which interpretation is still needed, is the sentence in the second part of the dream: "Have you categorated?" This speech had been actually made, like all speeches occurring in dreams (with the exception of some cases where the speaker is not seen and where interpretation shows the speech to be the spoken thought of the dreamer). Its actual occurrence, however, was only demonstrated in the dream of the "girls' closet."

The boy's master did not allow the children to go to the lavatory during lessons. They were supposed to perform this business beforehand. Thus it happened that the boys would ask each other before class: "Have you been outside already?" which is represented in the dream by: Have you categorated? i.e. urinated. This supplies the final and indubitable proof that "to categorate" means to urinate. But also the interpretation of the circumstance that in the dream Fritz is seated next to Kohn—which we have interpreted in the light of a sense of guilt—finds definite confirmation in a second determination. Leaving class during lessons was punished and such a punishment had been inflicted upon Fritz. The connection between the question: Have you categorated? and the comparison of Fritz with a culpable and bad boy, expressed by his sitting next to Kohn, clearly shows the affinity of "category" to a prohibited act.

Briefly summarized, this dream informs us that the dreamer has directed his sexuality into homosexual channels, and that he is inclined to gratify his sexual instinct by means of infantile scoptophilia, which, however, he feels as something prohibited and is for that reason about to repress.

II
The Dream of the Girls' Closet

This dream, which faithfully mirrors the psychic situation of the preceding one, was analysed seven weeks after the dream of the 'category'. Fritz spontaneously related it to the analyst with the remark that he had again dreamed the same thing, only different. On account of its great clearness and distinctness, the interpretation of this dream will be abridged, and in the main confined to references to the correspondence between the present and the previous dream. For the sake of greater clarity, the separate parts of it and the associations proper to them will be numbered.

(1) *I was at school. The master said: "A boy who is coddled will turn into a girl." (2) Then I thought to myself: "Now you'll be able to have a look at the closet of the girls." When we left school* (3) *the girls came to meet us. Before the girls had come,*

some one told me—correction: *I suddenly knew—that the girls, too, had to turn into boys. As the girls come to meet us* (4) *I see one already who has short red boy's hair and short grey trousers that don't reach to the knees and a grey jacket. As we walked out through the gate there was already* (5) *ice in front of the gate. When we were half-way home, I thought to myself I could go back now and have a look at the girls' closet. On the way back I at once began to slither on the ice. However* (6) *the master caught me, and said:* (7) *"You should go there beforehand." The master stopped me by holding his outstretched arm towards me.*

Associations and Analysis: a. Aunt Ella always says, "Not even girls are as coddled as you."

b. The master always says to us, "When girls chatter much, one says they are like geese. What shall one say about you?"

Interpretation: A girl is an object of disdain. For the complement of this thought compare the homosexual inclinations of the dreamer in the dream of the "category." Upon this, or rather upon its narcissistic component (pride of penis) is founded the scorn of the female sex.[3]

(2) *I often wish to have a look at the girls' closet.* Once I had to carry library books into the girls' classroom and I very nearly did look at it. But Franz was with me then, and so I couldn't. I said to Franz at the time, "Come and let's look at the girls' closet," but he didn't listen to me.

Interpretation: We see the sexual instinct in action in the form of scoptophilic instinct directed towards the business of excretion. The same was shown in the dream of the category. What we could there only gather by the aid of interpretation we here learn without effort. The fact that here Fritz has directed his scoptophilia towards the female sex shows that his sexual attitude is still oscillating. The previous dream, too, begins with heterosexual curiosity. But here, in the same way, there ensues a turning from it towards his own sex, and a depreciation of the female, which is even more distinctly shown in (4). At this point it may be remarked that the uncertainty of sexual inclination is probably decided in one direction or the other only at puberty, and that up to that time modifications of the sexual development are not altogether precluded, even though abnormal instincts may, perhaps, already have come clearly to expression.

(3) *The girls came direct to the fourth class where they had no business to be. They came to meet me.* (Fritz attends a preparatory school for boys and girls. The two departments are joined by a corridor.)

Interpretation: It is significant that Fritz gives in his association merely a clearer account of the dream-situation, but no reminiscence of reality. The surprised criticism which he passes on the situation with the words: the girls had come to meet him in the fourth class, where they had no business to be (Fritz is in the fourth class) shows that this coming to meet him has a meaning different from the one represented which refers to place. It is merely the pictural expression of the concept "to come to meet" in the mental sense. The feeling of surprise indicates that in reality things are the other way about, that the girls do not meet him half-way. This refusal on the part of girls is, however, to be looked for in the dreamer's mind itself, for actually girls are very fond of him as he is a good-looking boy. But they had no business with him because he has no business with them. Again, at the critical homosexual point, we obtain the abnormal element by the reversal of a sentence, just as in the dream of the category at the point "When one categorates one gets thirsty."

For the active desire of the dreamer to see the female genitals, the meeting in the dream signifies a wish-fulfilment. Fritz has by no means completely finished with the female sex, and the homosexual decision still lying in the deepest stratum of the unconscious is for the present unable to neutralize his curiosity about the female genitals.

(4) Marie F., of the fifth class, has *red hair*, though it is not short. She is the sister of one of my schoolfellows. Short red hair and a suit like that of the girl in the dream is worn by a schoolfellow of mine named Karl, whom I can't stand.

Interpretation: The last sentence in (3) "Then I suddenly knew[4] that the girls had to turn into boys' is realized in the girl dressed as a boy. The identification of a girl with a disliked schoolfellow indicates a refusal of the girl (homosexuality). Further determination is only required for the circumstance that the girl appears in boy's clothes. Following upon the sentence in (1) in which it is said that boys turn into girls, we gather from the masquerade of the girl a complete reversal of all sexual relations. A determination of her disguise which emanates from a more superficial stratum is supplied by Fritz in his supplemental remark: "If I were a girl I could have a look at the girls' closet." The analyst here hazards the deduction that the disguise of the girl in the dream serves the purpose of satisfying Fritz' wish according to the principle of the mountain that comes to Mohamed. Since he cannot become a girl the girl comes to him as a boy. To what little purpose it actually is, as things remain essentially the same, is expressed in the remark that the girls had no business to be in the fourth class. That the part played by the trousers is not a solution but an obstruction of the problem is apparent in the following conversation between Fritz and the analyst.

Analyst: Have you ever seen a girl in boy's clothes?

Fritz: Yes, Josephine. She was doing gym, and so that one shouldn't look under her skirts she had put on a black pair of boy's trousers underneath. Once a girl was sliding down the inclined stone in the park; she didn't have trousers on and one saw under her skirts.[5]

(5) *"I should like to skate now."*

Interpretation: The dream occurred in a January without frost. The ice is in the first place the fulfilment of a wish from the day before. In reality it contains the element of prohibition, for the boys were strictly forbidden to slither in the street in front of the school-building. This idea of prohibition gains in clearness by the fact that Fritz makes use of the opportunity when everybody has left the school to slither back on the ice to look at the girls' closet, because now no one would be likely to disturb him. To slide on the ice therefore means to tread forbidden paths. This clearly appears from what immediately follows.

(6) *a*. Once two boys escaped from the Hyrtl Orphanage. They were *caught* and punished by the police.

b. I should often have liked to look into a girls' closet, but I was *afraid* that a girl might be inside and report me.

(7) *"You should have gone there beforehand."* The master says that when we want to leave the room during class.

Interpretation: This portion also contains the idea of prohibition. The gesture with which the master stops him, Fritz may have noticed in policemen who stop wheeled traffic with outstretched arms at street-crossing. It means: Stop!

Theoretical Remarks.—The dream analyses submitted here afford us an insight into the sexual life of boys during the latency-period. We find the instinct of scoptophilia and the related one of exhibitionism active and establish the fact that the choice of an object, which in these dreams is already clearly pronounced, proceeds towards its development along the path of the excretion-libido also. This originally auto-erotic libido is likewise woven into the process of transference, and it appears that this is possible owing to two conditions. One condition is obviously contained in the magnitude of the quantity of libido attached to specific organs (by which organs it is at the same time qualified as a specific organ-libido). It is possible that not all the libido mobilized during the business of excretion is specifically supplied by the excretory organs, and that a part of this libido is undifferentiated and capable of being displaced from one organ on to another, and therefore also of being transferred to a foreign object as soon and as long as this displaceable quantity of libido invests an erotogenic zone which is biologically intended for a choice of object other than the auto-erotic one.

If this condition is given, then the capacity for transference of the excretion-libido is finally rendered possible by a second factor which consists in the *means* of object-selection, in that the eye (or some other organ mainly directed towards the control of the outer world) is placed at the service of the auto-erotic excretion-libido (or rather, its displaceable component), so that the sexual scoptophilic instinct contributes to object-choice by way of the excretion-libido in that it occupies itself with the process of excretion in other people.

The relation of this problem to that of narcissism, i.e. to the problem of the capacity for transference κατ ἐξοχην will be discussed on another occasion. Here it is merely remarked that the projection of the excretion-libido is at the same time the path of its repression, in that the auto-erotic sum of pleasure is rendered valueless (or at any rate replaceable) in such a way that the asocial excretion-pleasure returns to the subject, by way of the social scoptophilic instinct in a form which shows itself to be of equal value with all other forms of erotic valuation of non-auto-erotic objects. When in the course of development of the sexual instinct, under the governance of other erotogenic zones and the ego, the specific pleasure in the excretory processes of the love-object has been rendered valueless (by the excretory organs—in obedience to increased knowledge—now being valued merely as specific sex-features), then the process of development of the excretion-libido has found its normal termination. If it remains fixated on the way, perversions corresponding to the moment of fixation will result (scoptolagnia, exhibitionism, coprolagnia, etc.).

Finally I will mention that observations urge me to the conclusion that the sexual life of boys during the latency-period has the character chiefly of scoptophilia directed towards the excretory processes, and that this bodily function supplies the greater part of the sexual phantasies during the latency-period, because it brings their interest in the sexual organs into a connection which corresponds to the boys' knowledge and, moreover, is of necessity permitted by the educational powers.

Notes

1. Fritz is here mistaken. The schoolmistress could for her purpose not have read the column "Situations Vacant," but only "Situations Wanted." This error may be of significance as a result of distortion on the part of the censorship, but was not further analysed.
2. Cf. the following dream. In order not to deter qualified persons from child-analyses I wish to emphasize the fact that this curiosity of the boys soon subsided and gave place to the calm of acquired knowledge. Later on this knowledge in no way irritated the children, and the disturbing character of sexual curiosity was able to yield to ordinary interest in personal matters.
3. This remark is at the same time directed polemically against the hypothesis of Adler, who endeavours to explain the tendency of wishing to be a man as a "manly protest" arising out of the social valuation of the sexes or out of the desire for power, and not out of instinctual propensities.
4. Here, too, we refer to dream-technique as on p. 76. Fritz corrects the sentence "Then someone said" into "Then I suddenly knew" (Cf. *supra*). He does not see the speaker and confirms in the correction what we had determined by the interpretation on p. 76, namely that speeches by an invisible speaker are thoughts of the dreamer's.
5. On this occasion Fritz obtained the impression of the redness of the genital mucosa. Cf. p. 77.

4

Psychoanalysis of Philosophy and Psychoanalytic Philosophy

There is very little literature on the subject of this paper. But the fact that in that little nearly everything with which philosophy is concerned is touched on by psychoanalysis points to the extent of the border zone in which philosophy and psychoanalysis clash and the extraordinary liveliness that prevails in the relation between the two intellectual fields when their interests overlap. So far as psychological problems are concerned, the limitation of interest to the border between philosophy and psychoanalysis seems very intelligible, not only because the psychology of the conscious has historically been a part of philosophy, but also—and above all—because the boundaries of the psychology of the unconscious have not yet been fixed, with the result that on many points the authors are unable to decide which field to attribute things to. Apart from this purely scientific uncertainty, which is partly attributable to the authors' insufficient familiarity with one subject or the other, but partly also to the nature of the material itself, there is sometimes a cautiousness in the attribution of the material that clearly betrays its link with affective attitudes. If the authors have also displayed undeniable courage in descending into the depths, it cannot be overlooked that many of them—to adapt a phrase of Freud's—feel uncomfortable in the atmosphere of the depths and show a strong tendency to return to the surface,

---

Translated by Eric Mosbacher. *Jahrbuch für psychoanalytische Forschungen* 6 (1914).

where they meet with understanding from their old fellow travelers in their old mother tongue.

The relations that psychoanalysis has hitherto had with philosophy are mainly threefold in nature: we have to deal with the psychoanalysis of the philosopher (his characterology and motivation); the psychoanalysis of the philosophical system (the mechanisms and aims of philosophic thought); and, finally, there are the autonomous philosophic achievements of psychoanalysis itself insofar as psychoanalytic investigation has discovered laws the demonstration of which is also possible outside the specific frontiers of psychology and can be carried out by nonpsychological, e.g., epistemological or biological methods (in relation to determinism or the problems of time and reality, for instance).

Speaking quite generally, work of the first two types presents itself as the application of psychoanalytic findings to specific material, while the third appears to be represented exclusively by propositions put forward by Freud himself in various passages in his works. There are meager references to these in various authors.

In the basic position they adopt to the psychoanalysis of the philosopher and the philosophical system, the authors are in full agreement with each other and with the guidance given by Freud in specific instances (7, 2). According to this, the decisive characteristic of the philosopher is his turning away from the reality of the objects of the outside world that challenge the libido while simultaneously displacing libidinal cathexis to the thinking function. The reality of thought takes the place of objective reality and, because of its affective charge, assumes the characteristics of a material object. This characteristic classifies the philosopher with the obsessional neurotic.

Otto Rank and Hanns Sachs (6) distinguish three types of philosophical personality: the intuitive observer type, i.e., which is really that of the artistic metaphysician (Plato, the mystics, the speculative natural philosphers); that of the synthetic speculator (the positivists—Comte and Spencer and the empiricists and Locke); and finally the analytic thinker type (Kant, Spinoza, and above all Descartes and Hume). With this division they claim to establish only a heuristic division without any desire to diminish the multiplicity of the varieties that occur. It must, be pointed out, however, that as the context shows, this division does not really apply to the personal conditions for philosophical thinking, but rather to the classification of the types of philosophical systems from the viewpoint of the destiny of the libido.

The other authors who are relevant here, Hitschmann (4) and Alfred Freiherr von Winterstein (5), refrain from making any kind of motivational classification and trace the destiny of philosophical development solely from the point of view of the results of the development of infantile psychical constellations.

Philosophical systems emerge from the psychoanalysts' critique as systems of projection of intrapsychical processes and of screen ideas that have been given a rational facade in accordance with the principle of wish fulfilment, and are of other than biographical value only to the extent that by revealing a psychical process of some kind they reflect the general laws immanent in them. The general or special knowledge gained in the process of system formation can be verified by the methods appropriate to the particular field and constitute the objectively valuable content of the philosophical system. They are exempted from psychoanalytical criticism because of lack of technical qualifications.

Both Hitschmann and Winterstein correctly found the link with Nietzsche, who is shown by quotations to have been the only prepsychoanalytic thinker who recognized reflections and motivations of an affective constellation in the nature and content of the philosopher's thought.

Following are quotations from works mentioned in the bibliography.

From Hitschmann:

> That the dark, blind and not really knowable force that holds sway behind consciousness, knowledge and our wishes is Schopenhauer's will, which we psycho-analysts call the unconscious. That Schopenhauer is thus a predecessor of the discovery of the unconscious, which in the psychoanalytic view also perpetually wishes and drives. . . . (p. 128)

> The superficial observer, faced with the great emphasis on the will in Schopenhauer's life and works, is bound to be struck by the paradox that, as has been repeatedly pointed out by pupils and critics, this discoverer and admirer of a strong will to live became an advocate of quietism—a negation of the will. Nevertheless psychologically this

is readily intelligible as a result of the conflicts in the human psyche, the struggle between the primal drives and the inhibitions which the ego of civilised man puts up against them. This combating and repressing is directed against the blatantly egoistical and sexual drives, in which it therefore most plainly manifests itself; and at the same time it becomes typical of the whole attitude of the personality towards drives and the reaction to them in relation to the outside world in general. Thus the psycho-analyst will not be in the least surprised at finding that when he comes across a powerful drive a strong tendency to fight it also becomes perceptible. (p. 128)

That Schopenhauer's sex life was probably poor and unsatisfying can be assumed from this, as from other passages. If sexuality is typical of the rest of the psyche in so many respects, one of the roots of the deficient enjoyment of life that culminated in his pessimism can be detected here. (p. 130)

We are confronted . . . by the psychological fact that caused the drive-tormented Schopenhauer to become a profound metaphysician capable of expressing enthusiasm about the lofty pleasure procurable from pure knowledge liberated from the will; the fact, that is to say, that there were few to rival his ability to repudiate the will and repress the drives in such a way as to escape from the terrestrial. (p. 131)

. . . Nietzsche himself vigorously rejects this idea of pure, disinterested knowledge in philosophy and a similar disinterestedness in the appreciation of art, which he denounced as "nonsensical and absurd". (p. 133)

In this connection we must emphasize as self-evident that in our view also, though in a different sense, no such thing as "will-less knowledge" can exist. Schopenhauer deluded himself in maintaining that the will (the unconscious) can ever be still and leave thought uninfluenced. . . . (p. 133)

We must regard this whole idea of holiness, renunciation, approaching the state of the fakir and the penitent, as the expression of phantasies of pleasurable pain, masochism being closely associated with sadism. The intensity of these self-punishment trends can derive their intensity only from great guilt feelings, from which the strong wish for salvation arises. (p. 143)

It is thus clear that, in Schopenhauer's metaphysical values, the world, being merely imaginary, implies a form of being of inferior metaphysical value. His epistemological valuation of the objective world is at the same time a metaphysical, and a pessimistically metaphysical, valuation of the world (p. 150)

It must be emphasised as highly significant that this feeling that the world is mere dream and illusion is a surprising symptom typical of

> melancholic patients; here too it seems to arise from a wish to escape from the intolerable reality of life resulting from depression. (p. 150)

If one sums up the results of Hitschmann's observations, they turn out primarily to be that psychoanalysis of the philosopher Schopenhauer and his philosophy shows that the fundamental propositions of that important mind are projections and reactions of psychical attitudes: the paramount urge to think and philosophize is shown to be a form of the process of libido repression and a result of that repression; the pessimism is a consequence of an unhappy and unsatisfied instinctual life, and the ethics a reaction against antisocial trends, while the metaphysical position as a whole reflects an unconscious deliberate denial of that painful reality. The basic proposition of Schopenhauer's philosophy, the definition of the world as will and imagination, is thus to be understood as a projection of the philosopher's split personality.

Winterstein runs through the whole history of philosophy, using the psychoanalytic method of interpretation and explanation for the purpose of reducing all types of philosophers and philosophic systems to the psychoanalytically decisive factor. Psychoanalytic criteria are applied to an extraordinarily comprehensive range of material, and the different aims of the philosophemes are traced back etiologically. The construction of the work is not clear, the material escapes from the framework. The interpretation is essentially based on assured psychoanaltyical findings, and this leads the author to the problem of constructing a psychoanalytically based philosophy, and he comes down in favor of a realist-dualist position. Philosophically the whole work is admirably well-informed, and its special value lies in the fact that the problems subjected to psychoanalysis are selected by a philosopher, thus by an expert able to approach problems under the specific conditions in which they arose. The following points that he makes are worthy of note.

> . . . The philospher's teaching is conditioned by unconscious wishes. . . . (p. 175)
>
> . . . The mingling of wish material with established knowledge is demonstrable. . . . (p. 176)
>
> Contempt for the external world begins with Socrates. . . . The individual becomes asocial and seeks consolation in the innermost recesses of his being. . . . (p. 179)

> . . . The assumption of another world, which often arises from an unconsciously motivated tendency to devalue existing reality, may underlie the Buddhist nirvana, for instance, Plato's world of ideas, or Kant's thing-in-itself. The true psychological content peeps out from behind all these fictions in more or less concealed form. (p. 177)

> Plato's "intellectual matching" tallies with the visual type of the Hellenic people. . . . (p. 180)

> At the pinnacle of ecstasy, in Plotinus, for instance, the "looking on" that is aspired to is replaced by a crudely sensuous "touching" (phylogenetic regression to sense of touch, regression as wish fulfilment), a pleasurable "grasping of the absolute," and that absolute is itself the real "maternal depth", and the all is one, where the difference between subject and object is abolished. (p. 183)

> . . . Introversion. . . . Over-valuation of the purely spiritual because of the failure of reality. . . . The Socratic equation of insight and virtue. . . . (p. 183)

> "Eros" is the aspiration for a metaphysical reality in which there is neither place nor time. . . . Philosophising means (1) wanting to die, entering the unconscious, introverting; (2) remembering infantile pre-existence. . . the lasting peace of Plato's ideas is the unchanging nature of the imagines that is characteristic of the unconscious. . . while the physical world is that of restlessness, of coming into being and passing away, meaning the libido's perpetually changing cathexis of objects. . . . Does this not recall Freud's remarks about serial object choice following the maternal pattern? (p. 184)

> Plato's ideas theory—apart from the intellectual superstructure—is a libido theory. . . . (p. 185)

On the idea of God:

> Apart from the fact that He represents an elevation of the father, a personification of psychical phenomena . . . a projection of the wish-fulfilling, all-powerful, all-wise endopsychical authority of the unconscious. . . and a symbol of our conscious, our highest sexual repression, our moral personality, in short, our ideal. (p. 189)

On God's relationship with the world:

> Two systems can be distinguished: an emanation system and a creation system. The former is a projection of libidinal processes that are perceived endopsychically, as it were, a representation of the drives that have remained in the ego in the narcissistic stage and lead to object choice, and the continually repeated regression to that point of departure. (p. 190)

On creation theory:

> . . . God created the world out of nothing . . . if one bears in mind that mankind originally pictured the body, matter (note the etymological connection with *mater*), as feminine, negative birth-giving, while mind, knowledge, was regarded as the male, positive, creative principle. . . . Chinese uses the same sign to indicate "woman" and "negation." (p. 192–93)

In explanation of three beliefs: (a) in preexistence; (2) the transmigration of souls; and (3) the eternal return of the same thing, (1) is analogous to *déja vu* . . . memory of an (unconscious) phantasy or dream. On (2), the transmigration of souls takes place to the same extent as the migrations of the libido, and (3) is endopsychical perception of periodicity.

On the problem of Spinoza:

> Behind Spinoza lay the importance of the father. . . . He did not dare demand love of him. "God does not love us, but we, who acknowledge God, love Him. But because all mankind forms part of the infinite understanding which is an attribute of the eternal substance, a part of the force that perceives God everywhere and loves Him, it can be said that our love is part of the love with which God loves Himself." (Spinoza.)

Thus, as we can see, in addition to the general psychoanalytical criteria for judging philosophers and philosophy—wish fulfilment, projection of psychical processes and constellations, and turning away from reality—factors which are also brought into sharp relief by Hitschmann—Winterstein also draws attention to the etiology of philosophemes in partial drives—voyeurism and tactile gratification. The significance of the philosopher's relationship with his parents as well as the part played by sadomasochism in the conception of ethical principles is adequately appreciated by both authors. Under the same auspices Winterstein extends his discussion to the philosophy of the present day.

So far we have been dealing with psychoanalysts interested in philosophy, while Häberlin and Putnam must be classified as philosophers interested in psychoanalysis. Both are anxiously concerned to safeguard from psychoanalysis some of the principles and beliefs they brought with them, and they achieve their purpose by denying the competence of psychoanalysis on some personally important point. Thus Putnam (5): "We must decide to declare ourselves in favour of this or that philosophy of life . . . ," and, as he complains that psychoanalysts are determinists, he claims that ". . . it should be realised that the essential in any development is the independent energy we have frequently mentioned . . ." (p. 108). Similarly Häberlin (3) begins by safeguarding his philosophy against all scientific criticism by appealing to its practical importance and ends by appealing to his "conviction" that the "culturally important phenomena of experience cannot be derived from sexuality, but . . . from deeper-lying trends. . . ." That obviously cuts all roads to a cultural adaptation based on the new psychological discoveries.

C. G. Jung's *Symbols of Transformation* have been discussed at length elsewhere (Ferenczi). The writer believes that the position in relation to psychoanalysis adopted in that work can be called an attempt at a synthetic generalization of psychoanalytic discoveries. Insofar as it contains nonpsychoanalytic assumptions or modifications of psychoanalytic findings, it follows a path that leads from somewhere other than psychoanalysis and does not end in it, with the result that, like other philosophies and philosophising discussions, it constitutes a self-contained object for psychoanalytic investigation.

In the context of this paper discussion of psychoanaltyic philosophy must be restricted to a few observations. Determinism has been demonstrated in psychological events, and there is a psychological approach to the problem of time, which has acquired a relationship to empirical science because of the discovery of the special position of the phenomenon of time in the unconscious. In the two principles of psychical events we find the psychical reality which has served as background to all ethical systems and calls for the overcoming of the asocial, animal pleasure principle concerned only with the present in favor of a socially tamed instinctual satisfaction based on time and foresight. The psychobiologically desirable relationship between the principle and the reality principle is then realized by way of repression and the psychical achievements that follow it. Thus the mechanisms discovered by Freud in the process of psychoanalytic investigation are transferred to a basis on which the psychological problem is subjected to that of biological adaptation.

Works Cited

1. Freud, S. *Leonardo da Vinci and a Memory of his Childhood.* Standard Ed., Vol 9.
2. ———. *Psycho-analytic notes on an Autobiographical Account of a Case of Paranoia.* Standard Ed., Vol. 12.
3. Häberlin, P. "Über die Tragweite psychologischer Erkentnisse und Theorien." *Schweizer Zeitschrift für Gemeinnützigkeit,* no. 4 (1913).
4. E. Hitschmann, Schopenhauer. "Versuch einer Psychoanalyse des Philosophen." *Imago* 2.
5. J. J. Putnam, "On the significance of philosophical views and training for the further development of the psycho-analytic movement." *Imago* (1912), 1: 101–18.
6. O. Rank, and H. Sachs. *Die Bedeutung der Psychoanalyse für die Giesteswissenschaften.* Wiesbaden: Bergmann, 1913.
7. Winterstein, A., Freiherr von. "Psychoanalytische Anmerkungen zur Geschichte der Philosophie." *Imago* 2.

5

On the Psychology of the Alcoholic Occupation Delirium

I

Most sufferers from alcoholic delirium are inaccessible to psychoanalytic self-criticism, and chance has so far denied me cases of the better human material rarely to be found among them.[1] The present paper is therefore not a psychoanalysis of the alcoholic occupation delirium; it consists rather of an application of established psychoanalytic principles with a view to gaining an understanding of the clinical picture. The conclusions are based on limited observations, and it would therefore be as well if criticism were restricted to the correctness of those observations and of the approach to the problem.

Clinical psychiatry has hitherto taken a number of detours by which it has evaded the psychological problem of the alcoholic psychoses; it has applied itself to the investigation of the various blood pictures, or demonstrated that there are different frequencies of abuse of alcohol, assuming that different toxic metabolic intermediates account for different alcoholic psychoses. While I do not underrate the value of such investigations, I fail to see that they throw any light on the clinical picture. This approach to the problem opens no path toward understanding the psy-

---

Zur Psychologie des alkoholischen Beschäftigungs-delirs. Internationale Zeitschrift für ärztliche Psychoanalyse. (1915). Translated by Eric Mosbacher and Marius Tausk under the editorship of Paul Roazen.

chology of the alcoholic psychoses and, if one wishes to circumvent the psychological problem, one is left ultimately with no alternative but resorting to 'constitutional factors' for the semblance of an explanation. That, in fact, is the target set in the literature on the subject.

The leap from the biochemistry of the central nervous system to the form and content of a given mental disturbance is impossible to make. The two lie poles apart, and in between lie an inconceivable number of problems with which, in the course of the ages, religions, philosophies, and sciences have wrestled inconclusively. The gap can be bridged only by a question mark, and no answer can be given. But thanks to Freud we are now in a position to trace back the psychological causations of psychical phenomena without the risk of finding the way blocked too early by the *ne plus ultra* of speculation about the creation of the universe out of primordial chaos.

The psychoanalyst—though the psychoanalyst alone—recognizes in the various forms of alcoholic mental disturbance psychical factors which in other forms of mental disturbance his science has long since succeeded in defining and tracing back to a psychological prehistory. Exploring the psychological factors in other, not yet analyzed, disturbances therefore seems an obvious task. The fact that functional disturbance can be caused either by a known or an unknown toxin on the one hand or by a psychological impediment on the other is no reason why we should refrain from inquiring into the psychological mechanism of the disturbance and its specifically psychological background. This must be mostly explicitly stated, in view of the circumstance that certain clinicians wish to bar psychoanalysis from the exploration of mental disturbances for which an organic etiology has been established.

All the knowledge accumulated by clinical psychopathology provides no access to an understanding of the alcoholic mental disturbances, or for that matter of other toxicoses.

Most toxicoses make their appearance as states of confusion. The chief symptoms are temporal and spatial disorientation, total misconstruction of the environment. Clinical observation also notes ideas of persecution as a secondary symptom of the toxic psychoses, almost invariably accompanied by hallucinations (though the relationship of these to the confusion is never indicated), and anxiety, which dominates the clinical picture so far as affect is concerned. In the specific case of cocaine psychosis, the clinical picture is dominated by ideas of persecution and visual paresthesias (glass ball, macropsy). Then there are the two great alcoholic psychoses. In hallucinosis orientation is maintained, but there is great anxiety and fantastic hallucinations, while in delirium tremens complete disorientation, hallucinations of all the senses, and the characteristic occupation delirium occur. The affectivity of the patient suffering from occupation delirium is described as trivial and facetious.

From the psychoanalytic point of view, we shall for the time being disregard the question why different senses are predominately or at all affected by hallucinations in different psychoses, and in particular we shall disregard the special case of the cocaine psychosis, on which no work has been done yet. It remains an open question whether Bonhöffer's conjecture that alcoholic hallucinosis affects individuals of the "acoustic" type is correct, and whether the 'sensory type' in general is the determining factor in the choice of the type of hallucination.

Psychoanalytic theory would seem to have a ready explanation to offer for the occurrence of anxiety in the toxicoses. The poison paralyzes the inhibitory apparatus (theories of the inhibitory function of the cerebral cortex and the cortical site of attack of the poison), as is well known in regard to ordinary alcoholic intoxication, and it is also well known that the elimination of inhibitions leads to the break-through of suppressed affects (*in vino veritas*). If disorder of the inhibiting apparatus mobilizes such affects, which are not allowed to or cannot obtain their discharge through the intact remainder of the personality, the affect awaiting discharge is converted into anxiety.[2]

The activation of the hallucinatory mechanism must be considered to be a regression from the stage of ideation to that of the perceptory system. The relationship of this regression to that of instinctual life remains, so far as I am aware, totally unexplained.

What I have said so far, however, throws no light on the specific nature of the occupation delirium. For a clue to the problem I am indebted to a colleague, the medical student Fräulein I. Zimmermann, who informs me that there are occupation dreams the characteristic of which is that the dreamer is vainly struggling with some occupation, and that there is a similarity here with the alcoholic occupation delirium. This type of dream was unknown to me, though I subsequently learnt that it had been noted by Pilcz, though this author of course carefully refrained from applying Freud's method of dream interpretation to elucidating it.

It will be intelligible to the psychoanalyst that Fräulein Zimmermann's communication led me to assume that an understanding of the psychology of occupation delirium might be obtainable from an analysis of occupation dreams. Some of these that came to hand at the right moment yielded the following:

(i) The manifest content of the dream is trivial occupation with ordinary jobs the dreamer normally does in the course of earning his living or domestically. The purpose of the job is usually only very hazily present in the dreamer's consciousness; the actual effort being expended is on something that generally has no relation to that purpose. Attention is concentrated on some action which seems highly important, but is obviously of minor significance in relation to the objective. Often there is actually a feeling of surprise that the activity so absorbing to the dreamer should really lead to the goal of which he is conscious in the dream.

(ii) The affective situation in the dream is tinged with mild anxiety. Attacks of severe anxiety are rare. The dreamer has the feeling he has to hurry, because another task is awaiting him. Often this is something that cannot be delayed, but cannot be started before the task on which the dreamer is engaged has been finished. For all his busy haste, however, he makes no progress, but keeps finding himself back at the beginning, or actually doing something else, though it is not clear to him whether it is the same thing or something else; or sometimes he feels he ought to be doing something else, though he cannot stop what he is doing.

II

Specimen of an occupation dream:

It is early morning. The dreamer feels he should be helping his mother with her heavy domestic duties. He decides to be good today, a resolution he often made as a child but did not always keep. Also he has a feeling of doubt about being properly grown up, he feels rather like a child again. He finds himself turning the pages of a big book, wondering vaguely in the back of his mind how he got out of bed and whether this is the job he had been going to do. Then it seems perfectly all right, looking at the book is what he should be doing, and it is connected in some way with the fact that the tap in the kitchen needs polishing. He goes on turning the pages faster and faster, as fast as he can, but the pages stick, and the more he turns the more there are of them. He has a slight feeling of anxiety. He takes some rags into the kitchen; this somehow arises out of turning the pages of the book and amounts to the same thing. The tap is still dirty, but it is now clear that the big book contains the last few weeks' accounts, which have to be added up or checked. He has a feeling of relief. He starts adding up and makes good progress, and for a moment he feels fine, until he remembers the tap again, and realizes that he must hurry. The obvious connection between the adding up and the tap and being a good boy now disappears again, and he has to start adding up all over again. He hurries, but realizes that the adding up is really learning French. This he is really good at, he feels delighted, and has a great sense of relief. He learns quickly and well, and the words come tumbling out of his mouth or out of the paper. Sometimes he feels it is not really French he is doing at all, he is no longer nine years old of course, but all the same the learning goes very well indeed. He has difficult and interesting foreign words to pronounce, which at first he does very well, but then it gets a little more difficult, and sometimes he stumbles over a word. He repeats a word, but this time it sounds different or has a different meaning. He feels slightly anxious and awakens.

Analysis: The dreamer was a twenty-three-year-old student, whose major subject was Romance philology (French). He consulted me after failing with a prostitute to whom he went to find out whether his fear of being impotent was justified.

The beginning of the dream led straight to the period of the patient's childhood which was decisive for his troubles, which was when he was aged four. He was a precocious boy and had then, or even earlier, fully realized the state of dissension that existed between his parents, and he passionately took his mother's side against his father. Whenever he saw his mother weeping, which was often, he felt deep pain and sympathy and approached her in order to comfort her, and he always quite consciously expected her to admit that her tears were his father's fault and that she would make him her ally against the latter. But this expectation was always disappointed. When he asked why she was weeping, she always replied: 'Because my children upset me.' Though the boy was not aware of having done anything wrong and could not help feeling that this answer was grossly unfair, it produced in him a feeling of deep contrition which, however, seemed to him to be artificial. His uncontrolled sobbing always ended by producing a state of ecstatic emotion in his mother in which she hugged and overwhelmed him with tears and caresses.

Basically he was not deceived about the true state of affairs, and he regarded these scenes as the outcome of a tacit agreement between him and his mother; that is, if he acted as if he genuinely believed the reason she gave for her unhappiness, the reward for his "discretion" would be these caresses.

However, the boy was already dominated by a mature sense of guilt, because he had long been aware of sexual wishes and aggressivity directed at his mother and his siblings and of a sense of impotent rage against his father, and he felt his attitude toward his mother to be a *sacrificium intellectus*; he felt he was being bribed. He grew uncertain in appraising his feelings, in which he knew there was an element of dishonesty. To the boy's immature mind there was no way out of the conflict, since he was unwilling to renounce the pleasure of his mother's passionate embraces, while on the other hand his 'complicity' with her seemed to put a stamp of approval on his behavior and gave him a welcome excuse not to allow his ever-recurrent scruples to develop into a resolution to take the only morally correct course and renounce them.

The consequences for the next stage of the patient's development that followed his œdipal fantasy were far reaching. In the first place he found a way of avenging his father, whom he loved as well as feared, for his mother's disloyalty to him. Exploiting his assumed complicity with his mother, he concluded he had a right to be like his father, since his mother covered up and concealed the latter's behavior. So the boy found a way of converting his identification with the lucky possessor of his mother into real activity: he became disobedient, and treated his mother and his siblings violently and tyrannically, just as his father did.

His mother, who was obviously totally unaware of any complicity with him, complained about his naughty behavior to his father, who punished him severely. The boy naturally considered his mother's behavior to be a breach of faith; and, as he in any case unconsciously regarded his complicity with her as a demonstration of her lack of character, because it showed her love to be venal, since he could buy it by his 'discretion,' at the age of nine he started suspecting her of betraying his father with other men. With this his prostitution fantasy, which made his mother and later all women accessible to his secret wishes, was complete. In his deep feeling of guilt he now turned to his father, who accepted him as a welcome ally against the wife whom he now hated more than ever. But the boy had scruples about this alliance too, because this time he was betraying his mother, and again disloyalty was visited with retribution, for his father was a moody and brutal man who soon let the boy feel that his loyalty did not safeguard him against severe and unjust punishments.

Torn between love and hate and successful in neither, the boy's self-esteem collapsed. His disastrous love policy, which he ascribed to his own 'wickedness', led to guilt and self-recrimination. The next phase was that of good intentions. When he awoke early in the morning, after a night of violent scenes with his parents, his first thought was: today I am going to be good; and, indeed, for a few days he would be good, coöperative and patient.

On such days he felt an especially deep sympathy with his mother, to whom the big household was such a burden, since they could not afford a maid. At such times he would have liked to take all her work off her hands. One night he found himself half asleep in the kitchen without knowing how he had got out of bed. Apparently he had made up his mind in dream to polish the kitchen tap to give his mother a pleasurable surprise in the morning, but he did not carry out this purpose, because his mother was still in the kitchen. She kissed and hugged him for his good intentions and put him back to bed.

Puberty found the patient in the same state, since there had been no change in the family relationships. His masturbatory fantasies showed the extent to which his mother's passionate embraces had conditioned his attitude to loving. He imagined scenes characterized by the uninhibited passion he had experienced with his mother, and in accordance with his aggressive nature these were violent defloration fantasies. He indiscriminately involved all the more attractive women he knew in these, but occasionally in dreams he had intercourse with his mother.

His agonized struggle with masturbation, in which he made up his mind to be good as often as he failed, lasted for four years. This was followed by a period of continence only occasionally interrupted by masturbation. He went with a prostitute for the first time at the age of nineteen. He had intercourse with her twice, but in spite of this demonstration of his potency he was henceforward troubled by mild anxiety about it. He went with prostitutes from time to time solely for the purpose of testing his potency, as he intended either to marry or to have an affair with a decent girl, though this idea was associated with a fear of impotence he could not get rid of, though his potency never failed him with prostitutes. His explanation of his fear of impotence was that his long practice of masturbation might have done him harm.

There was another thing that struck the patient at that time. Intercourse never satisfied him completely; a day or two later he nearly always had to masturbate, and only then did he find himself "at peace." His explanation was that going briefly with a prostitute was not enough; he needed a woman for many hours or nights to satisfy his quickly recurrent desire, but lack of funds prevented him from immediately resorting to a prostitute again, so he was left with no choice but to masturbate.

At the age of twenty-one he met a girl, a fellow student, whom he liked, and he gave up masturbation completely. He wanted the girl to give herself to him, but she permitted him only to manipulate her genitals and refused intercourse. Her "bourgeois cowardice" roused his indignation, they had frequent quarrels and the girl was several times on the point of breaking off the affair. Though he had often been on the point of doing so himself because of the way in which her "rotten bourgeois prejudices" let him down, when she left him after a quarrel he found her absence intolerable. In the end, being able to tolerate her withholding herself no longer, he threw her out of the room. After three days the feeling that the breach was final gave him a sense of relief, and he began wondering whether to resort to a prostitute again. But he felt this would be degrading to the girl with whom he had quarreled. The desire to go to a prostitute became more pressing, but the fear of impotence, of which he had been free during his affair with the girl, revived again, and it was this that ended by sending him to a prostitute. This happened about ten days after the breach, and he was impotent for the first time in his life.

He fought the consequent depression for a few days, and then sought medical advice. The dream which is being analyzed here occurred during the night after the second analytic session.

The following explanations of dream fragments that do not seem to have been determined by the patient's life history as already described were produced without any particular difficulty in the course of the next few sessions.

The feeling of doubt about being properly adult; the feeling of being rather like a child.

He accounted for this by his continued struggle with masturbation. Adults did not masturbate. Only during his love affair had he had the sense of a certain male maturity. But the way in which he had had to make love to the girl had not permitted him to feel completely adult and masculine. Whenever he had masturbated the girl, it had made him feel puerile. Her keeping him in this puerile situation accounted for his great anger with her.

Turning the pages of the big book.

There was a magnificently illustrated big book in his parents' house which he used to look at while his mother sat beside him and explained the pictures. Those had been very pleasurable occasions in the boy's life.

At the age of sixteen he had struck up an acquaintanceship in a park with a retired official, who had engaged him in obscene conversations and suggested taking him to a waitress with whom he could have intercourse at his expense. The patient agreed, but reluctantly, because he felt ashamed of the idea of somebody else's getting him a woman. The man took him to a low tavern and came to terms with the waitress, and then they went back to his flat. But waiting for the woman to turn up enabled the patient's moral consciousness to gain the upper hand, and he told the man he was not going to wait any longer but was going to drop the whole thing, he was going home to work. "Today we're going to read a book with just two thick pages," the man replied. He was referring of course to the female genitals with the two labia. The patient was not to be detained, however, and went home.

It now struck him that this idea of a two-leaf book had often disturbingly occurred to him while masturbating his girl.

The connection between looking through the book and the kitchen tap.

In the patient's family the children's term for "penis" was 'tap.'[3]

If the tap was a penis and the book a vulva, the connection which was felt to exist in the dream became intelligible, as intelligible as the patient's wondering whether turning the pages was really what he wanted to be doing; for he did not want just to 'turn the pages' with his girl friend, which was a thing one did with one's fingers, as the patient had really done; he had wanted to establish connection with the "tap," i.e., engage in coitus.

His taking rags to the kitchen, which somehow arose out of turning the pages of the book.

He had often masturbated into handkerchiefs and rags, which were thus substitutes for the female genitals. "And amounted to the same thing."

There is no more doubt about the meaning of this identification. The kitchen tap was still dirty.

This was no surprise. The dream picture meant that he was trying to connect the female genitals with the penis (taking rags into the kitchen, where the tap was). The tap was still dirty because it had not yet been brought into contact with the rags by which it should obviously have been polished. Incidentally the patient explicitly remembered that in high school jargon *putzen* (cleaning) and *scheuern* (rubbing) both meant "masturbating."

We can now interpret the dream fragments dealt with so far. The patient dreamt that he was masturbating his girl friend, a simple wish-fulfilment dream, since this sexual activity, in spite of all the resistance he put up against it, gave him pleasure. The wish had been roused by the lack of the pleasure to which he had grown used. It made him feel puerile, and he compared this method of obtaining satisfaction with masturbation, in which he used pieces of cloth instead of the female genitals. This unworthy activity reminded him of his old struggle with masturbation, for the wish to masturbate in the dream revived the old resistance which in the past had cost him so many unkept good resolutions. The connection with the time in his childhood when the promise to be "good" had been a token of his love for his mother was established by means of the tap. He wanted to polish it to show his mother how good he was.

As, however, the tap was already a conscious penis symbol at that time, we must bring the somnambulant walk into the kitchen into the picture in order to complete the interpretation. The boy had evidently had a masturbation dream, or an equivalent dream of having to urinate, and he had reacted to the stimulation of the penis by attempting a demonstration of his love for his mother. In connection with this part of the dream the patient produced memories from still earlier periods, when his mother had handled his penis and washed it when giving him his daily bath. That this memory was also operative in the dream can be seen from the fact that the tap had to be cleaned ("polished"). In this connection the patient later confessed that having his penis handled by women gave him particular pleasure. This was also how he had reached orgasm in his affair with the girl student. This association of "turning the pages" connected masturbation (though by another person) with his own genitals, though it seemed originally to refer to someone else's. But the whole complex of wishes seemed to be the agent of some idea of a love object.

The circumstance that in the dream the patient was continually aspiring to reach the tap and clean it permitted the analyst to suggest that he wanted to handle his penis, i.e., masturbate, that it was the memory of mutual masturbation with his girl that made him want to do this, and that his continual failure to reach the tap indicated an inhibition against the autoerotic act. The patient's comment on this interpretation was that in his high school days he had often begun masturbating but that his scruples had gained the upper hand and he had stopped. He would pick up a book to distract himself, and his favorite method of doing so was by learning French vocabulary. He had often succeeded in quenching the urge to masturbate by this means, but sometimes he had failed, and masturbation had then ended in ejaculation, resulting in the revulsion that he feared so much.

This explained the "learning French" dream fragment; it was a way of distracting himself from the desire to masturbate. Hence his sense of relief in the dream when he started learning French. 'This he was good at, he felt delighted', delighted, that is to say, that he had succeeded in diverting himself from the wish to masturbate. But he was not allowed to enjoy his virtue long. Learning grew more and more difficult and finally broke down altogether, for the wish that it was intended to suppress again returned to the assault. The only means of defense against it left to the patient was fear, which roused him from sleep; the forbidden pleasure had been warded off.

Exactly the same interpretation applied to the preceding dream fragment, in which the patient was doing addition, accompanied by a feeling of relief, until he became aware that he ought to be doing something to the tap, whereupon the adding lost its value. Its place was taken by learning French, just as this had taken the place of turning the pages of the book, which occupation had been frustrated by inhibition when the pages stuck and their number increased so alarmingly.

The patient had little criticism of the suggestion that he could assume that he was again engaged in a struggle against masturbation. His eventual complete acceptance of it gave him the relief well known in psychoanalysis.

For the purposes of this study, the only still uninterpreted aspect of the dream that arises is the repetition of the phenomenon that the dreamer starts work at a moderate pace, which then gets faster and faster. This phenomenon is well known to us from waking life; it is constantly connected with the fear of being unable to finish in time. There is no need to elaborate on the extent to which "not being able to" is identical with "not wanting to," and the application of this identification to repressed sexual wishes.

The occupations in which the patient engaged in his dream, according to our interpretation so far, had different and even opposite purposes. "Turning the pages" turned out to be symbolic masturbation of the female genitals, while adding up and learning French symbolized distraction from the sexual wish. The conflict, however, is apparent rather than real. This follows from the theoretical consideration that the meaning of distraction here is equivalence and this could be the starting point for an inquiry into whether these occupations too do not—in contrast to first appearances—stand for sexual activities. The conclusion seems the more irresistible in view of the fact that both the addition and learning French culminated in anxiety. It would follow that the relief at first afforded by each change of occupation was due to relief at diversion from fear, just as in normal life we feel relief when we succeed in displacing an idea that causes anxiety by a harmless one. The dream censorship is momentarily deceived by the new idea, but the affect struggling to emerge soon finds a route leading toward discharge in the new idea, which is obviously suited to this purpose. Once more the censorship is faced with the danger of being overborne which it again obviates by the formation of anxiety.

However, there is no need of theoretical deductions or conclusions in order to identify the occupations that occur in this dream as symbolical representations of sexual activities. We have only to recall that we obtained the meaning of the occupations of cleaning, rubbing, turning the pages of a (two-leaf) book, not from interpretation of the dream, but from the dreamer's stock of conscious memories, i.e., from an undeniably sexual vocabulary, partly general and partly specific to the dreamer (turning the pages or reading a two-page book). Let us add that 'learning French' was a phrase familiar to the dreamer as referring to a sexual perversion, the attraction of which was not entirely unknown to him, though he had never practiced it. It can further be recalled the *rechnen* (calculating) in obscene jargon means masturbation ($6 \times 6 = 36$) and finally the *arbeiten* (working) is an obscene word for coitus, though it is sometimes used for masturbation; in any case it stands for active sexuality. Which meaning it has in individual cases can be determined only by analysis.[4]

With the knowledge now acquired, the dream can now be translated as follows. The dreamer, deprived of his girl, relapses into his old wish to masturbate (throughout the dream he is supposed to be cleaning the kitchen tap). At first he prefers masturbation with another subject (turning the pages), but that too is masturbation ("it amounts to the same thing"). He then begins calculating. But that too means the same thing ($6 \times 6 = 36$); in other words, the wish to masturbate repressed by the idea of turning pages now reappears in the disguise of calculation. At this point the patient added a new piece of interpretation: last week's bills stood for settling accounts with the girl. Checking them (*revidi-*

eren) he translated by "seeing her again" and "adding up," by "bringing them together." Here there is an evident turning to object love. That (i.e., coitus) he is good at, he says to himself in the dream, expressing his wish in regard to the matter, and feels a sense of relief accordingly. But it soon turns out that he fails to achieve it, for in the background there remains the desire to masturbate which, under the mask permitted by the censorship, might lead to an ejaculation. This it is necessary to prevent, and accordingly inhibition sets in, which in turn leads to anxiety.

The rest of the dream can be translated in the same way. What we are faced with, in short, is a conflict-fraught wish for sexual satisfaction. The wish to masturbate conflicts with adult male pride, while the wish for coitus conflicts with the patient's habitual masturbatory attitude which, however, became fixed because of the patient's rejection of coitus. Recalling his relations with his mother, we have long since attributed this rejection to oedipal fantasy.

III

After learning about occupation dreams, I felt completely cut off from access to understanding the alcoholic occupation delirium. The chief feature of the occupation dream is the anxiety that arises from the dreamer's realizing that he cannot possibly finish what he is doing. In contrast to this, the alcoholic delirium patient shows the facetious euphoria of a man of trivial interests who is doing his usual work in the best of spirits; the only striking feature is the extraordinary haste and an industriousness unusual in a man more given to drink than to work.

It was clear to me that, if anxiety could not be shown to be present in occupation delirium, there was no analogy between it and the occupation dream. Delirium patients answered direct questions about anxiety in the negative, often with humor and self-assurance. Also I failed at first to obtain any evidence that these patients had any feeling that they would never get finished, as in reply to direct questions they always said they did not worry about it. Catamnestic questions at first yielded no information about their affectivity. The patients who happened to be at my disposal had no interest in affectivity, or must have had an idea of anxiety different from mine. Not till I came across a case of abortive alcoholic delirium in a young woman who could be made to concentrate on self-observation while in delirium and gave sensible and coördinated information about her morbid condition did I obtain access to an understanding of it.

The important features in her case history were that she was unhappily married, took to drink because of dissension with her husband, and took no pleasure in sex. "I am glad when he leaves me alone," she said, typically. In this, as in the rest of her life history, she conformed to the pattern of the overwhelming majority of alcoholic psychotics. The unusual clinical feature of the case was that the patient often realized with astonishment that she was delirious, and thus behaved as one does sometimes in dream when, just on the point of awaking, one realizes with astonishment that one is dreaming. Thus her condition was not sharply marked off from ordinary consciousness, and her delirium was not complete. It was not difficult to pull her out of it, and when she was reporting her delirious ideas as reality and suddenly realized that they were delirious she would feel ashamed of herself. The abnormal condition would persist on this low level for two days, and the patient would then give a completely informative catamnesis.

I made contact with her in the delirious state while she was piling laundry. Every so often she wanted to move a completed pile aside. This cost her a visible effort, and she began hurrying. I obtained the following information from her about this phase.

In her delirium she found herself confronted with a large quantity of freshly ironed laundry. She had no clear idea how it had got there, but had the feeling that she had ironed it herself. Now she wanted to pile it. At first the work went ahead very well but, strangely enough, the unpiled laundry did not diminish; in spite of the work she had done, there was as much there as there had been when she began. So she started hurrying. At the same time she had a feeling of competence and efficiency, of being a "good" person. Gradually, however, she began feeling mildly anxious, because she saw that she could not get finished. Whenever she wanted to move a pile aside, the anxiety increased; she then had a feeling of tremendous helplessness in the face of the weight (resistance) of the pile, though this did not really seem to her to be very great and she knew from experience that she could manage it. It was this anxious sense of impotence in the face of the pile that she felt to be the most disagreeable thing about her delirium. She also said that she actually had not moved a single pile, but that while trying to do so she invariably forgot what she was doing; and that she found herself just as often piling the laundry as trying to move the finished piles without ever really knowing how she changed jobs. She always had the feeling of competence when she began piling, and anxiety set in when she started hurrying after a time, and the anxiety was greatest when she was unable to move the piles. There was never an overwhelming attack of anxiety, but a hazy, dreamlike transition to a change of job. She gave similar information about the other activities which provided the content of her delirium.

The resemblance between occupation delirium and occupation dreams could not have been more striking. Later I succeeded in obtaining details by questioning patients either in delirium or catamnestically. My failure to obtain better answers previously had been due to the way I put my questions, which I eventually succeeded in adapting to the patients. It is noteworthy that in no single case was the anxiety extreme.

The course of the alcoholic occupation delirium in general is that the patient sets about some task with confidence, in the best of spirits and with the humor characteristic of the self-confident, uninhibited, tipsy state. After a time the work ceases to go ahead. Either the task becomes interminable ('the more washing I do, the more there is to be done', the hoops a cooper had to fix increased to an unmanageable pile), or the task (burden) becomes, often contrarily to the patient's expectation, one with which he feels unable to cope.[5] The patient then starts hurrying in order to get finished, or makes a tremendous effort to move a heavy object or to hold up something that is about to fall, when the sensation of physical resistance[6] is felt very plainly. The mounting sense of impotence in the face of the task to be done is accompanied by mild anxiety, which keeps increasing for a time. But before it reaches a pitch comparable, say, to that which causes a dreamer to start from his sleep, the patient changes his occupation or begins it afresh. Each change of occupation or each restart is accompanied by a sense of relief. Also the delirium may be interrupted; the patient may allow his attention to be engaged by someone and give facetious replies, the cheerfulness of which I assume to be attributable to the sense of relief (saving of anxiety) resulting from distraction from the development of the anxiety connected with the activity on which he was engaged, while at the same time the anxiety is dissimulated under this smiling disguise. The catamnesis of one case showed beyond doubt that being spoken to by the physician interrupted both the anxiety and the delirious activity. Instead of occupations there may be endless journeys, the destination of which is never reached. Whatever it is that the patient has to do is of unpostponable urgency.

The following are additional reasons for regarding alcoholic occupation deliriums and probably all other occupation deliriums as occupation dreams.

My analyses have shown that individuals who have occupation dreams suffer from fear of impotence. The occupation dream is a fear-of-impotence dream. It is a complete reflection of the dreamer's waking condition. The latent ideas demonstrably present in the dream which lead to changes of occupation correspond to the inhibitions which in waking life inhibit the dreamer from obtaining full sexual satisfaction. (The fear of impotence that in the male completely or partially inhibits erection or unduly delays or precipitates ejaculation has its complete counterpart in the female who anxiously awaits the expected and desired orgasm but is left unsatisfied and disappointed.)

The occupation dream also seems to be a reaction to real lack of sexual satisfaction; it is associated with continence. Of the individuals whom I was able to observe, I can also report that when they had sufficiently frequent or regular intercourse they were either not impotent at all or not seriously impotent. Though they hardly ever attained complete physical satisfaction, they rarely failed to attain orgasm. But these patients are unable to tolerate continence, and as soon as unpleasure sets in they become nervous, anxious, and ill-humored, and fear of impotence is prominent among their symptoms. Analysis of the psychical details connected with their sexual intercourse shows regularly that to them coitus is to a large extent a substitute for masturbation and the only real one, while masturbation is badly tolerated and only sporadically practiced, against very strong resistance. During coitus these patients are concerned with themselves and not with the love object, which provides them only with the illusion of object satisfaction, the autoerotic act being forbidden by their sense of guilt. The love object is simply used to obtain self-satisfaction. Deeper analysis shows a strong homosexual-narcissistic fixation of the libido; this applied in the case of the patient whose occupation dream we analyzed above. More or less pronounced paranoid traits are also found in these cases.

All these so characteristic features of dreamers of occupation dreams recur in the prehistory of alcoholic delirium patients and alcoholics in general. Without exception they are either people whose sex life consists of sporadic intercourse with fleeting acquaintances—generally prostitutes—or they live in perpetual dissension with a partner, whether married or not. The psychical value of their sexual relations is minimal; these are characterized by the crudest sensuality and lack of erotic or moral respect for the other sex. With many alcoholics coitus is infrequent and is generally practiced under the influence of alcohol. The women are often frigid and 'glad to be left alone', and the men are impotent in one way or another, though complete impotence is rare, except when drunk.

All this points to the conclusion that the alcoholic's relationship to the other sex is disturbed, but the disturbance becomes very plain if one looks at the occasions that so often cause individuals whose behavior is otherwise normal to take to drink. The prehistory of alcoholism consists of disappointment in love, loss of the woman one loves, fear of impotence as a consequence of venereal disease; in the case of women, it is loss of their husband's love or loss of respect for him. Alcoholism following physiological impotence due to advancing age belongs to the same category. Thus the alcoholic's relationship to the other sex is either disturbed in advance, or such disturbance follows some experience. Alcoholism has then to fulfil a twofold task; to daze the mind so that the painful reality is forgotten, and to provide a surrogate pleasure. Now, not everyone who has had an unhappy love experience becomes an alcoholic. A predisposing factor for the addiction may be a strong oral libido.[7] (What we have said about predisposition of course also applies to seduction into drinking.) A second component in predisposition to alcoholism is revealed by the social behavior of the alcoholic. Drinking generally takes place in the company of one's own sex. Men drink with other men in taverns; their wives drink with friends or neighbors; mother and daughter sometimes take to drink together. The solitary drinker is a transient phenomenon.[8] It can be observed that drinking in solitude lasts only as long as does narcissistic pleasure in the suffering imposed by the other sex. This narcissistic-homosexual pleasure is soon displaced by the pleasure of object homosexuality. The table at the tavern takes the place of the woman the drinker wishes to or has to forget. The predisposing factors for alcoholism are narcissism and homosexuality.

This provides an explanation of the fact that the two major alcoholic psychoses, hallucinosis and delirium tremens, can end in paranoia. The predisposing factors for alcoholism and paranoia are the same. The alcoholic gets his paranoia by a circuitous route, by way of the poison which re-enforces his homosexuality and his narcissism by encouraging aversion from the other sex because of the fear of impotence, by favoring association of individuals of the same sex, by encouraging more than normal enjoyment of affectivity, and thereby endangering or greatly diminishing the inhibitions erected against the repressed homosexual-narcissistic trend. The instincts belonging to this constellation return from repression and are worked up by the mechanism of paranoia.[9]

One should not be led astray by cases of men and women, usually married couples or lovers, who drink heavily together. They get on well together only while drinking together. Alcohol is of course a liberator of all instincts, including the heterosexual instinct, and the supply of heterosexuality liberated is sufficient to make possible the establishment of a transient contact with the partner of the other sex. But the supply is small, the love is of short duration, and the usual end of these drinking bouts is a fight.

The homosexuality we are discussing is of course condemned to remain unconscious. The table in the tavern constitutes its sublimation, paranoia its working up into pathological symptoms. It is just sufficient to upset relationships with the other sex or to create a vulnerable spot for disturbances, to which the individual reacts by a surrogate formation able in one way or another to satisfy the unconscious wish.

One other observation takes us a little further into the problem. It had long since struck me that alcoholic psychotics never masturbate, either in hallucinosis or in delirium tremens, while masturbation is frequent or at any rate occasional in all the other psychoses. The alcoholic psychotic does not regress to autoerotism; his libido, in so far as it can be activated, remains object libido.

This gives us a clue to the understanding of the occupation delirium. To the alcoholic the way back to crude homosexuality is blocked; he has worked up his homosexuality in the way we described above. He does not practice autoerotism. Occupation delirium can thus only be a coitus-wish delirium. This, like a dream, represents the fulfilment of a wish the sufferer is not fully capable of fulfilling in his normal waking life and is totally incapable of fulfilling in the state of toxicosis. He took to alcohol, after all, because the other sex had left him dissatisfied. His dearest wish would have been to achieve a satisfactory love relationship with the other sex. Now he drinks and alcohol liberates his libido, but at the same time it makes him impotent. So the delirious patient, with his judgment destroyed and his appetites unleashed, like a dreamer impeded by sleep from the real satisfaction of his wishes, represents his perpetually unsatisfied wish for satisfaction with the other sex as having been fulfilled. This gives him a sense of competence and self-assurance, the 'this-I-am-good-at' feeling experienced by the patient whose occupation dream we analyzed. Both in the delirium and in the dream, 'working' is equivalent to engaging in coitus. But the work never gets going, in the delirious situation real coitus must not and cannot be attained. When the libidinal tension is at its height anxiety steps in, indicating inhibition of the dreamt-of wish. Alcoholic occupation delirium should be regarded as a coitus-wish delirium strictly analogous to the occupation dream, and its appearance in the form of a fear-of-impotence delirium accords with the sexual set up of the patient, whose potency, hampered by internal and external resistances, is totally inadequate to the demands of his increased libido.[10]

Notes

1. I am indebted to Professor J. Wagner von Jauregg's clinic in Vienna for the cases I was able to observe.

2. In a discussion of this subject at the Vienna Psychoanalytic Society Freud remarked that anxiety was a pathological discharge of libidinal affect. I agree completely. The idea of pathological discharge is consistent with my view of conversion of affect, which represents a morphological way of regarding the matter, while Freud's refers to the mechanics, the dynamics, of the process.

   Attribution of responsibility for the development of anxiety to toxic damage to the consciousness, which turns out to be adequate to cope with the incursion of affect resulting from the elimination of inhibitions is of course not inconsistent with psychoanalytic theory on the origin of anxiety. The inability of the conscious to cope is brought about in this instance by the toxic influence; in the absence of the latter, resistance does the work of preventing the repressed from coming to consciousness.
3. Tausk: *Zur Psychologie der Kindersexualität. Internationale Zeitschrift für ärztliche Psychoanalyse*, 1913, p. 451. "Fritz: 'It (the penis) is a water supply too; there's a tap, and a pipe, and the water flows out.' " A tap is a very common penis symbol among boys.
4. When the present paper was discussed by the Vienna Psychoanálytic Society Professor Freud and Dr. Hanns Sachs called attention to the phylogenesis of the dream symbol of 'working'. We are indebted to Dr. Hanns Sperber of Uppsala for uncovering this symbolism (*"Über den Einfluss sexueller Momente auf Entstehung und Entwicklung der Sprache'* Imago I, 5, 1912, Vienna, Hugo Heller & Co.). This paper was previously unknown to me, but it provides ample and acute corroboration of Freud's discovery that symbolism is a residue of the primordial language to which civilized man regresses in certain conditions, chiefly in art, in dream, and in mental illness. Sperber's work was done independently of psychoanalysis, which gives it the value of independent evidence.

   The author first asks what could have led to the development of language, and finds the answer in the need to communicate. He sees its origin in two primitive selfish situations, the child's drawing his mother's attention to his need of food and the male's need to draw the female's attention to his need to mate. He gives good reasons for rejecting the assumption that social reasons ("warning cries") were primary factors.

   The cry of hunger hardly comes into consideration as a factor leading to the development of language, as it belongs to earliest infancy and does not inherently contribute to further development since, apart from reflex sounds, the child learns language from adults. The chief source of language formation must be looked for in sexuality. Its origin lies in the alluring call.

   The further development of language was vitally affected by the invention of tools. Sperber says: 'I believe that primitive activities carried out with the aid of tools were accompanied by sounds that resembled alluring calls in that they had a sexual accent. By that I mean that in the fantasy of primitive man activity with tools bore a certain resemblance to activity of the sexual organs; that working with tools was to a certain extent seen to be a replica of the sexual process, and that affects consequently appeared similar to those that accompany mating, though of course of lesser intensity, but causing tension in men's minds. This tension had necessarily to be discharged in a way similar to sexual tension, i.e., by the emission of sounds.'

Sperber strikingly demonstrates the sexual accentuation of all work intended to promote the fertility of the soil. The psychology of the development of language from this source can be deduced from the resemblance between the fertilization of the soil and the sexual fertilization of animals and man. The comparison can be shown to have arisen autochthonously everywhere in the world. In all languages we find a 'mother earth' who is 'worked, tilled, ploughed' by means of a tool which is compared with a phallus. The 'womb' of earth receives the 'seed', and 'bears' just like the womb of woman. The words most closely connected with agriculture plainly show the sexual origin of language. The terms used for methods of reducing the size of grain are identical, perhaps in all languages, with terms that mean *coire.* The Latin *molere,* the Greek *myllein,* the English 'mill' and 'grind', mean both *coire* and 'triturate'. *Pinsere* is related to *pisti,* meaning *coire:* the Latin *pilum,* 'pestle', recurs in the Low German and Danish (borrowed) *pil,* which means penis, Sperber also shows that words for all activities that involve cutting with blunt tools have also meant or still mean coitus. Thus *ficken,* or *fickeln* (to cut clumsily), *fuxeln, fegeln* (hence probably *vögeln*), *gixen, fummeln, finken* and *futjen,* all words known to mean coitus in obscene speech, in various dialects and speech areas mean cutting or sawing with a blunt instrument and also *coire.*

Sperber adduces very extensive evidence from all fields of activity and speech areas, supplementing these few examples in all directions and in very convincing fashion. He explains the 'desexualization' of originally sexually accented activities as follows: 'With the invention of the first tool a word was invented that was first so strongly accented sexually that we must ascribe to it a double meaning, i.e, both to perform the sex act and to describe some job, e.g., digging. This word was learnt by the next generation a long time before the mating urge was felt by it, and the sexual significance of the word consequently receded and acquired the quality of a secondary or figurative meaning, as it were. And, though the sexual accentuation of the work might easily on occasion occupy the foreground, in general it would more and more fade into oblivion as men more and more habituated themselves to it and it became commonplace. When a new kind of work was discovered, however, the situation was different. This could take place only under the influence of sexual tension [Sperber's view coincides completely with Freud's concept of the sublimation of the sexual instinct]. Whenever a new kind of work was invented, the man using it was not in a calm frame of mind which would have enabled an existing word to be transferred to it, but in a state of excitation, an exclamatory mood; and it is obvious that his exclamations would have sounds different from those which other individuals had created perhaps several hundreds or thousands of years previously to designate an older method of working:

Sperber's paper should be read in full; to go on quoting from it seems inappropriate. The passages we have drawn on, however, furnish us with an important explanation of two facts to which our attention had not been directed. The first is the fact that to the present day new popular language formation, in so far as it creates new verbs or nouns, is almost exclusively concerned with new designations for sexual intercourse and the sexual organs (*Zumpf, Zumpel, pimpern, remmeln, titschkerln,* etc.). The second has an important bearing on the subject of the alcoholic occupation delirium. This is clinically described as trivial, in contrast to the sublime and fantastic activities which are sometimes the subject of hallucination in other psychoses. Professor Wagner-Jauregg drew attention to this characteristic of triviality when this paper was read to the Vienna Society for Neurology and Psychiatry. Sperber's paper makes it clear that work symbolism stands for 'trivial' occupation. It originates from the circumstance that it was the trivial occupations that were first invented by man and received the sexual accentuation of the creative impulse that led to the invention of the new working method. Patients suffering from alcoholic delirium who, with very few exceptions, belong to the working class, merely restore their 'trivial' activity to the libidinal level at which it was originally consciously learnt and acquired. The work which was a sublimation of the sexual instinct now becomes an expression of that instinct. It is simply a regression of sublimation. It is certainly no chance that terms descriptive of work such as *schustern, flicken, bohren, rammeln, putzen, pudern, stemmen* (cobbling, patching, drilling, ramming, scrubbing, powdering, chiselling, etc.) are popularly used for coitus. If our dreamer used more sophisticated occupations as sexual symbols, it was because he accommodated his sexual instinct in those higher activities.

Had he been a coachman he would have 'driven', which would then have had the same meaning as turning the pages of a book. Whether an occupation in a dream represents a form of a sexual activity in any particular case must of course always be established by individual analysis.

My further comments on Sperber's paper are that what he has to say on the origin of nouns from sexually accented work is not relevant in the present context; and that work symbols are also used secondarily to represent masturbation, which can be of vital importance in an individual case in the interpretation of dreams and for the understanding of mental disturance.

5. Here is an observation I made after I had finished this paper. A

patient in delirium felt very alarmed because he believed himself to be naked in a tavern. His clothes lay scattered about the room; one item of clothing was on a table, another on a chair, etc. Whenever he tried to pick up one of them, he either dropped it, or it mysteriously disappeared, or someone took it from him, or it had suddenly grown too small and he could not put it on, or he would notice while putting it on that the rest of his clothes had disappeared or had been taken away. (Here again we note that the occupation is trivial, though in this instance an exhibitionistic component is also present.)

6. Federn: *Über den Flugtraum. Jahrbuch für psychanalytische Forschungen*, 1915.
7. Freud: *Three Essays on the Theory of Sexuality.* [*Standard Edition* 7.]
8. Lenau *Der einsame Trinker:*

Ach wer möchte einsam trinken
Ohne an die Brust zu sinken
Einem Freund in Wonnedrang.

(Oh, who wants to drink alone without collapsing blissfully into the arms of a friend?)

9. Freud: *Psycho-analytic Notes on an Autobiographical Account of a Case of Paranoia.* [*Standard Edition* 12.]
10. I must also mention that I have recently succeeded in demonstrating anxiety in the animal hallucinations experienced during delirium tremens. All the creeping, crawling, scurrying, multiplying creatures (vermin, mice, rats, snakes, frogs, toads, lizards, cats, dogs, and more rarely, big animals such as horses and elephants) rouse anxiety in the patient. The 'little men' often hallucinated instead of animals belong to the same category. The interpretation of these hallucinations is by no means assured.

6

Diagnostic Considerations Concerning the Symptomatology of the So-Called War Psychoses

For a time, particularly during the first half of the war, authors used the term "war psychosis" quite indiscriminately. Some did so perhaps in the expectation that mental disturbances arising out of war experiences would show specific clinical characteristics; others used it without any particular theoretical premises and without any particular sense of responsibility. Recently I have had the impression that most authors have decided to use it merely to indicate the situation that was the immediate occasion of the illness. The fact that the war or a particular wartime event provides the content of the disturbed mental production is of course irrelevant in so far as such content is worked up into a mental disturbance of an already familiar type.

I was myself at first unable to form an opinion whether or not specific war psychoses existed. The special difficulties presented by the type of patient encountered in the Russian theater of war at first confronted me with cruder tasks, which had to be tackled

---

Diagnostische Erörtungen auf Grund der Zustandsbilder der sogenannten Kriegspsychosen. Weiner Medizinischene Wochenschrift, 1916. Originally read at the Second Conference of Medical Officers, Lublin, January 19, 1916. Later experiences made revision and expansion necessary. An important part of the theoretical discussion of paranoia *cum* melancholia was added after a discussion at the Vienna Psychoanalytical Society. Some of the cases quoted and the description of acute anxiety paranoia are also subsequent additions. Translated by Eric Mosbacher and Marius Tausk under the editorship of Paul Roazen.

before any diagnosis was possible. In the first instance my efforts were of course devoted to classifying cases into clinically established diagnostic categories, even though some of the phenomena with which I was confronted struck me as new and incomprehensible in the light of my clinical teaching.

The difficulties in the way of diagnosis in certain—and very numerous—cases could be reduced to two main factors: ignorance or insufficient knowledge of the patients' language and its nuances—they came from all the language groups of the monarchy—and the social and cultural characteristics of the level of their prewar life.

Better knowledge of the many foreign languages involved, and in particular adaptation to the awkward and unreliable process of examining patients with the aid of interpreters, soon resulted in many apparently new and incomprehensible phenomena turning out not to be problematical at all. The second factor, however, remained important in shaping the clinical picture and continued to make diagnosis difficult. Though at the conclusion of my observations I was generally able to decide that the clinical picture belonged to one of the known groups, I often had to add the qualification that that was what the illness appeared to be in an individual of his particular social stratum or cultural group. I had to remind myself that a training in a university hospital of a big city, with relatively sophisticated patients, had its disadvantages; the most primitive forms of the various mental diseases did not occur among them. It is hardly possible to exaggerage the primitiveness of certain popular classes. A peasant from Lower Austria represents a high standard of cultural development in comparison, for instance, with a Ruthenian peasant, whose interests and outlook on life we can describe in words but cannot enter into with emotional understanding. It was for that reason that a number of cases of schizophrenia seemed for a time quite inaccessible for me. A number of these patients presented a picture of euphoric feeble-mindedness associated with the behavior of a manically excited, stupid child of five or six. What looked like the 'talking past one' that was such an impressive feature might just as well have been due to nonunderstanding, dull-mindedness, or stupid malice. The incommunicativeness of these people, the poverty of their ability to convey what is going on in their mind, even when normal, has to be experienced before the difficulties involved in making a differential diagnosis can be appreciated. All the ways in which schizophrenics living in European cultural conditions communicate their abnormal bodily sensations, e.g., when they say they are electrified, hypnotized, influenced, and so forth, are not available here. The brooding about the change in identity and personality that is so characteristic of schizophrenia does not occur. These patients do not brood; they are totally bewildered by the morbid phenomenon taking place inside them and are incapable of putting anything about it into words. Many create the impression of delirium tremens; others look so exactly as if they were in the manic phase of a progressive general paralysis that it is impossible to fall back on the picture of schizophrenia in all its manifold forms that one acquired in hospital. Only the variety of symptoms in these patients, the changes and the multiplicity of the phenomena which present themselves, point to the multiplicity of internal processes which are worked up into the numerous morphologically different symptoms so characteristic of schizophrenia. It is important to stress this multiplicity, because we are often faced with phenomena which do not conflict with the patient's situation and can easily be taken for the unimportant outcome of psychical processes adapted to the environment. It is a relief to one's scientific conscience when one comes across a definite, clinically characteristic, symptom, such as when a patient suddenly gives his neighbor a terrible box on the ear for no reason whatever and then takes no further notice of him, or wets his bed or smears it with feces, because, if general paralysis has been more or less excluded, it is then possible to diagnose schizophrenia.

These patients are mentally as unproductive in illness as they are in health; they present nothing but crude expressions of affect—depression, cheerfulness, or anger; and to the extent that these states of mind are insufficient for diagnostic purposes, the psychiatrist is faced with the apparently often insuperable difficulties referred to above.

Among the approximately 1,500 cases which were referred to me in the course of seven-and-a-half months, mostly directly from the front, there were only four cases of typically pure paranoia, and these were German-speaking trained craftsmen. Melancholia was fairly frequently represented, several times associated with suicide attempts. It generally took an unproductive, stuporous form. In about one third of the cases it was accompanied by anxiety, but was always unproductive. In the case of peasants of the type described above, the patient would present the appearance of a sad, sick domestic animal. Acute amentia, which in the majority of cases followed catastrophic explosions, always presented a clear picture, of course.

As regards the so-called functional mental disturbances, such as neurasthenia, hysteria in all its forms, anxiety and obsessional neuroses, my observations are not in agreement with those of Laudenheimer,[1] who says that these do not occur among peasants and unskilled workmen, those prone to them being chiefly brain workers and members of the higher social classes. Among the patients whom I had the opportunity of observing, hysteria (in the form of tic, convulsive fits with *"arc de cercle,"* or twilight states) was as frequent among peasants and unskilled workmen as it was among the more educated.

It is not the training of the intelligence, but what Freud calls the vicissitudes of the sexual instinct that are relevant in these cases and, when instinctual development has been disturbed, the roots of the disturbance have to be looked for among conditions far more primitive than lack of education. Otherwise the outbreaks of mass hysteria among peasants in the Middle Ages would be inexplicable. It is also a long-familiar fact that hysteria occurs in our own time among peasants belonging to all cultures.

I propose to discuss a phenomenon that presents a diagnostic problem in a sense quite different from that which I have just mentioned. If we refer to the descriptions of psychopathological conditions in our textbooks, we find that symptoms of different psychoses occur in each that is dealt with as a diagnostic unit. In particular, paranoid symptoms, for instance, occur in almost every instance, and melancholic features are nearly always present in all cases and in all psychoses. Broadly speaking, however, we can regard melancholia, paranoia, schizophrenia, etc., as units, in spite of the occurrence of symptoms belonging to other clinical pictures.

Clinical psychiatry has hitherto restricted itself to describing the symptoms under each main classification as primary or secondary, but has had no or only very superficial explanations to offer of the psychical mechanism of the individual symptoms. There are authors who believe that by using a metaphorical or a comparative description of a psychical disturbance they have uncovered the cause and essential content of a symptom.[2] There are others who try to rationalize and explain symptoms which can be observed as occurring independently and without fixed correlation with others as having a conscious connection with other coexistent symptoms;[3] to say nothing of those authors who look for a specific organic cause of the illness, completely disregarding the presence of individual symptoms in nearly all the psychoses.[4] Now, so long as symptoms could be tidily classified and the diagnosis based on the chief symptom turned out to be prognostically correct, subsidiary symptoms could be ignored without psychological scruples, and a case could be diagnosed as melancholia, for instance, and the subsidiary paranoid traits could be disregarded. These were merely subsidiary, and were noted as such for the sake of completeness.

I owe to the war a number of cases which simply refuse to fit in with this psychiatric system. To the extent that they were occasioned by the war they are "war psychoses."

First of all, there were some cases in which melancholia was fully developed in every respect with all its characteristic symptoms but coexisted with a no less fully developed paranoia.

The first case I saw was a shoemaker from northern Bohemia, aged thirty-four, married and the father of two children. Alcoholism and syphilis were denied and could not be demonstrated. The symptoms of melancholia were depression, self-reproach for masturbation, dishonesty, offensive behavior to others and treating his wife and children badly, since in former years he had sometimes drunk wine or beer on Sundays instead of laying the money aside for his family. He expected very severe punishment indeed for his sins. He had recently attempted suicide and was now obviously dissembling the thought of suicide. He did not believe he would ever feel better again. In addition to this he presented the following picture of a well developed paranoia. He had noticed for some time that he was an object of general hostility. Wherever he was, in the street or with his unit, he was the subject of whispered remarks, and he was watched and looked at suspiciously. He had heard his name suddenly called out several times, and people had spat in front of him. A very striking feature was the extent to which he was worried by a pea-sized boil above his navel. He never stopped asking whether it would heal or whether he would not die of it, and he was greatly concerned that it should be treated and dressed every day. Hypochondria of this kind is of great importance for the diagnosis of paranoia (Freud).

The second case was that of an officer of aristocratic birth, who had led a very unscrupulous and dissipated life and was responsible for several broken lives; I was able to confirm that this was true. His sins, however, were probably attributable to the hypomanic phases which alternated at irregular intervals with his melancholic phases. When I saw him he was deeply melancholic, inconsolable, full of remorse and bitter self-reproach. His thought processes and affectivity were severely inhibited. There was also a complete system of ideas of reference and delusions of being watched, without hypochondria but with a pronounced resistance to the idea of leading a better life and a continuous readiness to suspect others.

Of the many other cases that came my way I select the following: 'Leopold K, infantryman, aged thirty, unskilled workman, at the front since July, 1915. No previous illness. According to a letter from his company commander, a brave and dependable soldier.'

About a fortnight previously the patient had suddenly changed, became apathetic, inhibited, and lost his appetite. "His mouth says what his heart does not feel." He said things such as "The lieutenant ought to be killed by a shell," or "We ought to desert to the Russians, as so many have done already." Such words "came to him" when he was under stress and he felt he could not stick it. He reproached himself bitterly for having said these things, but insisted that he said them only under "compulsion", without really feeling them. All the same, he had been accused of having these evil intentions. He believed he deserved severe punishment, though he had neither done nor intended anything wrong.[5] His comrades reported a suicide attempt made by the patient a few days previously. He had no more desire to live. Furthermore, he felt that recently he had become an object of suspicion, was being watched mistrustfully as if he were a traitor, a disloyal soldier, a spy. He had also been looked at askance because he wrote so few letters. What sort of man was this who had no one at home to write? But whom was he to write to and what had he to say? He had no feelings. His mother had abandoned him, and he did not know where she was. Before the war he had had a girl, but he no longer knew her address.

The following were noteworthy details from his life history. He was an illegitimate child, brought up by foster parents. He was allowed to see his mother only on Sundays, which hurt him very much and gave him a low opinion of women. Since his seventeenth year he had not seen his mother. She had married a man who was a total stranger to him. He had never had a lasting affair with a woman, he had kept changing and had never been really in love. But when he believed he was going to be transferred to another unit because of the bad things he had said, his first thought had been: "What will become of me if I never see my mother again?"

Salomon H, aged twenty, by civil occupation a waiter, who had been in the front line for fourteen months, had a week previously been ordered to fetch a number of men belonging to his unit from various taverns. He had carried out the order willingly. Next day, however, he had suddenly begun to feel he was a pitiful wretch who deserved no love, was heartless and worthless. He violently reproached himself, but at the same time felt he was being persecuted and watched by his comrades. They looked at him askance and suspected him of harboring the most evil thoughts.

Franz S, aged fifty, sergeant, civil occupation railway official.[6] The first impression created by the patient was of complete melancholia. He reproached himself severely for not having loved his wife sufficiently and not having carried out the orders of his superiors conscientiously enough. Now he had sunk low and was going to sink lower still, his wife was completely estranged from him, he was so worthless that nobody wanted to have anything to do with him. He reproached himself for having given in to his weakness and allowed himself to be sent to hospital. He should have stayed at the front. He presented the picture of a profoundly depressed, utterly disconsolate individual. His thought processes and affectivity were severely inhibited.

In the course of repeated examinations a fully developed paranoia appeared. He had been called up to the infantry, and had had to supervise fifty-year-olds building huts. He had noticed that the officers had hinted that he should not associate with other ranks, because by virtue of his education and civil occupation he really belonged to the officer class. When he had been talking to [other] sergeants, the inspecting officer who came to see them would be only a second lieutenant, but when he had refrained from associating with the sergeants the inspecting officer was always a lieutenant. This was a reward for maintaining his status, just as when the officer was only a second lieutenant it was a punishment for demeaning it. His present humiliation was a punishment for not having sufficiently heeded these hints by his superiors. His wife, having kept her position as postmistress, was now totally estranged from him, as she would not live with a man of inferior status. He had realized that his wife had become *getrennt* (estranged) from him when he was transferred to the *Train* (pronounced *trenn,* i.e., army service corps). At the ticket window at Lublin station he had realized he had one last chance of reconciliation with her. The booking clerk had had in front of him a rubber stamp pad which was covered with *Kompost* (compost). *Kompost* meant *komm zur Post* (come to the post office). He should have taken this obvious hint and turned back instead of going to hospital. Then he would have 'gone back to the post office', i.e., to his wife. But now all was lost.

During the examination he objected to my desk's being painted yellow. A doctor *der etwas weiss* (who was worth anything) would have had a *weiss* (white) desk. He himself had used to be white, but was now black. He drew this conclusion from the fact that there was a very dark-skinned gypsy in his ward.

At a clinical demonstration to the medical officers of the Lublin garrison he suddenly jumped to his feet and said: "Sir, I wish to report that I am a deer, a buck." When asked to explain, he replied: "I have been shot like a buck and I am now jumping down from one level to another."

He also said that before leaving for hospital he had asked his commanding officer to transfer him from the service corps to a unit at the front. The commanding officer had not replied, but next evening there had been *Gewehr und Geschützfeuer* (rifle and gunfire), and he had known his request had been granted. The outburst of fire had meant *Ich gewähre und beschütze* ("I grant and protect").

The patient's life history showed that before his marriage he had lived with a girl with whom he did not feel in love while the affair lasted. He had left her to marry for financial and social reasons. He had not been in love with his wife while living with her, but had felt that the woman he really wanted was his former sweetheart. He now felt that he had not loved his wife as much as she deserved, and since he had been separated from her he felt very much in love with her.

I refrain from mentioning the many other symptoms of the same type which the patient produced.

What should the clinical designation of these cases be? Melancholia or paranoia? Or paranoia *cum* melancholia? The last, I think, is the best description of the syndrome. It is not a mere mixture of the two conditions. The symptoms are present alongside each other, each in a state of full development, though affectively they conflict with each other at many points. How, for instance, is the self-belittlement and self-contempt of the melancholia to be reconciled with the megalomanic idea of being the center of attention? Attempting to follow the old pattern by relating the symptoms to each other according to their conscious content and thereby to rationalize them would surely lead to failure.

My clinical training gives me no clue to these strange syndromes. It would be easy to become famous by laying claim to the discovery of a new psychosis, though one would run the risk of being told that it had been known for a long time. However, I am avoiding this risk by announcing that it has indeed been known for a long time, though not in the sense that any author has ever drawn attention to a psychosis of the type described. But every psychiatrist has seen melancholic and paranoid mechanisms side by side, and the only outstanding feature about the cases I have mentioned is that they show large-scale development in both directions and thereby force themselves upon our attention.

We have thus reduced the problem to the question of the extent to which these disturbances usually occur together. In the psychoanalytic treatment of the neuroses they are found together in every possible proportion.

We cannot, however, remain satisfied with the mere statement of facts. If the coincidence of paranoia and melancholia is not universal but occurs only in a notable number of cases, the question arises of how this can come about. Are we confronted with two independent, isolated, psychical mechanisms having no connection with each other? That would seem theoretically improbable. Such isolation and independence is psychologically hard to conceive, and the frequency of the coincidence seems rather to point in the direction of an easily possible and therefore readily established connection between the two forms of illness. However, on the basis of current clinical views and practice, the path of further investigation would seem to be blocked. For, according to the textbooks, melancholia is a state of primary dejection to which the content of the patient's mind is adjusted, and it is therefore useless to look to it for an explanation of the illness. And paranoia? Practically all that clinical teaching has to say about it is that it is a form of insanity; and it has similarly refrained from posing the questions of which component of psychical life is involved in the specific symptom and which specific functions must be disturbed for a specific symptom to be generated to the exclusion of other symptoms; and what laws of normal psychical functioning cause the disrupted parts of the psychical mechanism so to be put together again that they invariably produce the same typical disturbances. Instead we see clinical psychiatry forcing diversity into terminological pigeon-holes. There was a time when this had a value that should certainly not be underrated. But nowadays there are things in the same pigeon-hole which have long since established their right to a genealogy of their own.

I consider it imperative to indicate the deep exploration of the psyche that would be possible if the psychoanalytic method were applied.[7]

I maintain, in agreement with Freud, that melancholia is a pathological reaction to the loss of love objects in the outside world, whether these are humans, animals, or things. The model of melancholia in the normal psyche, according to Freud, is the normal mourning over the loss of a love object; melancholia can thus be regarded as pathological mourning.

Now, we see that melancholia also arises in association with events in which there is no real loss of loved objects in the sense that these are destroyed or withdrawn. Clinical psychiatry notes that there can be very numerous and apparently very disparate occasions for the appearance of melancholia, including physical illness. The very fact that physical illness can lead to an outbreak of melancholia enables us to take a wider view of the problem of the conditions in which this mental disturbance arises and at the same time to regard it from a more elevated point of view.

As Freud, following a verbal suggestion by S. Ferenczi, points out in On Narcissism: An Introduction [Standard Edition, XIV, p. 69], a man plagued by organic pain and disagreeable sensations to a greater or lesser extent withdraws not only his general interest from the outside world but also his libidinal interest. 'The patient withdraws libidinal cathexis into his ego.'

Thus in the case of physical illness there is a loss of libidinal relationship with the outside world, just as there is when a real love object is lost. Libido is detached from the outside world. This detached libido has to find re-employment. Psychoanalysis tells us that unemployed libido can succumb to pathological elaboration.[8]

Detachment of libido can thus be due to either external or internal causes. "External causes" boil down to real object loss. An example of an internal cause is physical illness, in which libido is withdrawn to the ego.

We cannot proceed with the discussion of melancholia, i.e., the working up of detached libido into melancholia, without considering the mechanism of paranoia as described by Freud.

Let us assume, in accordance with psychoanalysis, that paranoia is a defense against the break-through of the unconscious homosexual-narcissistic component, as demonstrated by Freud in the Schreber case. The army provides all the conditions for mobilizing this component, in particular the close and exclusive contact with individuals of the same sex on active service. In the case of paranoia the individual is forced by the onslaught of unconscious homosexual libido to detach this libido from homosexual objects in order not to succumb to the sexual perversion. The amount of homosexual libido involved exceeds the amount that is socially acceptable, and because this amount is pathological it is worked up pathologically. In accordance with the narcissistic disposition of the homosexual, it is allotted to the ego, is used for the magnification of the ego and appears symptomatically in the form of megalomania. The delusions of reference and of persecution represent an attempt—reversed and projected into the outside world—at fighting off the homosexual object by perceiving it as hostile.

The problem in melancholia is why the detached libido is not used for magnifying the ego, for increasing self-esteem, for defiant self-assertion in the face of the outside world,[9] but rather for reducing self-esteem to the point of self-annihilation, for diminishing the ego, to quote a verbal remark of Freud's. I found the answer to the problem in an observation made some time ago and confirmed by Freud to the effect that the melancholic's self-reproaches are only seemingly directed against himself; they are really intended for the love objects he had abandoned.[10]

"They are the criticisms of the love object that made the patient give it up." (Verbal comment by Freud.)

This remarkable process of assuming the sins of others is explicable only by Freud's view (expressed in a verbal comment) that the melancholic identifies himself with the abandoned love object, so that criticism of the latter seems to be directed at the patient himself.

In the cases under discussion we are confronted with a twofold pathological mechanism of working up the detached libido, the paranoid and the melancholic.

Now, Freud's view that the paranoid mechanism is a specific method of warding off homosexual libido can be regarded as psychoanalytically firmly established. It is a specific form of libido characterized by the sex of the love object which is subjected to the paranoid mechanism. Part of the object libido, according to Freud, irrespective of the object's sex, is, provided that there is no regression to narcissism, pathologically applied to the production of anxiety. It should be added that Freud says in On Narcissism: An Introduction that narcissistic libido when pathologically magnified and provided it has not been converted into homosexual libido, appears, exactly like anxiety, in the form of hypochondria. We find anxiety and hypochondria typically, though not invariably, connected with melancholia or paranoia.

The question that now arises is which part of the libido is worked up into the melancholic mechanism.

The cases of paranoia *cum* melancholia on which this discussion is based seem to offer an approach to the solution of this problem. A striking feature of all these cases is that the melancholic self-reproaches always refer to persons of the opposite sex, wife, mother, or sweetheart. Corroboration of the psychological classification of this fact is provided by the observation I have repeatedly made that mania may also be an attempt to ward off the melancholic mechanism by contrast of mood after a repulse suffered by the heterosexual libido. This is confirmed by Freud, and other authors have corroborated it, and it also follows, if my memory is correct, from a paper by Hoch in New York. I now hazard the conjecture that it might be the detached heterosexual libido which is pathologically applied in part of the symptomatology of melancholia. The withdrawal of libido from the heterosexual object probably also accounts for the feeling of lovelessness of which the melancholic complains. The familiar symptom of loss of feeling for nature also seems to be connected with the heterosexual libido situation, for it appears with striking frequency as a sequal to heterosexual love disasters, both in normal life and in the transference neuroses. It will perhaps be possible to explain other melancholic symptoms by their closer or more distant relationship to heterosexuality. I most certainly do not claim, however, that this explains the whole symptomatology of melancholia, which undoubtedly has more widespread and perhaps deeper roots originating in different soil.

The task of attempting to explain how this double illness of paranoia *cum* melancholia comes about is greatly aided by the simple and transparent conditions in which it makes its appearance. Apparently what takes place is that in a unisexual environment the homosexual-narcissistic component is re-enforced. This entails a detachment of heterosexual libido. Part of the latter then becomes a floating surplus not worked up in such pathological mechanisms as anxiety and paranoia, and it is used to produce part of the melancholic symptoms. The re-enforcement of homosexuality becomes primary and brings about detachment of libido from heterosexual objects and from objects which by displacement of affect have acquired libidinal connections with heterosexuality. The conditions in which part of the libido in one and the same subject is worked up pathologically, as is the case with anxiety, while still directed toward external objects, for the time being remain obscure, as do those in which other parts enter the narcissistic constellation and are then worked up into paranoia or into certain melancholic symptoms, depending on the sex to which they are tied. We must content ourselves with noting that such interrelated partial processes can take place and assuming that in certain conditions which cannot be more closely defined components of the libido (narcissistic or object-directed, homosexual or heterosexual libido and also libido that has regressed in various degrees) having certain characteristics can succumb to various specific pathological mechanisms.

The question arises why the melancholic identifies himself with the abandoned love object and why, if our hypothesis is correct, this identification is applied specifically to the heterosexual object. The answer may lie in a still unpublished conjecture of Freud's (which I quote here with his special permission) which has the additional advantage of explaining how paranoia and melancholia can appear simultaneously. According to this hypothesis, a predisposition to melancholia should be expected in individual's who make their object choice on the narcissistic pattern and therefore deal with the heterosexual object on a homosexual basis.[11]

This proposition and its implications for the theory here presented require some further elucidation. In the Schreber case Freud has shown that in homosexuals object choice is of the narcissistic type. The homosexual loves his own sex, in his homosexual object he loves himself. However, as Freud shows in On Narcissism, heterosexual object choice may also be of the narcissistic type. But, while libido detached from the individual's own sex can be allotted to the ego and used for its magnification (it was allotted to an object by a pathologically magnified ego in the first place), it seems that libido vested in a heterosexual object lacks this property and cannot in all circumstances merely be withdrawn into the ego. The identification mechanism peculiar to the narcissistic constellation causes the loss of the external love object to appear in the form of loss of self-love, and in melancholia this assumes pathological dimensions, in the form of the total collapse of narcissism, self-love, self-confidence and self-esteem.

That we are confronted in the present cases with a narcissistic position of the heterosexual libido seems to be indicated by the fact that these melancholia patients are simultaneously suffering from paranoia, the narcissistic-homosexual disease par excellence. This circumstance suggests that a disturbance of homosexual relations in these individuals has also implicated that part of the heterosexual libido that is narcissistically employed.

The whole picture we have built up is strongly supported by the fact that the anamneses of melancholics generally show disturbances of love relationships with the opposite sex dating back to childhood. These patients complain that they have never been able really to fall in love. The criticism that this complaint is an outcome of the manifest melancholia does not conflict with the view that this disturbance is due to the patient's narcissistic-homosexual disposition.

It was this that led to this specific symptom at a very early age. Further evidence for our view is provided by the fact that melancholia often appears in men and women during the period when sexual life is becoming atrophied as a result of aging processes and the individual is losing his value as a love object and subject. The physiological diminution of heterosexual love relations may in these cases provide the impulse for the reenforcement of homosexuality, and the formation of melancholic symptom-formation may develop from that secondary position. An indication of the presence in some cases of an organic factor or substratum that might partly or wholly account for the psychical mechanism we have described is perhaps provided by the fact that during their illness women melancholics so often produce secondary masculine sexual characteristics (growth of beard).[12]

It might be concluded from the above that paranoia and melancholia are essentially correlated processes and should therefore always be found together. This, however, is by no means the case. Even the keenest observer must admit that some cases impress one as either pure paranoia or pure melancholia, though sometimes the coexistence of the two forms of illness may not be detected because of inexact observation. Nevertheless the coincidence of the two syndromes has been observed often enough, and gives the clinical picture in the cases here described quite specific features.

The special conditions in which these cases arose perhaps afford an explanation of those instances in which the coexistence of melancholia and paranoia is not demonstrable. I assume that in cases which have developed into pure paranoia the quantities of heterosexually cathected libido were so small from the outset that their detachment led to minimal symptom-formation, which was therefore unnoticed; or alternatively that in the course of a long, slow, insidious development of paranoia the heterosexual libidinal cathexes were worn away and bit by bit displaced by homosexual and narcissistic cathexes, with the result that at any particular moment only a minmal and therefore very ineffective amount of detached heterosexual libido was available for melancholic symptom-formation. The special conditions and pressures of life in wartime lead to paroxysmal processes and allow no time for such a slow demolition of heterosexual positions. A sudden and catastrophic collapse of heterosexual libido follows a sudden and catastrophic collapse of homosexual libido. Large amounts of heterosexual libido cathexes not previously suspected of being insecurely based may be shaken in a short space of time, often within a few hours. It seems natural that this process should bring to light both directions in which the disastrous development has taken place, and that the connection between the antagonistic libido positions should be shown by the collapse of one seeming to be the immediate consequence of the disturbance of the other. (I cannot at the moment offer a plausible explanation of pure melancholia from this point of view. It would be of the greatest theoretical interest if melancholia were observed in a conscious, declared homosexual. I have not encountered such a case.)

To support the view that we are confronted here with interrelated partial processes in the working up of specifically qualified libido, I wish to draw attention to a clinical picture of which I have failed to find a description in the psychiatric war literature to which I have had access. It has a better claim than any other to be called a war psychosis, because the conditions in which it appears could hardly arise to such a marked extent except in wartime.

I refer to an acute psychosis the affective feature of which is intense anxiety and the content of the ideation is persecutional. I would suggest the use of the term acute anxiety paranoia for this psychosis. It often set in with an anxiety dream or a brief delirium, but there may be no such prelude. Sometimes it begins with hallucinations, generally acoustic and rarely visual, but hallucinations may be absent altogether. Generally there is a brief prodromal phase of depression or apprehensiveness, generally lasting for a few hours but in a few cases for two or three days. Often, however, the illness erupts suddenly, on guard duty or on patrol, after an explosion or a fright. The 'fright neurosis' noted by several authors should probably be included in this group, but this is only a special case, characterized by the event that triggered it off. I propose to pay special attention to the condition in which hallucinations and states of confusion are lacking as these apparently are accessory symptoms only. In a very large number of cases the individual's affected are those who feel themselves enclosed among comrades speaking a strange language with whom they cannot communicate. In these instances we are almost entitled to talk of a solitude neurosis. The following is a typical patient's story.

He was the only Czech among a lot of Hungarians. Suddenly he noticed that they were suspecting and persecuting him. He heard them saying he was a traitor and a spy; they wanted to get rid of him, kill, poison, or execute him. Often patients believe they have been sentenced to death. Generally they are not aware of any bad intentions, but often admit that at the time when they first had this sense of being surrounded by hostility they had been doing exceptionally heavy work, or there had been talk of imminent war perils, or they were worried because they had not heard from home for a long time and were homesick for that reason.

In many cases this psychosis clears up with a change of environment. The paranoia, for instance, disappears when the patient finds himself among his fellow-nationals again, or being cared for and looked after in hospital. Psychoanalysis enables us without difficulty to recognize in this clinical picture, taking into account the occasion and circumstances of its appearance, a reaction to a suppressed desire to escape from the difficulties and dangers of military duty. The paranoid symptom is, as always, explained by the threat of homosexual-narcissistic components from the unconscious. A surplus of libido seems to have been worked up into anxiety.

There are cases which cannot be placed at all unless resort is had to psychoanalytic method, unless one contents oneself with using the suffix "form" (e.g., "hysteriform" etc.), or even less responsibly describes the clinical picture as 'mixed'. If psychiatry is to ignore psychoanalysis, I do not know what it will have to say about the following case.

A sergeant was ordered to buy some supplies on his way home on leave. As he did not want to spoil his leave, he asked a comrade to do it for him. The latter was negligent, and allowed the shopkeeper to smuggle some summer *salame* into the purchase instead of the winter *salame* that was ordered. On his way back from leave the sergeant collected the goods and discovered what had gone wrong. Within a few days he produced the following psychosis. He reproached himself severely for his neglect of duty, could get no peace, withdrew into himself, wept a great deal, and could not sleep. He suffered from terrible anxiety on the ground that the military authorities would now demand compensation on an enormous scale from his relatives and his financée, and pursue, harass, and ruin them, in spite of their total innocence in the matter. He felt he had ruined himself and his family. Also, though nobody but he yet knew anything about the matter, he noticed that he was being watched and looked at mistrustfully; and remarks that he overheard could be interpreted only as hints about his guilt and the punishment that awaited him. He wanted to go and see the mess officer to explain the matter, incriminate himself, and clear the whole thing up, but this officer himself went on leave before the interview could take place. The patient contemplated suicide and was totally disturbed and incapable of carrying out his duties. At the same time, however, he had the positive feeling that the whole thing was not worth talking about, that nothing would happen to him, and that the military authorities neither could nor would take any action against his family. Nevertheless he was defenseless against the onslaught of anxiety, remorse and ideas of persecution and reference.

Is this melancholia, paranoia, obsessional neurosis or hysteria?

Clearly a psychiatry that cannot explain the mechanism of individual symptoms as originating in the unconscious, does not understand the problem of infantilism, and can give no information about the mechanism of self-love and self-esteem, of love of one's own and the opposite sex, of the development and vicissitudes of all these forms of loving and the reactions of the ego to disturbances of these love relationships (knowledge of which can be gained only through psychoanalysis)—such a psychiatry, confronted with these cases of "war psychosis," will soon come to the end of its stock of names. To listeners who feel uncomfortable in this scientific impasse I can point only to the free road of psychanalysis.[13]

Notes

1. Laundenheimer-(Alsbach), *Anamnesen der sogenannten Kriegsneurosen. Feldärztliche Beilage zur Münchner medizinischen Wochenschrift,* No. 38, 21.9. 1915.
2. For example, Stranski, who considers that the term 'intrapsychical ataxia' solves a problem of psychomechanics. Similarly Berze with his 'primary weakness of psychical activity'.
3. Delusions of grandeur in paranoia, for instance, are attributed to a conscious search by the patient for an explanation of the persecution to which he feels he is subjected, which results in his concluding that he must be an exceptional personality if he is the object of so much attention. But megalomania occurs in general paralysis without delusions of reference.
4. Textbook descriptions of dementia praecox in particular often include reports of various findings in the brain at autopsy. But which of the innumerable symptoms present in all psychoses are attributable to these anatomical findings?
5. When the obsessional symptom is considered in conjunction with the situation that occasioned it, anyone familiar with Freudian psychoanalysis will have no difficulty in recognizing in it a rejected unconscious wish. It would obviously be meaningless in this instance to attempt to rationalize the delusions of reference and of being watched with the aid of conscious statements which the patient himself regarded as being alien to his own feelings. I was able to observe a whole series of similar cases associated with war experiences likely to stimulate revolt of the instinct of self-preservation against military duty. (See also concluding remarks on "acute anxiety paranoia".)
6. I give this patient's paranoid symptoms in detail because they provide an outstanding example of the use of verbal instead of concrete ideas

(Freud's *The Unconscious,* [Standard Edition, 14:161]) and also a conscious translation of verbal ideas into the language of concrete ideas. The fortunate circumstance that the patient made this translation spontaneously provided an indisputable demonstration of the complete analogy between pathological symptom-formation and the mechanics of dream formation as discovered by Freud, and of how impossible it is to understand symptoms without a knowledge of the mechanism of dreams, and how the opponents of psychoanalysis bar the way to psychopathology by rejecting freudian theory, and the interpretation of dreams in particular.

7. What follows should for the time being be regarded as amounting to no more than a working hypothesis based on experience in analysis of the neuroses. The validity of this experience for the explanation of the psychoses cannot always be demonstrated, though a high degree of probability alternating with certainty would seem to point to it. In so far as assumptions are used here which psychoanalysis itself does not yet regard as absolutely assured, they are all of a kind that fit in well with established psychoanalytic views. But even if future work should show them to be erroneous, I believe that as an attempt to present the psychoanalytic approach they open perspectives of psychological investigation in comparison with which the outlook from the position of clinical or organological psychiatry is like having a blank wall in front of one's eyes.
8. The normal psyche avoids this by transferring the free, i.e., detached libido to other objects, either by displacement of affect or by withdrawal into the ego. The latter mechanism however, as is made clear in Freud's *On Narcissism: An Introduction*, leads only to a temporary state of affairs, 'because man, if he is not to become ill, must eventually love again'; he must again transfer to the outside world that part of the libido that was withdrawn into the ego.
9. The established clinical picture of anxiety melancholia shows that part of the detached libido is used for the formation of anxiety. Freud's theory of the way in which anxiety is produced explains this.
10. In so far as these may be lifeless objects, the latter are probably to be regarded as representing living ones. Whether these are human or animal may make no difference. As an example that may serve as a piece of evidence supporting the theoretical consideration in this paper, I may quote the case of Eduard H, who succumbed to a psychosis consisting of a combination of paranoia, melancholia, and anxiety after the loss of a stallion to which he was devoted. The paranoid mechanism was attributable to the stallions' representing a homosexual love object in the patient's unconscious. The remainder of the detached libido seemed to have been absorbed partly in the mechanism of melancholia and partly in that of anxiety. I should like to draw attention at this point to the later discussion of the possibility of partial processes in the symptomatic working up of pathologically inhibited libido.

11. The mechanism of identification is typical of the narcissistic constellation and is the essential mechanism by which the psyche comes to terms with the outside world, as I have shown elsewhere (my paper to the psychoanalytic congress at Munich, 1913), and as Freud agrees. Thus in melancholia, as in paranoia, a regression to the narcissistic stage takes place. The mechanism of identification belongs to a stage of development of the psyche in which the individual has not yet established the correlation between subject and object or, as Freud says, has not yet made any object choice. At this stage the individual experiences the libidinally colored outside world, not as contrasted with or separate from his self-feeling, but as part of the latter, as belonging to it. This is narcissism, and the thought mechanism or way of dealing with the outside world associated with it is identification. As Freud has shown, in certain predisposed individuals, i.e., those who have undergone a fixation in narcissism, the way back to this stage remains regressively open in the event of a failure of object libido, and sometimes it is taken pathologically. The result of this regression is what Freud calls the paraphrenias, or narcissistic psychoses, as distinct from the transference neuroses, in which regression to narcissism does not occur, but the whole pathological process takes place within the constellation of object-directed libido. Paranoia and schizophrenia belong to the first group, while hysteria and obsessional and anxiety neuroses belong to the second. The extent to which melancholia should be included among the narcissistic psychoses should be clear from the present paper.
12. It is well known that the reproductive, i.e., specifically heterosexual, functions disappear during melancholia (amenorrhea in women, *impotentia coeundi* in men). Psychoanalysis puts the sluggishness of the digestive organs in melancholia into an intelligible relationship with the inertia of the sexual functions; it explains it merely as a partial process related to the latter [Freud, *Character and Anal Erotism, Standard Edition,* 9:169].
13. A week after reading this paper a copy of the *Wiener Medizinische Klinik* of January 23 1916 (no. 4) came to hand with an article by Fritz Mohr, of Coblenz, entitled 'Some Basic Considerations concerning the War Neuroses' (p. 89). I was delighted to find him in close agreement with me on several points. I quote verbatim:

> P. 89. What is the clinical picture of the neuroses among men on active service? Pure types, as depicted in the textbooks, of neurasthenia, hysteria, obsessional neurosis, fright neurosis, tics, etc., are rarely found. Nearly always mixed forms are encountered, among which, however, sometimes neurasthenic and sometimes hysterical or other features may predominate. This is also the opinion of the majority of the colleagues whom I have consulted. (Oppenheim and Noone are also of this opinion.)
>
> P. 91. This makes it clear that the psychology of the conscious which many observers take as their starting point is not sufficient to explain all these processes. . . .

'But, if one explores more deeply, it turns out that unconscious instinctual impulses are active which, just because they are unconscious, cannot be controlled, purely infantile defense mechanisms against unpleasure such as I have previously described. They emerge with the certainty of a psychological experiment as soon as feelings of unpleasure exceed a certain degree. How soon the point is reached at which the tendency to reduce unpleasure causes the flight into illness or a multiplication of the symptoms depends on the momentary and permanent psychical constitution of the patient. The latter has to be taken into account if any understanding of the structure of a neurosis in Oppenheim's (*sic*) sense is desired. This, however, has occurred far too rarely in regard to the war neuroses. This remaining content with psychologically inadequate explanations has of necessity led to the continually observable tendency prematurely and excessively to invoke hypothetical molecular changes in the cerbral cortex and other hypothetical physiological explanations.

The essential point about all these processes, however, is that they are all connected in varying degrees of intensity with affective and instinctual life, in which their chief source lies.

My only regret was that the author should have produced such a sensible and promising paper out of the current stock of Freud's views, theories and terminology without even hinting either at Freud's name or at psychoanalysis. No doubt the reason for this discretion is to be found on p. 92, where Mohr recommends "psychotherapy by reasonable analysis." It will not be surprising if "reasonable" in this context turns out to mean 'non-sexual' or "almost non-sexual," as authors always fall back on "reason" when they wish to spare themselves the acknowledgment of any debt to Freud or psychoanalysis. It is regrettable that all that "reasonable" analysts know about the unconscious and everything connected with it comes from "unreasonable" psychoanalysis—an embarassing situation for "reasonable" analysts, I must confess.

7

On the Psychology of The War Deserter

I

What I have to say on this subject is bound to be restricted in some respects by the circumstance that this is not a suitable time for discussing military institutions or political conditions. The military view of the deserter differs from the psychologist's, who is not concerned with whether or not the consequences that follow from his investigations harmonize with the requirements of the army, or the political situation.

As I know from firsthand experience, the attitude of patriotism in arms to the crime of desertion is pretty candidly based on the theory of deterrence. It follows from this practical principle that when deserters are tried in court psychological considerations will be taken into account only in exceptional cases, that is, when the judge has an overwhelming impression that the accused is mentally ill. The extent to which this impression will depend on the personal qualities of the judge, who will rarely have had psychiatric training, is easy to foresee. For the same reason it is impossible to count on all the mentally ill and only these being sent for psychiatric examination. Also I found plenty of confirmation for my supposition that men not submitted for psychiatric examination were sentenced after being declared fit to stand trial

---

Zur Psychologie des Deserteurs. Internationale Zeitschrift für ärztliche Psychoanalyse, 4 (1916). Delivered at the Ninth Medical Officers Seminar, Belgrade, March 3, 1917. Translated by Eric Mosbacher and Marius Tausk under the editorship of Paul Roazen.

on the same shaky grounds as those on which others were sent to the psychiatrist as being mentally ill, or suspected of being mentally ill. It is, however, to this indiscrimination, often accompanied by the best of intentions, that I am indebted for the great variety of cases sent me for examination, and I can face with the greatest equanimity the criticism that my observations were restricted to pathological cases and therefore biased.

To the best of my belief, my subject has no scientific history. I am not aware that any previous work has been done on the psychology of the deserter, either in former wars or in the present one. I regret this, since it puts my work at a disadvantage. For, though I can be certain that for my own approach to the subject, i.e., the psychoanalytic, no information or support is to be expected from earlier workers in the field, I should have preferred it if other observers had at least left a description or classification of actual motives for desertion, no matter from what standpoint. That would have provided a broader base for my observations, made sounder judgment possible on the extent to which all the possible or at least all the typical cases have been included in my observations, and I should be less exposed to criticisms of my classification's being prejudiced or arbitrary. However, I have my reasons other than that for renouncing in advance any claim to have investigated the subject completely. My only purpose is to make my audience acquainted with a topical and very tragic subject and with an interesting method of psychological approach.

This method has been called psychoanalysis by its founder, Professor Freud of the University of Vienna. His theory, to which the Vienna neurologist Dr. Josef Breuer made important contributions in the initial stages, has met with more—though not better—enemies than friends. A substantial literature is available which will enable you to inform yourselves about the full range of this science. I shall acquaint you with only a few aspects of the theory directly connected with my subject.

I shall not be able to go beyond presenting the problem as it emerges from the facts and my apporach to these facts. Apart from the military and political situation to which I have already referred, any attempt to find a solution, and in particular to apply it to the administration of justice during this war, is limited by existing legislation, which cannot be expected to be changed soon and lays down lines from which the judge dealing with the crime of desertion cannot depart. But if the courts are again to be faced with the sad necessity of deciding the fate of individuals whose duty it is to participate in the destruction of human beings and human values, it is my hope that what I have to say may reach the ear of future legislators.

You will long since have realized that I am going to subject the psychological principles imposed on the courts in dealing with the crime of desertion to not very benevolent criticism. I can understand that all of you, apart from feeling that deterring men from committing this crime is a practical necessity, also have a sense of idealism which leaves little room for sympathy with the deserter. The deserter tries to escape from duties and ordeals imposed on all comrades, he is interested only in saving his own skin in the dreadful devastation that has come over the world, and you indignantly ask what right he has to think only of his own safety and leave his comrades in the lurch. You believe the deserter to be selfish and cowardly, and I do not deny you your right to that opinion. In the course of what I have to say I shall even show that there is a sense in which it is in perfect harmony with his psychological situation. Nevertheless I shall try to persuade you to replace your opinion, which is equivalent to a condemnation, by an insight inherent in which are a great many universal human values which could be of greater value to the country than the killing off of a few deserters.

Practically every week for nearly a year and a half in the capacity of expert on mental and nervous diseases I had to report to the court on deserters' fitness or unfitness to plead, and I have therefore seen a great many cases.

I feel I must account to you for my attitude in the matter, just as I had to account for it to myself.

I began this work with the greatest aversion. I had already escaped once from the professional necessity of sitting in judgment on others, and I now found myself in the position of being compelled to take part in the judicial process in the capacity of physician. Perhaps some of the judges here present are conscious of the fact that to many the apparently impersonal application of the law involves insoluble personal conflict, while to others it is a pretext for giving rein to appetites for power of various kinds, and that if only the just sat in judgment there would not be enough judges to go round. I admit, however, that there is also an unhealthy or, shall we say, sentimental, side to this attitude toward the office of judge which should play no part. There are certainly judges—and it is a good thing that they exist—who are able to carry out their duties without being hampered by the thought of how many psychological and educational potentialities they are sentencing to death when they deliver their verdict. I also admit that the judge must set aside his scruples about pronouncing judgment in the safety of a courtroom about a man's duty to stand up to an artillery barrage.

There was another factor that diminished my pleasure in the work, this one unconnected with the relationship between the judge and the criminal and his crime, and thus free of personal and therefore insoluble problems. Instead, it was connected with the objective relationship between the law and the crime of desertion, which makes it a less insidious and more productive subject of discussion. Laws do not change as quickly as men's views and ways of living, and many social or personal values are given legal sanction which later, so it seems to us, it would be better to remove from public regulation, with the result that legal compulsion in the matter is felt to be an anachronism and an unjustified restriction. This applies in particular to certain aspects of sex life, and also to a number of factors that originated in superseded forms of power structure and social status. Also we cannot fail to observe that newly engaged values of human society and personal life are not given legal protection quickly or extensively enough, with the result that legal powers seem sometimes too wide and sometimes too narrow. I must remind you that our penal code dates from the beginning of the nineteenth century, so that, when you compare social conditions now and then, even those of you who are not lawyers will be able to draw logical conclusions about its appropriateness.

There are also problems and doubts connected with the historical attitude toward desertion. When military service was entered into on a contractual basis, as it was in the days of mercenary armies, the psychology and moral evaluation of the crime was different from that of an age in which a certain category of men, i.e., the able-bodied, fit to bear arms, are liable to conscription;

and in considering this matter of conscription the historical phases of popular habituation to that institution must be taken into account. The great mass of the less fit or unfit who have been conscripted in this war had long since accustomed themselves to the idea that they had a right to exemption from it, and in view of that were not able to adapt themselves smoothly to the present surprising extension of conscription. Our legislation could not of course anticipate the form taken by this war, but insistence on the letter of the law imposes an obligation on the individual that he was not brought up to fulfil.

Those were more or less the thoughts with which I approached the task that devolved upon me, until I realized that it was limited to deciding whether or not the deserters whom I should have to examine were responsible for their actions and therefore punishable according to law.

This reflection, however, promptly involved me in a new conflict, which arose when I noted the few psychological considerations which have a place in our more than century-old legislation in regard to establishing guilt or innocence or the question of penalty.

Paragraph I of the penal code says that crime requires evil intent. This statement has an appealing simplicity and is certainly calculated to reassure even the most conscientious and least assuming. The next paragraphs, however, cause the psychologist a lively disquiet, which remains with him to the end.

Evil intent cannot be assumed, the law goes on, if the person committing the act was wholly deprived of reason at the time, or was in a state of mental confusion or complete intoxication (unless he became intoxicated for the purpose of committing the act), or was acting in justified self-defense. In this legal terminology we can discern two psychologically quite distinct factors that exclude guilt. According to the first, an individual is not guilty if he commits an act while deprived of his senses and power of judgment, because in that condition he is not capable of forming an intent. According to the second, if he is acting in justifiable self-defense he is considered capable of forming an intent; but his is not described as an evil one.

We are confronted with the fact that the law has quite definite ideas of good and evil. The commentaries on justified self-defense make it clear that the psychological category to which it belongs is that of "irresistible compulsion" (the two ideas do not coincide, but overlap), and elsewhere we are told that "irresistible compulsion" applies to safeguarding the legitimate interests of oneself or of others. Then again we learn that among those the defense of whose interests constitutes "irresistible compulsion" and excludes guilt, "beloved persons" occupy a preferential position. On the other hand, such exculpating love can be pleaded only in relation to specified persons, i.e., close relatives or legitimate love partners. In other words, the law claims a complete knowledge of love and its effects. As you are aware, not only does homosexual love not exclude guilt on the ground of irresistible compulsion, but it is in itself guilty and punishable. As you see, the law-maker has some remarkable assumptions and interferes with the mechanisms of nature with some remarkable results.[1]

All these factors are confusing. To the psychologist who thinks in terms of history, the notion of what is evil is less assured. It has varied at different periods and in different countries at the same period. I must desist from pursuing this subject further, because it would lead to endless commonplaces.

However, there are certain peculiarities about the attitude of the law in the matter of intent which cause the psychologist to wonder about the etiology of certain legal stipulations. For instance, the law adapts the extent and nature of the punishment to the age of the offender; it treats the young up to a certain age with greater leniency, as if they were less capable than their elders of the psychical act known as 'intent'. This assumption, however, is certainly wrong. Very young children, including those declared by the law to be incapable of committing a crime, are perfectly capable of forming an intent. Punishment by domestic educators is, after all, based on the belief that the child acts with intent. The child does not lose his capacity to form intents and carry them out in any other way than an adult. Ignorance of the law cannot be pleaded to exonerate a child, since this is no defense to an adult who has committed an illegal act; and I do not believe that anyone who understands children would seriously maintain that they have no knowledge of evil. That can be assumed only in the first two of three years of life, and then only within limitations. In general, children have a much stronger sense of wrong than adults, most of whom have dismissed the idea of the omnipresence of a punishing God; and, in so far as evil means the same as malice, children are certainly capable of every kind of malice. The proclivity to such feelings does not depend on age; if anything, it decreases with age.

If we assume in accordance with psychology that all the conditions which determine punishability and accountability in the adult are also present in the child, we can explain the leniency of the law to children only by assuming that the legislators were poor psychologists. The assumption is probably correct. Nevertheless we cannot bring ourselves to judge children by the same yardstick as adults, even though the age limits accepted by the law need a good deal of adjustment in the light of psychological consistency. If we seriously ask ourselves what makes us so lenient in this respect in spite of our psychology, perhaps all of us—and for the sake of the general validity of my theme I shall assume all of us without exception—will admit that it is our love of our own children and our own childhood that makes our attitude to the youthful offender more tolerant. We are governed in this instance by an entirely subjective emotional urge which is certainly not justified in all cases by the seemingly objective plea that the child is capable of improvement; it may, indeed, be true in only very few cases indeed.[2] The adult too has time for remorse and improvement, if he is capable of these things, after committing a crime, but he is not spared the penalty for that reason.[3]

In laying down the nature and extent of the penalty the law takes into account the magnitude of the crime. But sometimes it lays emphasis on the intention and sometimes on the result. Attempted murder is less severely punished than murder, but a hostile act resulting in death is treated as homicide even if the intention was no more than to penetrate the skin with a fingernail. But if all the death wishes felt by children, even if only the conscious ones felt in moments of anger and hatred and released in acts of aggression of various kinds, were punished as attempted murder, the state would soon not have enough soldiers left to be able to set about killing its enemies. We may note in passing that premeditated killing in a duel was once considered a noble action, and still enjoys a preferential position in our penal code. I shall also not elaborate on the fact that all these considerations which may seem obvious to you in relation to crimes against the person can equally well be applied to crimes against property. But this is not the time to talk our economic system to pieces.

You will soon see the connection between what I have been saying and the deserters about whom I am going to talk to you. I ask you only to bear in mind the confusion that exists in the relations between even this simple psychology and the law. I shall later indicate to you some psychoanalytic ways and means, not of disposing of the problem, but of mitigating your discomfort at my manner of presenting it.

Before I undertook the task of making psychiatric reports on deserters for the court, the ideas that I had of these people did not go beyond those of a patriotic high school boy whose fitness for front-line service had not yet received its baptism by fire. I imagined deserters to be defiant individuals who refused obedience to the Emperor, or cowards who trembled for their lives while their comrades were being killed or were bleeding to death all round them, gladly sacrificing their lives and that of their nearest and dearest for their country.

I gained a faint idea of what these glad sacrifices were like from men who had taken part in assaults. I discovered that they did not sacrifice anything, let alone gladly, but that they were generally the victims of a crazy, mindless fear that knew that there was no way back and could see no way forward, but could only hear, and that their valor consisted in surviving an inconceivable ordeal.

I discovered what deserters were like from my own observations.

There were three points that emerged from them that forced the psychology of the deserter upon my attention and led me to attempt this study.

In the first place, by far the majority of deserters do not belong to combatant units, and desertions take place, not from the really dangerous, fighting front, but from non-combatant units in the back areas, from army formations employed on guard or labor duties.

Secondly, deserters on the run often endure hardships unquestionably more severe than any military duty or danger, in spite of which they return voluntarily to their duty only in very rare cases indeed. I have known deserters who spent months living like wild beasts in the forest, suffering from bitter cold and starvation and constantly exposed to the most wretched of deaths which, however, they prefered to facing their duties with some guard or labor company in the back areas. Some of them would sneak into a village at night to beg a kindhearted peasant for some bread; others would hide in a village, living in agonizing fear of discovery or being given away. One man, a German, made his way on foot in the depth of winter from Warsaw to Lublin, suffering indescribable hardships and stress. It is premature to conclude that liberation from military duties, in particular in back areas, compensates for all this suffering. It should be borne in mind that, with very few exceptions, all these deserters come from the lower levels of the population, accustomed to heavy labor. They are peasants, unskilled and manual workers, to whom army service does not very often mean an unaccustomed burden, a restriction of freedom of movement and of opportunities of enjoyment that contrasts intolerably with the civilian life to which they were used.

Thirdly, a good half of all the deserters I saw created the impression at first sight of being mental cripples, dull, feeble-minded, emotionally infantile and lacking in decision. If the criticism is made that as a forensic psychiatrist this was the only sort of case I saw, my reply is that the other half of those I saw did not create this immediate impression; they might have been as normal mentally as most of the men drafted to serve as hospital orderlies. Also I have been assured by reliable sources that among cases not certified by me there were as many feeble-minded as apparently normal cases among men executed for desertion. There was an extreme instance in which one of our pathologists found a microcephalic brain in an executed deserter.

There was one overriding impression that I carried away from the multiplicity of my experiences with these people, and that was of unqualified human wretchedness, and that applies to every deserter I met. I state this fact entirely without sentimentality. It would ill become me to appeal for sympathy with these socially almost worthless individuals at a time when the most valuable are being condemned pitilessly to manure the soil with their flesh and blood.

The term "psychoanalysis," of which I have told you nothing tangible yet, gentlemen, indicates quite literally that we are concerned, not with synthesizing impressions, but with separating psychical phenomena into their component parts. Closer examination of the personality of all these deserters showed a variety of reasons for the wretchedness common to them all. No great skill was required to discover this. All I had to do was to question the men to find out that there are various motives for desertion, and that deserters can be classified in various categories accordingly. If you accept the fact that an appropriate method of questioning and some practice enables one generally to unmask lies and get the man to tell the truth, though a few cases remain sterile from the point of view of scientific investigation because the low-grade mentality of the man under examination makes even the most elementary rapport with the physician impossible, the two respects in which my conclusions are probably most vulnerable to criticism, the reliability of these men's statements and their psychological accessibility, are eliminated at the outset. The only other criticism that remains open is that of the validity of my method. As I present my findings I shall introduce you to some freudian psychoanalysis, though only with the few principles of that science that are relevant to the quite crude present study.

My first category consists of sufferers from pathological disturbances of consciousness (fugues),[4] hysterical or epileptic disturbances about which they can generally give no information whatever. In the course of apparently normal existence they had been taken over, as it were, by an alien ego. Some of these patients had absolutely no memory of what had happened during the attack; they did not know they had left their place of duty, all conscious intention of leaving it was completely alien to them, and when they found themselves in a strange place they did not know how they got there and were as surprised as on awakening from a dream. A few had not lost their memory of what happened during the attack, but they had usually just wandered about aimlessly, in a manner they were unable to explain, wherever their promptings took them. In such cases we speak of a pathological urge to wander. I must leave this whole category of deserters out of my considerations. Epileptics cannot be analyzed, and hysterics of this type cannot be analyzed with any prospect of success while under examination in a military hospital pending a court-martial.

The second category also consists of restless, wandering souls. But these neither suffer from confusion nor have memory gaps. They are fully conscious of their actions, which they carry out rationally and deliberately, and are not unaware that they have left their post illegally. Sometimes there is a defiant emphasis on their rebellion against military duty and perhaps also on the dangerous consequences of such rebellion. These men were usually industrial workers, but two were students. Their past history often includes punishments for repeatedly absenting themselves from wherever they ought to be. The question why they deserted produces answers which can be interpreted either as intolerance of compulsion in general or aversion to an occupation unsatisfying to or conflicting with personal needs. Closer examination of the latter turns out to be a mere pretext for escaping from compulsion in general. The immediate occasion of the desertion is attributed to such things as a power-conscious non-commissioned officer's having shortened the men's off-duty time by drill or putting them to work. Once I was told that a sergeant, whether rightly or wrongly, had ordered men who had beards to shave them off. 'That was the last straw', I was told. Another man deserted because he was transferred from boot-repairing to army transport. Another, by civil occupation a stableman, had somehow managed to smuggle himself into a German horse transport column, because he 'had a greater sense of human worth doing a job he knew'. When chance threw him together with his old corps, he was arrested as a deserter. His 'ideal' reason for deserting was not believed.

In the face of the huge compulsion by which the world is now being throttled, these reasons for desertion look merely petty. When I pointed out to these men that their comrades had to live under the same restrictions and frustrations but did not desert, I could rely on their full agreement. Sometimes I could see the reasons just given for their desertion losing their sharp outlines in the face of this consideration and giving way to surprise and dismay. Sometimes I would be told that it was 'everything' that got too much for them and caused them to absent themselves from their unit, and also that it had been stupid and over-hasty, but now it was too late.

The typical biographies to be extracted from these men lead us quickly to psychological soil of a kind very familiar to us from psychoanalysis. The deserter's misdeed turns out to be a characteristic behavior pattern. All these men have been 'fugitives' since childhood. Some had run away from home innumerable times. Others had never kept a job, or had continually changed it. One was an adventurer who had traveled half the world over and done many different jobs. Those who had been to school had been truants and bad examples to their fellows. They had 'always been like that'. Why? One had a strict father, the other a stepmother. They could not bear it at home. They had stayed away from school because the teacher treated them unfairly. Father had not allowed them to learn the trade they would have liked, they had had to learn something that gave them no pleasure. One had been badly treated by all his masters, another by his masters' wives, yet another by his master's children, or his companions or fellow-apprentices. "If only I could have taken over my father's business I should have settled down,' one of them said to me. As, however, his father had been unwilling to let him do this, he had kept running away from home, and the police had kept bringing him back.

What these cases show is that the motivation of desertion in this category originates in childhood and can often be traced to infancy, and that the characteristic experience of these people is the flight from family compulsion. You have only to accept the fact that "master" and "teacher" are surrogates for the father, that the master's wife is a surrogate for the mother, and that comrades, fellow-apprentices and classmates are surrogates for the siblings, and you will be able to see the complete picture. To persuade you to accept this assumption I shall have to introduce you to a little psychoanalysis.

II

Freud's great discovery, and in fact the basic principle of psychoanalysis, is that the child is father to the man. I must ask you to accept this familiar commonplace as a startling novelty in psychology, for that is how it is regarded by the vast majority of literate people, including the learned. This latter section of humanity cannot be told anything more novel and more startling than that their dignified personalities consist of residues of their infantile life which, partly unchanged and partly changed in accordance with definite laws, make up their present, apparently adult, image. The adult likes to regard the child as qualitatively different from what he thinks himself to be. He takes the child to be, not childlike, but childish, that is, he does not take seriously the expressions of children's affects and instincts, but regards them as provisional, as it were; since they are bound to "grow up," there is nothing for it but to wait until this phase is over. Psychoanalysis has, however, shown that it is never "over," but enters into the make-up of the adult personality, which must be regarded as nothing but the outcome of the vicissitudes to which the child's instincts have been subjected. The child loves and hates just like the adult, though generally with much greater force and seriousness than the adult, especially the adult in our flattened out, civilized life. This flattening out, in so far as it means convention, pettiness, and a blurring of emotional life, is an undesirable effect, though an inevitable one in view of the nature of the human material, of very important principles which govern the social adaptation of man and the maturation of his orientation to his environment. It is the great seriousness and the intensity of the child's psychical life which these principles make use of in turning him into an adult; and it is not the fault of the principles but of those who apply them—more rarely those to whom they are applied—that adults live so insecurely and discontentedly with the teaching they have received and pass on.

The outstanding characteristic of the instinctual life of the child is his inability to postpone or renounce the satisfaction of his wishes. The child lives according to the pleasure principle; he has to be educated to the reality principle. Freud describes these two opposite principles of psychical development as the factors the internal struggle between which produces the final result of the individual's development. The child not only demands immediate satisfaction of his wishes, he demands the satisfaction of inherently unattainable wishes and wishes which immediately or eventually would harm him or his environment. The child feels any restriction of his instinctual satisfaction to be a grave personal outrage. He cannot renounce pleasure-gain even if it involves danger. Nevertheless he has to be educated into satisfying his pleasure needs in accordance with the world of reality, that is, in ways which are practicable among contemporary people and in contemporary circumstances and will promote his mental and physical well-being. He has to learn that when he reaches for the moon he is asking for the impossible. If he tries to dominate his brothers and sisters, he has to learn that he has no more rights in the matter than they have and therefore he must either renounce the desire or try to outdo them in a way which human society, though it will not always help him, will not always obstruct, e.g., by working hard at school to show his superior brain power. In psychoanalytic terminology, he thus sublimates his crude tyrannical wishes and acquires a source of mental pleasure that takes the place of the pleasure of the domestic tyranny that has been renounced.

When he wants to be as big as his parents in order to be able to do things that they are allowed to do, he has to learn to wait. In short, he cannot have everything, and there are many things he cannot have immediately. When in his boundless childish rages he desires the death of some adult or child in his environment, he has to reconcile himself to the fact that that person does not die. He has to renounce the exclusive possession of his parents' love that he wants only because in his childish egocentricity he does not understand and therefore does not tolerate the right of his brothers and sisters to exist.

This education in renunciation and postponement fails in the case of some children, who remain unconsciously attached to their infantile wishes. They fail to acquire a useful substitute for the satisfactions denied them, for they want no such substitute. They want to satisfy their old wishes in their original form. Some of these, such as the fantasies of infantile ambition, death, and sexual wishes directed toward their closest relatives, are for internal or external reasons obviously unfulfillable in their original form. Of special importance are the death wish directed against the father and the sexual desire for the mother in the male child, which constitute the oedipus complex described by Freud. I shall not expand on this subject on the present occasion except to say this attitude toward the parents is a primary experience of the human male, and *mutatis mutandis,* of the human female, in whose case love is directed toward the father and the death wish toward the mother. Children who cannot escape from their infantile wishes are in psychoanalytic terminology said to be fixated on those wishes and objects. They find no acceptable substitute for the satisfactions of which they have been deprived, but keep trying to find one. These attempts must necessarily fail because unconsciously—the whole process as it develops sinks into the unconscious and therefore becomes incomprehensible to the individual concerned and impossible for him to tackle–these people desire only to achieve the old wish. They therefore never reconcile themselves to the world of reality in which their wishes are unattainable, and by running away from everything that is attainable they continue merely to demonstrate that what they want is always something different from what they are doing and can have.

When we look at our deserters of the second category, we see that they are fixated on the old wish to escape from family compulsion. As this wish has become unconscious, every dependent relationship in which they become involved rouses their unconscious rebellion against family compulsion, though the family constellation against which the rebellion is really directed is not present in their conscious mind. Anyone in authority, anyone who can or wants to give them orders, is felt to be a member of the family, only because they feel his authority. This member of the family is generally the father, who exercised authority in the family and tried to lead him from the pleasure principle to the reality principle by giving him orders and imposing punishment and the renunciation or postponement of satisfactions. Such a son identifies his teachers, his employers, his n.c.o.'s, with his father, and just as he wanted to run away from his father and did, so did he run away from his school, from his employers, and finally from the army which had taken his father's place.

The rebellion against the father had been displaced in his unconscious to those who succeeded his father in authority over him. But since the substitution resulting from this displacement is incomplete, it is the rebellion that calls the tune; the occasion that triggers it off can be absurdly trivial. Whenever the feeling of rebellion is activated, it turns readily into the impulse to run away. It is what the individual is used to, and so the act of desertion is liable to occur at any moment.

Is it not an irresistible compulsion if a man lives under a psychical constellation of such a kind? But no such grounds as this for excluding guilt are of course known to the law. The theory of the fixation and displacement of infantile wishes takes us deep into the problem of man's free will and responsibility when faced with human judges untrained in psychoanalysis. We shall certainly not try to tackle this problem now, but shall confine ourselves to noting that our deserters of the second category are suffering from psychical infantilism, that their reasons for desertion are infantile, and that they are not fully responsible adults. We shall, however, refrain from estimating the amount of responsibility attributable to them for the crime committed.

The fact that I have expatiated on this category of deserters, gentlemen, might create the impression that they were especially numerous among my cases. This was not so, for they represented only a small proportion. But, because of the simple psychical structure involved, this category is particularly suitable for an introduction to psychoanalytic principles at which, after this broad explanation, we shall only briefly hint when discussing the succeeding categories.

The motivation for desertion in the third category is fear of punishment for some offense. The offense is invariably trivial. Though penalties under military law are relatively severe even for minor offenses, they are still trivial in comparison with the punishment for desertion. Often they are also trivial in comparison with the severe hardships and stresses suffered by a deserter on the run. The most characteristic case is probably that of the German deserter we mentioned previously who made his way on foot from Warsaw to Lublin. He deserted because he had contracted gonorrhea. His commanding officer had threatened to 'break every bone in the body' of any man who caught a venereal disease. Any normal individual would not have taken a parade-ground threat of this kind too seriously, and he would certainly not have taken it literally. His action was, to say the very least, precipitate. Like nearly all deserters in this category, incidentally, he was a human wreck. The poor devil had psychical inferiority written on his face. His eyes were full of fearful expectation. When talked to at all sharply he was shaken to the core. By trade he was a baker's hand, and his father had a small street-paving business. With minor variations, in which the constant factor was always the same relationship between father and son, his life story resembled that of all his fellow sufferers in this category. His father was very strict; very strict with his family, that is to say; he did not apply to himself the moral principles he required of them. He often came home drunk and maltreated his wife and children in his beer-inspired frenzy, and the sound of his footsteps in the hall hushed the children into terrified silence. He would punish them for the slightest thing, and as between one drunken bout and the next he often forgot that he had punished them for something already, but not that there was something to punish them for, they were frequently beaten on several days in succession for the same often trivial misdemeanor. Fear of his father dominated this deserter's whole life. At school and during his apprenticeship he was dependent and insecure, always expecting punishment even when he was not aware of having done anything wrong. His chief characteristics were the ease with which he was shaken and his agonizing fear of punishment. Whenever he talked of the paternal maltreatment and the fear this caused him he was so shaken that he wept.

Here again, as in the previous category, we see a disturbed relationship between father and son. We also see its displacement onto surrogate father-figures and finally onto superiors in the army. The son's reaction is different in each of the two categories, however. While in the first he becomes a fugitive all his life, keeps running away from the father (or from the family), in the second he does not become emancipated to the extent of rebelling by daring to run away from him. On the contrary, he is completely dominated by his father, he has sacrificed all freedom in relation to him and lives in constant, helpless fear of him; and, if he finally manages to run away from a threatened and dreaded punishment, he is likely to be picked up as a deserter. Here we have another instance of fixation in an infantile attitude. Perhaps some of my listeners will already have drawn their own conclusions about the apparently normal lives of their fellow citizens from these two examples of fixation, and will have noted the extent to which the individual's social destiny depends, and necessarily depends, on his attitude toward his father, or to put it another way, the extent to which he must reconcile himself to the destiny with which his family has sent him on his way.

The problem of the applicability of the legal concept of irresistible compulsion and of the limits of human responsibility is even wider open here than in the case of the preceding category.

The reason given for desertion by the fourth category is inability to stand the strain of their duties. These are too much for them. Yet they tolerate the most fearful hardships and stresses of the life of a fugitive on the run almost with equanimity and with stubborn, unyielding endurance. This type of deserter is numerically very strongly represented. Most of them are older peasants, and all of them can be described as more or less feeble-minded. They are used to heavy labor at home, and the demands made on them by the army are often no greater, but these turn out to be too much for them. In these cases the etiology is not very far to seek. These men are simple, childish peasants at the lowest conceivable level of culture and education, unable to produce interest in anything outside the accustomed activities of their village life. Almost without exception they are illiterate. Their relationship to the idea of the state or nation is limited to the fact that they have always regarded the obligation to pay taxes as unfair, and they are unable to view the connection between their military service and the general purposes of the state in any different light. Their interests are completely infantile. They cannot transfer libido to any work the fruits of which they cannot physically take home. They have never taken any part in national life, they can neither understand it nor have any love of it, and they do not see why they should make sacrifices for something that is called the general interest in an enterprise not of their making. It is because these things are alien to them that they overrate the strains of military service, just as children overrate everything strange and unaccustomed, turning it into either very good or very bad. But the strains involved in being a fugitive on the run, which consist essentially in the exercise of primitive, innate capacities for self-preservation, seeking out hiding places and laying hands on food, are neither strange nor too much for them, though they are far greater than those imposed on them by their army duties.

There is an additional problem of responsibility in relation to the performance of duties that arises out of the peculiar nature of this war, which has caused masses of men to be called up for military service whose usefulness has long been questioned even by the military. The types we meet here in the guise of deserters are also encountered elsewhere, filling the hospitals in the guise of sufferers from lassitude and exhaustion, hypochondriacs, malingerers, "hospital bugs." Thus there are ways and means of evading military duty without coming into conflict with the law. Only the stupidest actually desert. In hospital they make themselves conspicuous by their absurd hypochondria and their vague complaints about all sorts of illness. The stupid cunning of their easily unmasked imaginary symptoms either infuriates the doctors or makes them laugh.

The fifth category of deserters that came to my knowledge is not very numerous. It consists of neurotics in the strict sense of the term. They suffer from various anxiety and obsessional ideas which the psychoanalyst easily recognizes as originating in the unconscious sexual life. One of these cases presented the picture of typical anxiety over beginning anything or any change of situation. This led to all sorts of compulsive actions. My conjecture that the man suffered from fear of sexual impotence was confirmed. Fear of the new or of beginning anything is a typical displacement to non-sexual activities and objects of the fear of sexual impotence. Information about displacement of the sexual instinct to non-erotic situations is readily obtainable by a closer study of psychoanalysis. This man deserted when he was given a new company commander. "He could not imagine what things would be like under him," and this idea worried him so much that he deserted. "What will it be like? How shall I manage?" are the typical questions which the sufferer from fear of sexual impotence asks himself whenever he is faced with a sexual demand. I shall not go into the question of the extent to which this neurosis may have been determined by unconscious homosexual inclinations, which may have been the real cause of his fear of impotence. I also include in the fifth category men who desert because of thwarted ambition. These cases are rare too. The ambitions involved are not very exalted, and the frustrations of them that lead to the desertion do not strike us as very grave. A stableman, for instance, deserted allegedly because he was pestered by his n.c.o. It turned out, however, that he could not tolerate his work not being considered as good as that of his comrade. He also presented a number of definite neurotic symptoms which caused me to put him in this category. You will readily believe that his behavior was childish, infantile. In the present paper I must limit myself to indicating that his neurosis was an unsuccessful superstructure erected on top of his psychical infantilism.

Deserters of the next category, the sixth, are very numerous. Their motive is homesickness. As the song that begins with the words *Zu Strassburg auf der langen Brück* says with such directness and simplicity,

> *Der Knabe, der das Schallhorn blies,*
> *Der trägt die Schuld daran*[5]

Homesickness plays a major or minor role in practically all categories of deserters. When things are going badly with a man, when he loses control of his life, he takes flight—in reality or in fantasy—to a situation or a time when life was good, when he did not have to fight the inclemencies of the outside world alone and with no one but himself to fall back on, when he was sheltered and protected. For everyone there has been such a situation and such a time—in his childhood with his mother. To the vast majority of human beings this relationship with their mother is of abiding permanence, as is shown by the legend of Antaeus. In fact, all these deserters—no single exception came to my notice—wanted to go back to their mother, or occasionally to their wife or sweetheart, who, as psychoanalysis shows, are to be regarded in a sense as a substitute for the mother, and certainly so in the case of all infantile men. They never want to go back to the father, or to a friend; no instance of that has ever come to my notice. Homesickness is homesickness for the mother. The need for maternal protection is always a factor present when desertion is contemplated, and it may provide the final impulse. Very often it is the only one. This category consists of sad individuals. They come from all classes of society and are usually very young. But most of them are peasants, because most soldiers are peasants and most peasants are childlike, i.e., have an especially strong attachment to their homes and their fields, their mother and their earth, which are symbolically the same, as we see in the phrase 'mother earth.' These men suffer from a sense of loneliness and abandonment. The clash with the military injunction which, like the Biblical one, says 'thou shalt leave thy father and thy mother' could not be more violent or more insoluble, and these men's only illness is that they do not want to do what the Biblical injunction and military law require. They refuse obedience, not out of defiance, but because of childlike suffering. They are still childlike. It is difficult to expect the law to take account of homesickness, but the psychologist cannot help taking this psychical phenomenon seriously.

There is, however, another possibility that I cannot exclude in this connection. I pointed out last year in a paper on war psychoses[6] that severe mental illnesses are often preceded by a sense of isolation, taking the form of depressive and anxiety states, which must be regarded as in part causing them. The heavy, homesick, depression that precedes desertion in many cases makes me believe that it is sometimes merely an unconscious flight from a threatening mental illness, a "solitude psychosis." Escape to the home, where one is never solitary, might perhaps represent salvation from the impending madness. By trying to avoid the Scylla of madness, of course, the deserter merely runs into the Charybdis of a court-martial.

For the sake of completeness I shall mention a seventh category, of which, however, I have no personal experience. I refer to men who desert for purely political reasons. These too are certainly of general psychoanalytical interest, but, not having come across any of them, I have nothing to say about them.

Keeping, however, to cases that came my way, I can conclude with an eighth category, in which the motive was lack of interest in the purposes of the present war, or opposition to war as such. We can imagine a mentally healthy idealist of high moral qualities rejecting a duty accepted by all others in complete disregard of the consequences to himself. Among those who sacrificed themselves for their convictions there have always been men who have been safe from being classified as pathological. I do not believe, however, that an individual of that kind, after doing military service for some time in a back area, would suddenly desert, and later, reduced to a physical wreck by the harrowing experiences of being on the run, would be referred to a psychiatrist for a report on his mental condition. The few cases I saw were definitely pathological, showed feeble-minded, eccentric, infantile ideas, religious sectarianism, anxieties, and pronounced delusions of being watched and symptoms of persecution mania. I must ascribe this group to dementia praecox.

Before concluding my observations with some general psychological conclusions, there is a legal consideration to which I must revert.

Desertion in the eyes of the law implies the intention to absent oneself permanently from one's military duty. I can state that this subjective condition, which is essential if the crime of desertion is to be legally established, is only rarely present so far as the deserter's conscious mind is concerned. All that is present in the latter is the intention to escape from the painful situation and the tormenting feelings which were the immediate occasion of his running away. Fear of the punishment for desertion is very soon superimposed on this, becomes the dominant factor, and kills the resolution to report back for duty when—as not infrequently happens—it arises after the stormy affects that led to the flight have died down. In some cases the intention to stay away from duty permanently arises as a *dolus superveniens* when the deserter is encouraged by his initial success to hope that his luck will hold.

The penal code nowhere states that criminal intent can be unconscious. On the contrary, many of its stipulations lead to the conclusion that criminal intent must be conscious.

The practice of the courts in cases of desertion takes no account of this, however. It proceeds as if every desertion were motivated by the conscious intention of permanently abandoning military duty. As a psychoanalyst I wish to state explicitly that this interpretation in fact harmonizes with the psychological situation. Almost invariably I had the impression that there was an intention—mostly unconscious—permanently to abandon military duty. The law, which is based on the old psychological view that only what is conscious can be called mental, ignores the fact that the roots, the preparation and the aims of everything that comes under the heading of purpose, intention, wish, and thus everything that appears in the form of conscious purpose, lie in unconscious mental life. Psychoanalysis therefore equates unconscious with conscious intent. But the extent to which the individual should be held accountable for his unconscious intentions is quite a different matter. Accepting an unconscious intention as the subjective criterion of the crime of desertion puts the criminal law in a position analogous to that which it takes in relation to the crime of homicide which I previously mentioned. In most cases of homicide in which the conscious intention to kill is lacking, psychoanalysis would say that an unconscious one was certainly present. Not so the law, which penalizes less severely the not consciously intended result of the action and takes no account of a possible unconscious intention to produce that result. If the equation of conscious and unconscious intention were taken into account in deciding the question of criminal intent, the impact of psychoanalytic psychology on the framing of a future penal code would be very far-reaching. But bringing this approach into harmony with criminal law as it has developed historically and with our present way of life would be a difficult task, which we must leave to a psychology of law which does not yet exist.

In enumerating the different motivations for desertion which I found, I have shown you, gentlemen, just as many types of human character. I have tried to show you that the deserters whom I examined, apart from the fact that a high proportion were more or less feeble-minded while a few were neurotic or psychotic, all shared the common characteristics of psychical infantilism. I must add that psychoanalysis has also learnt to interpret the psychoses from the same point of view. You will certainly have noted how the notion of infantilism shades imperceptibly into what we regard as normal on the one hand and into the pathological on the other. I have also been able to link this discussion with the question of the legal responsibility of the individual for his actions.

We have associated the notion of infantilism with certain characteristics of the infant's mind, his inability to postpone or renounce the satisfaction of his wishes. The explanation of this is firstly the intensity of those wishes, secondly his inability to understand and to admit the validity of the interests of others in addition to his own, and thirdly his ignorance of adult life—he has no reason to save himself for the pleasures and duties reserved for the latter. He has to be educated to all these things. He has to be induced to exchange the pleasure principle, which makes the child seem selfish to us, for the reality principle, through which he becomes a social being. This educational program often breaks down for the most varied reasons, most of which must be looked for in the methods used. When it breaks down, the individual remains infantile, asocial, retaining his infantile wishes, partly in conscious but chiefly in unconscious form. He thereby becomes to a greater or lesser extent unadaptable to the social life which the individual cannot do without ("no matter whether he wears socks one yard high").[7] The more unadaptable he is, the more numerous and more deeply rooted in his childhood the individual's fixations are, the closer his infantilism is to psychosis.

Because of their infantilism, our deserters are asocial in relation to the common fate which has overtaken human society in this war. I do not know how many of my listeners are taking part in this war because of an inner impulse, but I do know that many are doing so only because they are able to subordinate themselves to a compulsion that leaves no one unaffected. Though military service costs most men severe losses, both material and emotional, they do not desert. Partly they renounce the satisfaction of personal wishes, the importance of which they subordinate to that of the general situation; partly they postpone the satisfaction of those wishes because of a real expectation based on a real understanding. In other words, they behave like adults.

Permit me, gentlemen, to conclude my serious survey with some serious words spoken in jest. In this war there is a group of men who, like children, cannot renounce the satisfaction of their wishes and want to have everything their heart desires, and even more. They too manage to evade the general suffering, not to their own detriment, as the deserter does, but at the expense of society. They, however, are not asocial, but antisocial. We shall not honor them by calling them deserters. They are the war profiteers.

Notes

1. In this discussion of the law I am only tracing factual connections. I am aware that I am putting the text of the law on a par with various theories and practices of the courts.

2. It is this spontaneous attitude toward our children and childhood that probably makes it impossible for some of us to set ourselves up as judges over others; and perhaps this unwillingness deprives us of a number of good judges.
3. In this respect Austrian law incidentally lags behind that of a number of other countries, in which considerations such as these have in varying degrees begun to have an effect.
4. *Ausnahmszuständen*.
5. *Translators' Note*: "It is the fault of the boy who blew the horn." *Schallhorn* is a misquotation for *Alphorn*, alpine horn. The song purports to be sung by a Swiss soldier, serving presumably in the French army, who was standing on the "long bridge" across the Rhine at Strasbourg when a boy went by blowing a tune that reminded him of his native country lying in the mist to the south. Overwhelmed by homesickness, he plunged into the river and began swimming upstream, only to be seen by a sergeant and caught. He sings this song while expecting to be executed the same day.
6. *Diagnostische Erörtungen auf Grund der Zustandsbilder der sogenannten Kriegspsychosen*. [Diagnostic Considerations Concerning the Symptomatology of the So-Called War Psychoses precedes this paper.]
7. *Translators' note*: A modified quotation from Goethe's *Faust*, in which Mephisto says to Faust: *Setz deinen Fuss auf ellenhohe Socken, du bleibst doch immer was du bist,* "Even if you put on socks one yard high, you still remain what you are."

8

Some Comments on Abraham's Paper on "Ejaculatio Praecox"

Abraham's very instructive paper deserves careful discussion. I propose to make some qualifications and comments on his theory that ejaculatio praecox is attributable to excessive erogenicity of the urethra and fixation of the libido on micturition. To clarify the extent to which the observations that follow should be regarded as complementary to Abraham's paper, I propose to precede my remarks by a critical summary of the etiological factors and syndromes which the author regards as essential components of the pathogenesis and clinical picture of the illness.

His starting point is the observation that with these patients "the semen is not ejaculated rhythmically but is discharged passively." He regards this phenomenon as analogous to the voidance of urine in infancy, when the individual has no or very limited control of his bladder functioning; and he points out that enuresis plays an important part of these patients' case histories, and that the sexual pleasure value of micturition in infants has been established beyond doubt by psychoanalysis; and he concludes that neurotics suffering from premature ejaculation have been arrested at the infantile stage of libido and "gain sexual pleasure from the discharge of bodily products."

The consequence of this fixation of the libido is a lack of "virility in these patients." Fixation on urethral eroticism and pleasure in

---

Internationale Zeitschrift für ärztliche Psychoanalyse, 4, no. 4. Translated by Eric Mosbacher.

micturition result in the genital zone in the strict sense of the word failing to become the leading zone. This is also shown by the fact that in many cases the glans penis is insufficiently excitable and that there is often a particular erotogenicity of the perineum and the dorsal part of the scrotum, thus in the area which phylogenetically corresponds to the introitus vaginae and its surroundings. These men's sexuality is thus robbed of its real masculinity.

So far Abraham's argument would seem to be psychoanalytically unassailable. At this point, however, he postulates female frigidity as the female counterpart to premature ejaculation, pointing out that in frigid women excitation, instead of applying to the introitus vaginae, is confined to the clitoris, and that thus here too, as in the male suffering from premature ejaculation, "the genital zone in the strict sense of the word has not become the leading zone." From this analogy he concludes that premature ejaculation can simply be equated with female frigidity, since "the leading zone in the case of each sex has sacrificed its appropriate significance to that part of the body that represents the equivalent of the leading zone of the other sex."

This theory is open to a number of criticisms.

1. The author attributes premature ejaculation in the last resort to infantile urethral eroticism. If premature ejaculation in the male is the equivalent of frigidity in women, it should be possible to demonstrate excessive urethral eroticism in the latter. Abraham nowhere suggests that evidence for this could be produced. Personally I should not consider the chances of finding it promising.
2. Female frigidity is simply female impotence. No other form of female impotence is known to us. Is female impotence to be attributed to urethral eroticism in all cases or only in those in which excitation results from stimulation of the clitoris and not of other zones?
3. If frigidity of the introitus vaginae is equated with premature ejaculation, it follows from the etiology of the latter that both male and female impotence are attributable to fixation on the urethral zone and pleasure in micturition. The author cannot seriously maintain this.
4. Fixation at the leading zone of the opposite sex is a form of homosexuality and is of major importance in the development

of homosexuality in both men and women. The case histories of male and female impotence provide an abundance of evidence that makes it necessary to take homosexuality into account as a factor in impotence. The case histories of sufferers from premature ejaculation also abound in such material. Abraham neglects this aspect of the subject.

In the light of these criticisms, Abraham's simple equation of frigidity in women with premature ejaculation seems to me to be seriously mistaken.

In relation with the theme of urethral eroticism and pleasure in micturition, Abraham continues as follows:

These patients, he says, identify sperm with urine and in ejaculatio praecox behave as they did in infancy in regard to urination. They soil the woman lovingly with sperm just as they soiled loved persons with urine as a token of love in infancy. This is attributable to the infantile narcissistic idea that the excreta form part of one's body and are therefore an appropriate love gift. Unmanly behaviour, however, leads to contemptuous rejection by the other sex, and in accordance with the law of ambivalence in symptom formation premature ejaculation thus also serves as an expression of hostility to the woman, who is denied the expected reception of the sperm and the ensuing conception. This component of the symptom is also based on the equation of sperm with urine and the idea that the products of excretion are part of one's body. There is a fixation on the function of the penis as the organ of micturition. The pleasure taken by the patient in female manipulation of the penis is another pointer to the infantile pleasure in micturition, and is a residue of the child's habit of urinating with its mother's help and exhibiting itself to her in urinating. This whole group of symptoms is based on the pleasure of excretion as an expression of narcissism, on which there is an excessive fixation in these patients, resulting in a deficiency of object libido. Impotentia ejaculandi is also to be regarded as attributable to the patient's narcissistic purpose of denying the woman his sperm. The occurrence of premature ejaculation only when intercourse is attempted and not in masturbation is explained by the patient's resistance to the specifically male activity. What he seeks is satisfaction without effort, he wants to get what is to him the disagreeable business of coitus over and done with as quickly as possible. But this weakness and passivity conceal a reaction against an attitude of sadistic cruelty to the other sex, which is also shown by the patient's powerful castration complex—he fears losing the penis, which to him is a dangerous instrument for exercising fearful and forbidden impulses, and he therefore does not want to introduce it into the vagina. A factor in the development of the castration complex is fear of the father, who wishes to exclude him from intercourse with his mother; and also present is reaction to the idea that coitus is an act of cruelty carried out by his father on his mother, which the son, in his ambition to displace his father in his mother's affections, shows himself to be incapable of carrying out himself.

In this summary of Abraham's paper I have tried to present his symptomatology of ejaculatio praecox in such a way as first of all to group together the symptoms associated with urethral and excretory eroticism in immediate association with the aetiology assumed for them by the author, and within this grouping to arrange them in accordance with the closeness of their connection with that etiology, clearly separating them from the chance environmental factors that play a part in symptom formation. I hope that in this I have not in any way misrepresented him. Assuming I have not, I wish to express the view that he has not shown the path that urethral and excretory eroticism, in conjunction with "passivity," sadism, the castration complex, incest, etc., must follow in order to lead to ejaculatio praecox, because we see all these phenomena in nearly all neuroses, and very often without the presence of ejaculatio praecox. We shall therefore have to resort to other factors in the case histories to find an explanation. I shall therefore point out some conditions and syndromes which have invariably been present in my case histories of ejaculatio praecox and are very noticeable in the following extracts.

The patient in civil life was a senior civil servant and had been doing war service as an army officer for three years. He was aged forty-one, was married and the father of two girls, aged six and nine.* In spite of great external and internal difficulties, he had

*The older child had masturbated since before the age of one and suffered from enuresis. The apparent hereditary nature of this, and above all the fact that

been successful in his career. He came of a family of slender means and had had largely to support himself while at the university. His father was very strict, and he had been very much afraid of him. He still showed great dependence on his seniors and superiors.

The following is quoted verbatim from the handwritten life story he gave me, in which he characteristically writes about his own childhood in the third person.

> He was a lonely child. Always obstinately wanting to sit on chamber and producing motions. When his father took his mother and him for a walk in the woods in the early morning, he looked especially for a hollow treetrunk for the child to sit on and defecate. Once the small boy dirtied his feet with faeces, and when he got up from his chamber dirtied the whole room, with his father chasing him angrily.
>
> At the age of five the child went to a watering place with his mother. His mother got into a bath-tub wearing a chemise and took the boy with her. She played with him, making air bubbles under her chemise and letting the son slap them. I believe he also played with her breasts. He was left with a continuing pleasure in the corners of pillow cases,* which he used either for sucking or holding between his legs, which he enjoyed.
>
> Once, when a corpulent aunt took off her corset and showed her bosom, the boy, with a companion, looked on and enjoyed himself. He was rebuked and told to go away.
>
> I suffered from bed-wetting. For years I slept on a hard sofa mattress, and slept well. After wetting the sheet, I was capable of rolling from the sofa on to the floor and urinating there without awakening. Until my fifteenth year this was my greatest worry. Eventually masturbation came, and that helped. At first masturbation to me meant success in getting rid of enuresis.
>
> In my free time away from school I was continually told to do housework, and I complied only reluctantly. Dusting, drying up, going out

---

only one of the children suffered from enuresis, favor Abraham's assumption of a constitutional basis for the affliction. When the child was two and bathing with her mother she pointed to her genitals and said: "Papa bimbum, mamma no bimbum." An illustration of infants' alleged lack of interest in sex.

*We know from other analyses that corners of pillowcases stand for the penis. Identification of breasts and penis is also familiar. The patient equates all three, a not infrequent occurrence.

to get bread and milk at five o'clock in the morning, pushing my little sister in the pram, learning to knit, were all things I detested.*

At the age of nine I went to K. for the holidays. While playing with some boys and girls one evening, a bigger, strongly built girl took a piece of paper and drew what obviously must have been genitals—I cannot remember for certain. But I do remember her pointing to me and saying sympathetically: "He's only a baby and doesn't understand, and in any case he shouldn't."

In the second grade of high school I was led astray by a school-mate into masturbation. To the present day there is no one in the world whom I detest more than I detest him. During the summer term mutual masturbation with desk neighbors, through the trouser-pockets, began. I can still feel the huge, pleasurable excitement caused me by another's hand touching my penis. Nothing gives me an erection more quickly than my wife's holding my penis.

In the following year I must have masturbated ten times a day. Still, I was strong, and gladly joined every climbing expedition, irrespective of duration or altitude, hunger or thirst. At harvest time I zealously helped the peasants. In my struggle with enuresis I discovered that masturbation got rid of it.

A pretty, seventeen-year-old peasant girl saw me in my bath with an erection, and said that it was still much too small for her. If she had accepted me at that time, I might perhaps have been saved.**

During the singing lessons an enormous amount of mutual masturbation went on. I always secretly envied one boy who had a very big penis and could masturbate for a long time without ejaculating. Mine was smaller, and I had a phimosis, which hurt when I masturbated and made me ejaculate quickly.

After one excursion I waited for my friend in bed like a mistress and then we masturbated in my parents' big beds.

After masturbating I always felt full of the joy of life, sang, did the most difficult jobs, or committed to memory the most difficult things.

I went through a period of the most outrageous lying and kleptomania.

One day my imagination was terribly excited when in a drawer of my father's desk I found a small obscene book and some handwritten

*The patient was being emasculated. This method of upbringing fell on well prepared soil.

**Patients often make this kind of remark, and there are many indications that they may be right.

obscene poems, whereupon I set about finding out whether the writing was my father's or my mother's.* Next came the struggle for the key. My father must have grown suspicious, because he put the things in different drawers and eventually in the bookcase, but I always managed to force the lock and find them. Gazing for some time at Adam and Eve, plus reading the things mentioned above, led to a prolonged erection and then to quick masturbation and ejaculation. For years afterwards I visualized that writing so vividly in bed before going to sleep that a slight pressure of the blanket or squeeze of the penis between my thighs would induce an orgasm.

At that time I began letting flies creep over my thighs, the penis and the glans (Venus with a fly on her thigh.)**

One afternoon I went with my mother to visit my grandparents. It was very hot there, and I had a spontaneous erection. My erect penis made my light summer trousers bulge. My mother came over to me, took hold of it, and said: "What on earth have you got in your pocket this time?" I felt deeply ashamed of myself, she looked at me, and must have realised what was happening. She said no more, but was curiously amused.

At all events, an almost fierce and, I felt, justified desire flared up in me. Why, if my mother knows this, does she not let me sleep with her? Then I should be saved, I said to myself. It must be because my father forbids it. Next I began secretly falling in love with all my female relatives, my aunts, even my grandmother, and also the maid. They all must know that they could save me, I felt.

The degree of excitement that dominated me during my fourteenth and fifteenth years is also shown by the fact that at S. I attempted coitus with our bitch. Many years later, when I called on a friend of mine who was an assistant in the gynaecological department at J. and discovered that he was out and the room empty, I tried to have coitus with a preserved female pelvis, but ended by giving it up, because it was too hard.

During my last three years at high school I succeeded temporarily in suppressing masturbation by vigorous physical exercise and hard work.

---

*This literature was of course his father's. Another of those 'strict' fathers who want to have innocent sons.

**The mythological parallel was supplied by the patient himself. That the fly sitting on Venus represents the penis appears to be beyond doubt. This interpretation, applied to the patient, shows his homosexuality, and probably also the significance of creeping creatures as representing male genitals, which may be noted as a contribution to the interpretation of animal hallucinations in delirium tremens.

> At the university I masturbated only about once a week. Apart from my law studies, I used to hang about the medical school. The sight of shaved female bodies was disappointing. Pubic and axillary hair, particularly when seen through a transparent blouse, are still greatly exciting to me.*
>
> In my twenty-second year I went with a prostitute for the first time. Ejaculation took place before entry and with a few exceptions I have never since been free of ejaculatio praecox.
>
> At the age of thirty I met my wife. Masturbation ceased, but nocturnal emissions increased to an alarming extent. I married a year later. Premature ejaculation remained the rule, but normal intercourse became possible the second time. Often an involuntary emission occurred on the same or following night. Before going with my wife pre-coital excitement was so great that I had a kind of cold shivers and my teeth chattered.** Then a rapid hot flush occurred, and ejaculation *ante* or *intra portas*.
>
> I have not suffered much from sexual abstinence during the war, as I have nocturnal emissions twice a week.

The patient described his principal characteristics as follows: ambitiousness, resistance to work, proneness to violent outbursts of temper accompanied by offensive language, lack of quickness of wit, extreme sensitivity to the slightest personal affront, and in general a sense of puerility.

On the relationship between masturbation, involuntary emission and enuresis, on which the patient's manuscript is not quite clear, verbal analysis disclosed that when he began masturbating the enuresis stopped, but began again when he stopped masturbating. Involuntary emissions similarly took the place of enuresis or masturbation, and vice versa.

I add some of the patient's characteristic emission dreams.

(1) He was snuggling up against a woman. He could not remember who she was. A man, his father, was looking on. Even-

---

*I have referred elsewhere to hair's standing symbolically for the penis.

**Expectation, temporarily inhibiting libido, probably turned into anxiety.

tually a big blanket covered them and he pressed vigorously against the woman.* Emission and awakening.
(2) A whole series of dreams which the patient noted down end with the remark: "I awoke with an erection because of having to urinate."
(3) He dreamt that it was possible to have nocturnal emissions right or left, and awoke with an emission.**
(4) In the notes the observation occurs: "Why do I so often have nocturnal emissions after being given clean bed-clothes?"***

Looking through my case histories of ejaculatio praecox, I feel entitled to describe this as a typical case. It certainly very amply confirms Abraham's view of the prominent part played by urethral erotogenicity and micturition-libido in the pathogenesis of the illness, and it also reflects some of the essential characteristics of these patients as noted by him. In regard to the role of urethral erotogenicity in ejaculatio praecox, I should like to add that it sometimes appears after treatment for gonorrhea.

Unless chance has caused me to come across only cases of the same type****—which is hard to believe—I am surprised that Abraham pays no attention to the masturbation and involuntary emissions which play such a prominent part in my case histories. I have come across only one sufferer from ejaculatio praecox who assured me that he had never masturbated, because, he said, he had been "enlightened at an early age." But instead he suffered from almost daily involuntary emissions. All the other patients had been heavy masturbators for years, most of them into their

*The woman turned out to be his mother. The patient conspired with her as soon as they were out of his father's sight ("to hide under a single blanket" in German is "to plot.") The patient remembered masturbating under a blanket with incestuous phantasies. Also he had for years slept in his mother's bed, with his father in the other bed.

**The patient recalled urinating right and left, a game that small boys played.

***There was clearly a tendency to soil things, similar to the habit observed in infants of soiling loved persons and pleasing objects with urine.

****While I was reading the proofs of this paper, F. Löwenfeld's *Sexualleben und Nervenleiden* (J. F. Bergmahn: Wiesbaden, 1916) came to hand. On page 351 there is a case history, described as Observation 89, in which the factors to which I have drawn attention are very conspicuous.

thirties or forties, and all had gone through at least one, if not several, periods of frequent involuntary emissions.

While the case history I recorded above shows us the big part played by masturbation and involuntary emissions in the story of sufferers from ejaculatio praecox, here is an autobiographical fragment that tells us something about the inner lives of these patients. The following is from a manuscript written by a thirty-six-year-old playwright. He was married, but his relations with his wife, by whom he had one child, were unsatisfactory because—so it was assumed by his friends—of his numerous affairs with other women. He was not unsuccessful in his career, though he had to struggle with great resistances in his work, and managed to get down on paper only a fraction of what he planned. As he was unable to exploit his intellectual resources, it will not surprise us that in personal contacts or alone he was much more intelligent and more talented than in his work. The secret of his inhibitions in his work and of his unsuccessful marriage is disclosed in the following extracts from his diary:

> Where is the woman whom I embrace? I clasp her naked in my arms and am still searching for her. I suddenly notice that I am lying with my eyes shut.* Then I am unable to see her. I open my eyes. Yes, she really is pretty. But is that all when one is holding a woman in one's arms, a woman who has yielded herself completely and given herself to me? I say to myself: This is a human, a human being, a human female who is lying beside me. I too am human, a human male, who has just achieved the human male ambition, the desire of all human males, the subject of their songs, the thing for which they toil and steal and murder. And all this, mark you, I imagine, have to imagine, have to force myself to realize. Is this love? Love is something I have to imagine. What inexpressible misery! What inhuman, barren, empty misery, so inhuman that it does not even deserve to be called misery!

A later page of the diary recounts in calmer prose:

> Ever since I have been thinking, I have been sexually irritated. Hardly a minute of the day without my having sexual phantasies. When I go

*"I lie with my eyes closed and think about a thousand things, without realizing immediately that my thoughts are far away from the woman lying beside me. I compose poetry, or think about other women and of past or future affairs" [Verbal addition].

> with a woman, I have anticipated it all. It is only the wet conclusion which I deposit at her door. Often, only too often, I do it alone, because I cannot wait. Ravening phantasies have a numbing and stupefying effect on the mind. The hopelessness of expecting the 101st time to be any more successful than its 100 predecessors spoils what would have been worth waiting for. Sperm is poison in one's body. I want to give it to the woman, I win her, she comes. But before that I have already enjoyed her in a thousand ways, in the wildest imaginings. When I take her in my arms I no longer want to do any of the things I have thought of before.
>
> Her genitals are alien to me. I do not like seeing them. In my phantasy I lick and bite them. In reality they disgust me. They smell and are ugly. . . .
>
> In my mind I betray her. My mind wins her, my most beautiful phantasies entice her through every movement of my body. My love is an art, but my art is not love. "What a man he must be with a mind like that," she says to herself. Yes, the man has a mind, but the mind has no man. I squirt away my intellectual sperm at every street corner. Why doesn't she see that? The two things are connected. Women are stupid. The clever ones stick to lackeys and hussars. . . .
>
> Only when I have been doing hard, serious mental work for a long time without getting heated by my phantasies is the way to the "wet conclusion" longer. Being able to exercise mental restraint, not giving oneself away too soon, seriously and deliberately putting the last stone to the edifice constructed with great pains, react on the body and have a formative effect on it. But it is the body's fault that I can so seldom achieve such mental victory. . . .

This second case history needs supplementing by the following facts. The patient was "house-trained" before the age of two, and his education in cleanliness did not meet with any special difficulties. Analysis uncovered only two instances of bed-wetting after his second year. In his twelfth year he once wetted his bed when he dreamt that a goat was drinking milk from a plate. Analysis of the dream seemed to show that the goat was there to get rid of the milk, meaning urine, that the dream followed after the accident, and that its purpose was to undo what had happened. However, a nocturnal emission could not be excluded in this dream. On an earlier occasion, that could not be dated more specifically, he wetted his bed while dreaming he was urinating in the W.C. This was a simple dream of convenience.

An important factor in the case is that the patient never suffered from ejaculatio praecox in his marriage, but only in his adulterous excursions, and then only during the first coitus; the second always took place normally. Reasons for the prematurity given in analysis were fear of infection and of an extramarital pregnancy. In every case the coitus was preceded by a long and often tormenting period of expectation, filled with wild phantasies. A striking feature of the patient's character was his ambivalent attitude towards the male sex, a residue of his not completely overcome homosexuality. Another was the proneness to verbal aggression noted by Abraham. On the other hand, he showed toughness, energy and endurance in the most difficult situations, though cunning often took the place of real intelligence. After some unsatisfactory sexual experiences, his narcissism, originally strong, self-confident and worked up into intellectual aims, showed the melancholic reaction of self-mistrust and self-contempt.

Among his masturbatory practices, masturbation in the anus and perforating sheets of paper with the erect penis (defloration phantasy) were conspicuous. The reaction to his attempt to give up masturbation in his fifteenth year was an agonizing period of nocturnal emissions that lasted for many months.

From these case histories, which I could supplement by others more or less similar, a number of essential characteristics of ejaculatio praecox emerge which Abraham either fails to appreciate or, in my opinion, does not put in their proper place in the clinical picture.

Without detracting from his well-founded and very important observation that most sufferers from ejaculatio praecox have a strong fixation of the libido on micturition, there are many such patients in whom this cannot be shown to be present to a greater extent than in many neurotic who do not suffer from it. Ejaculatio praecox can have all sorts of causes, in fact all those which can also be shown to underlie other forms of impotence. The castration complex (fear of losing the penis, fear of infection) and fear of the strict father (with the Oedipal attitude or sibling incest in the background, or fear of "making a baby" for which one would have to answer to one's father) are very prominent. But a predominant part in this form of impotence is played by homosexuality. The patient simply rejects "male activity" because he feels female and is in search of the male, the penis and not the vagina. In these cases narcissism with all its expressions provides only the soil on which homosexuality grows. Identification with the mother is a mechanism never absent in this illness. Hence the "passivity." Ambivalence towards men, very often active homosexuality, masturbation, sensitivity to "the erogenous zones of the other sex," are only symptoms of homosexuality.

All these inhibitions of active male sexuality lead up to the same formula, namely that the patient does not want normal intercourse and therefore cannot have it. Apart from the homosexuality that rejects woman as a whole as such, the other cases show that the rejection applies, not to woman, but only to normal coitus, as Abraham notes. Such rejection can be caused by any perversion. I had a patient who did not suffer from ejaculatio praecox when practicing cunnilingus, but had it immediately when he wanted to terminate it with coitus.

Among the most striking features of the case histories of ejaculatio praecox are the persistent, hardly ever abandoned and sometimes excessive masturbation and the frequent involuntary emissions which, as Freud has pointed out, should be regarded as equivalents of masturbation. Involuntary discharge of semen during defecation, and sometimes also after urination, often occurs with these patients. Consideration of these phenomena reveals another aspect of ejaculatio praecox in which Abraham's theory of a fixation of urethral and micturition libido plays an essential part.

Any patient suffering from ejaculatio praecox will admit that he is constantly preoccupied with sexual phantasies, like the writer of the second autobiographical notes quoted above. These phantasies are generally completely conscious and of the most manifold content, but are predominantly concerned with the idea of a female object. They can easily be shown to be preliminaries to an attempt at normal intercourse, often in the form of unconscious phantasies. What is conscious is usually only precoital anxiety as a reaction to the phantasy of satisfaction which has been repressed in favor of the expected real satisfaction. Thus ejaculatio praecox represents the termination of a sexual phantasy; touching the female genitals has become only an equivalent to the intense final phase of a masturbatory phantasy, and a very appropriate one, the impact of which far exceeds that of the "reality" (produced with difficulty and seldom uncritically or without disturbance) of the phantasy and is therefore readily capable of leading to immediate ejaculation. At the same time it is a discharge of anxiety, an equivalent of anxiety, and its connection with the anxiety noted in Abraham's paper, which often precedes the premature discharge of sperm, becomes plain. This accords with Freud's view of the anxiety equivalent of any kind of symptom formation.

From this point of view it becomes intelligible that ejaculatio praecox generally occurs only at the first and not at the second coitus. In the latter the patient usually obtains stimulation and fore-plesure entirely from the object, he does not have to produce an introductory phantasy, he produces the entire charge leading up to the final outburst of end-pleasure thanks to the object and with the object. The entry and the movement of the penis have not been anticipated in phantasy, ejaculation does not occur when the phantasy is terminated by touching the genitals, but at the end of a real sexual act carried out with appropriate movements.

The practices by which patients try to prevent premature ejaculation show the importance of masturbatory phantasy, of "anticipation," in the explanation of the phenomenon. They are attempts to substitute conscious reality for phantasy, consciously to face the presence of a real object, a female body that can and will be entered and offers everything needed for pleasure from alpha to omega, and that phantasy is superfluous because it is all actually there, actually tangible, seizable, attainable. Only when the rejection of woman or of the normal sex act is so strong (as a consequence of perversion, anxiety, etc.) that a real woman provides no stimulus does the second coitus also end in ejaculatio praecox, as the whole thing up to and including ejaculation takes place in phantasy.

The conscious effort to face reality postpones ejaculation and often actually leads to the opposite phenomenon, ejaculatio tardiva or even impotentia ejaculandi, which shows that the patient is entirely dependent on his phantasy because he has grown used to it or because it gives him things which the object cannot give. That ejaculatio praecox occurs as the termination of a preliminary masturbatory phantasy is very plain from the passage in the first autobiography which says "that a slight pressure of the blanket or squeeze of the penis between the thighs after prolonged phantasy induced ejaculation." Phantasy has raised excitation to the point of terminal intensity, with the result that the slightest physical contact is sufficient to touch off the explosion.

On the other hand I have come across cases in which masturbation or fellatio by a woman does not lead to premature ejaculation. In these instances there is a powerful inhibition against such sexual practices because these patients, even in phantasy, are predominantly orientated towards normal intercourse, and to them masturbation or fellatio by a woman is an unworthy and unwanted waste of sperm. Most of these patients, when such abnormal experiments are made, experience an abnormally delayed ejaculation or none at all. They withhold their sperm, preferring to wait for the normal sex act, but when they attempt it ejaculatio praecox intervenes. Obviously, in spite of all their conscious intentions, they cannot wait.

This is a factor to which Freud has repeatedly drawn attention in the discussion of masturbation, namely that these patients cannot wait. Masturbation is one of those evil deeds which keeps generating evil.* The small boy began masturbating because he could not wait for the too distant day when it would be permissible for him to obtain object satisfaction. Masturbation spoilt him and deprived him of his remaining capacity for self-restraint. The familiar state of permanent sexual overstimulation by masturbation set in. Every approach to a woman roused the desire for immediate satisfaction. Physical contact with the object, a real attempt to achieve the sexual goal, represents the termination of a sexual act that took place in phantasy. The condition deserves the familiar name of "irritable weakness."

The process is unquestionably accompanied by physical damage to the inhibitory apparatus of the ejaculatory organs, as is shown by the completely pleasureless, often totally unnoticed, discharge of semen during defecation.

If a specific comparison between ejaculatio praecox and female frigidity is to be made, the point of comparison might be masturbation. For it is well known that in women who have practiced

---

*An adapted quotation from Schiller's *Piccolomini* (translators' note).

clitoral masturbation for a long time the *introitus vaginae* remains insensitive, whereas they show quite typical "irritable weakness" for other sexual approaches.

One of the principal symptoms of the "inability to wait," or "waiting weakness," is the involuntary emissions, particularly the frequent ones, from which all these patients suffer. Spoilt by masturbation, they cannot tolerate even slight sexual stimuli without discharging sperm. Moreover the emission dream furnishes an explanation for Abraham's observation that ejaculatio praecox occurs only when normal coitus is attempted, not with masturbatory activity. There is a very well known type of emission dream, which has not yet been described from the aspect under discussion here, which is characterised by "flight from emission."* It may begin, say, with homosexual images and then several dream mechanisms are produced which are plainly recognizable as attempts to escape from a sexual action (an endless journey, looking for doors, successive changes of symbols, often accompanied by a feeling of surprise) and eventually ends with emission accompanying a dream picture representing a normal or perverted sex act with an object or an act of masturbation. Analysis shows that the dream picture that leads to the emission stands for the dreamer's strongest sexual goal, and that the whole purpose of the dream was to prevent the appearance of the irresistible sexual objective, which is desired above all else, and that with its appearance ejaculation inexorably took place. Faced with this supreme objective the dreamer has no power of self-restraint, and when it appears he can wait no longer.

Ejaculatio praecox as the termination of a practically permanent masturbation phantasy is completely analogous to this nocturnal emission dream.

We can distinguish two opposing factors in the mechanics of ejaculatio praecox:

1. The patient rejects the female genitals, because of homosexuality, perversion, or anxiety.
2. The patient desires the female genitals.

*Cf. my paper on the psychology of the alcoholic occupation delirium.

The mechanism of premature ejaculation is set in motion by the preceding phantasy. Having regard to the basically positive attitude to normal coitus indicated by the predominance of the second factor, we are entitled to speak of "expectation weakness." Ejaculatio praecox is to be regarded as equivalent to involuntary emission and having the same relationship to masturbation as involuntary emission. To the extent that enuresis is a masturbation equivalent, involuntary emission and ejaculatio praecox are the same.

Abraham's concept fits this last type only. Psychoanalysis has every reason to be grateful to him for the description of this clinical picture. It applies to patients who either have never escaped from enuresis or—and these represent the majority of my cases—have regressed to micturition-libido through masturbation. These patients are strongly homosexual and show the symptoms, mentioned by Abraham, derived from the narcissistic—homosexual complex. My experience does not permit me to consider micturition-libido as the sole cause of ejaculatio praecox.

Finally I should like to point out that ejaculatio praecox is significantly reduced or even disappears altogether when the patient gives up his conscious or unconscious masturbation phantasies, from which I conclude that it cannot be fully explained unless masturbation and involuntary emissions are taken into account as factors in its causation, and that among the greatly disputed harmful consequences of masturbation it is to be regarded as a certainly harmful one.

9

On the Origin of the "Influencing Machine" in Schizophrenia

I

The following considerations are based upon a single example of the "influencing machine" complained of by a certain type of schizophrenic patient. Although in this particular case the structure of the machine differs materially, to the best of my knowledge, from all other varieties of apparatus of this sort, it is hoped that the present example will nevertheless facilitate psychoanalytic insight into the genesis and purpose of this delusional instrument.

My example is a variant—a very rare variant—of the typical influencing machine. The objection can of course be made that it is rash to draw general conclusions from the study of a single case, and that generalizations, to be regarded as scientifically valid, should be based on a larger mass of material. My justification is that I have simply not encountered any further case material in support of my conclusions, and that to the best of my knowledge psychiatric literature contains no descriptions of individual cases of the influencing machine phenomenon, such as would make my paper superfluous. There exist only general descriptions of the apparatus, and its regular features and functions are given only as perfunctory clinical illustrations. Clinical psy-

Psychoanalytic Quarterly 2 (1933). Translation from the German by Dorian Feigenbaum.

chiatry, interested only in general descriptions, lays no stress upon the significance of individual symptoms for the study of the dynamics of psychoses. Psychiatry has not hitherto sufficiently investigated the origin, the meaning, and the purpose of a symptom, because, not employing the psychoanalytical method, it does not even postulate such problems. Yet in principle, it is permissible to derive general conclusions from exceptional types. Variants and mixed forms stimulate inquiry into general types. The conformity of typical cases may have the ultimate effect of an impenetrable barrier, while a deviation from type, on the other hand, may be a window in the wall through which a clear view is to be obtained.

Deviations from the rule and ambiguous types compel the assumption that a given phenomenon may be of diverse origin. It is only when an unexpected departure from the accustomed occurs that one feels the necessity of investigating the uniformity which had previously characterized the phenomenon or at least had seemed to do. Inquiry into extraordinary causative factors has often stimulated inquiry into those ordinarily encountered.

It is to be hoped only that the example taken as a basis for the following conclusions will prove to justify them, and that the origin and significance of this variant example have been correctly conceived and formulated.

II

The schizophrenic influencing machine is a machine of mystical nature. The patients are able to give only vague hints of its construction. It consists of boxes, cranks, levers, wheels, buttons, wires, batteries, and the like. Patients endeavor to discover the construction of the apparatus by means of their technical knowledge, and it appears that with the progressive popularization of the sciences, all the forces known to technology are utilized to explain the functioning of the apparatus. All the discoveries of mankind, however, are regarded as inadequate to explain the marvelous powers of this machine, by which the patients feel themselves persecuted.

The main effects of the influencing machine are the following:

1. It makes the patients see pictures. When this is the case, the machine is generally a magic lantern or cinematograph. The pictures are seen on a single plane, on walls or windowpanes, and unlike typical visual hallucinations are not three-dimensional.
2. It produces, as well as removes, thoughts and feelings by means of waves or rays or mysterious forces which the patient's knowledge of physics is inadequate to explain. In such cases, the machine is often called a "suggestion-apparatus." Its construction cannot be explained, but its function consists in the transmission or "draining off" of thoughts and feelings by one or several persecutors.
3. It produces motor phenomena in the body, erections and seminal emissions, that are intended to deprive the patient of his male potency and weaken him. This is accomplished either by means of suggestion or by air-currents, electricity, magnetism, or X-rays.
4. It creates sensations that in part cannot be described, because they are strange to the patient himself, and that in part are sensed as electrical, magnetic, or due to air-currents.
5. It is also responsible for other occurrences in the patient's body, such as cutaneous eruptions, abscesses, and other pathological processes.

The machine serves to persecute the patient and is operated by enemies. To the best of my knowledge, the latter are exclusively of the male sex. They are predominantly physicians by whom the patient has been treated. The manipulation of the apparatus is likewise obscure, the patient rarely having a clear idea of its operation. Buttons are pushed, levers set in motion, cranks turned. The connection with the patient is often established by means of invisible wire leading into his bed, in which case the patient is influenced by the machine only when he is in bed.

However, it is noteworthy that a large number of patients complain of all these ailments without ascribing them to the influence of a machine. Many patients consider the cause of all these alien or hostile sensations of physical or psychic change to be simply an external mental influence, suggestion or telepathic power, emanating from enemies. My own observations and those of other authors leave no room for doubt that these complaints precede the symptom of the influencing apparatus, and that the latter is a subsequent pathological development. Its appearance, as many observers state, serves the purpose of an explanation for the pathologic changes that are felt as alien and painful and dominate the patient's emotional life and sensations.

According to this view, the idea of the influencing machine originates in the need for causality that is inherent in man; and the same need for causality will probably also account for the persecutors who act not through the medium of an apparatus but merely by suggestion or by telepathy. Clinical psychiatry explains the symptom of an influencing machine as analogous to the ideas of persecution in paranoia (which, it is known, the patient invents in order to justify his delusions of grandeur), and calls it "*paranoia somatica.*"

However, there is a group of patients that dispenses completely with any gratification of the need for causality, and complains simply of emotional changes and strange apparitions within the physical and psychic personality, without the intervention of a foreign or hostile power. It is particularly declared by some patients that their visions are not foisted upon them in any way but that, to their great astonishment, they simply see them. There also occur other strange sensations for which there is no evidence of an originator, especially, for instance, the complaint of a loss or change of thoughts and feelings, without the thoughts or feelings being "drained" from them or "foisted" upon them; and of a similar nature are complaints of a change of sensations in the skin, face, and extremities. This group of patients does not complain of influences originating from a foreign, hostile force, but of a feeling of inner estrangement. They become strange to themselves, no longer understand themselves: limbs, face, facial expression, thoughts, and feelings, have become estranged. These symptoms clearly are part of an early stage of dementia præcox, although they may also be observed in advanced stages as well.

In some cases it may be stated with certainty, and in others with strong probability, that the sense of persecution originates from the sensations of change accompanied by a sense of estrangement. These feelings of persecution are ascribed to a foreign, personal interference, "suggestion," or "telepathic influence." In other cases, the ideas of persecution or influence may be seen entering into the construction of an influencing apparatus. It is necessary to assume, therefore, that the influencing apparatus represents the terminal stage in the evolution of the symptom, which started with simple sensations of change. I do not believe that heretofore the entire sequence in the development of the symptom could have been studied completely from a single case. But I have observed the connection between at least two stages (of which I shall present an example later), and I have no hesitation in maintaining that under especially favorable circumstances it may be possible to observe the entire series of developmental stages in a single patient. Meanwhile, I am in the position of the observer of plasmodia who notes various pathological forms in the blood cells as developmental stages of a continuous cycle of growth, although he is never able to observe in any one blood corpuscle more than a single phase.

Recognition of the various symptoms as stages of a unified developmental process is rendered difficult not merely by inaccurate observation but by other factors as well. Patients conceal single stages behind secondary and correlative symptoms—each patient in accordance with his morbid disposition. Changes of feeling are covered up by a simultaneously or consecutively produced psychosis or neurosis belonging to another clinical group, such as depression, mania, paranoia, compulsion neurosis, anxiety hysteria, or amentia; and these clinical pictures, advancing to the foreground, conceal from the observer the more subtle elements in the development of the delusion of reference. It is, besides, very likely that in many cases not every stage of development reaches consciousness, and that one stage or another runs its course in the unconscious and thus leaves gaps in the conscious psyche. Finally, depending upon the rapidity of the pathological process and upon the individual disposition, some of the stages may be missing altogether.

Ideas of reference in schizophrenia develop equally with or without the influencing apparatus. In but one case[1] have I been able to observe electrical currents in the absence of the influencing apparatus to which those are usually ascribed—in the absence, in fact, of any hostile power whatsoever.

This observation was made in the case of a thirty-four year old man, Josef H., an inmate of insane asylums at frequent intervals throughout his life. He felt electrical currents streaming through him, which entered the earth through his legs; he produced the current within himself, declaring with pride that that was his power! How and for what purpose he did this he refused to disclose. Upon discovering these currents in himself for the first time, he was (he admitted) somewhat astonished, but he soon came to the conclusion that this manifestation had a special significance—that the currents served a mysterious end, regarding which he refused any information.

I shall now cite another instance, a singular case of "*paranoia somatica,*" having, as will later be seen, a significance of its own in substantiating the developmental process which I have assumed. The same example has already been cited by Freud in another connection. Miss Emma A. felt herself influenced by her lover in a singular manner; she maintained that her eyes were no longer properly placed in her head but were entirely twisted out of position, and this she attributed to the fact that her lover was an evil, deceitful person who twisted eyes. At church one day she suddenly felt a thrust, as if she were being moved from her place, which had its cause in the fact that her lover disguised himself,* and that he had already ruined her and made her as evil as himself.

This patient did not merely feel herself persecuted and influenced; hers was a case of being influenced by identification with the persecutor. If we take into consideration the view held by Freud and myself that in object-choice the mechanism of identification precedes the cathexis proper by projection, we may regard the case of Miss Emma A. as representing the stage in the development of the delusion of reference preceding the projection (namely, on to a distant persecutor in the outer world). The identification is obviously an attempt to project the feelings of the inner change on to the outer world. It constitutes a bridge between the feelings of an inner change without external cause and the attribution of these changes to the power of an external person, a kind of intermediary position between the feeling of

*This patient's words, "Sich verstellt"—taken literally, mean "moves himself from one place to another."—TRANSLATOR.

self-estrangement and the delusion of reference. This rounds out especially well, and substantiates psychoanalytically, the concept of the development of the symptom, up to its crystallization in the influencing machine. We are here concerned with the discovery, or rather the invention, of a hostile object; but for the intellectual process it is unimportant whether the objects observed are hostile or friendly, and the psychoanalyst, at least, will certainly have no objection to the equating of love and hate in this instance. Among the illustrations that may be given of the various forms or stages of the delusion of reference, the case of Staudenmayer (whose autobiography was presented before the Vienna Psychoanalytic Society some years ago) may be mentioned.

Staudenmayer—who, if I am not mistaken, was declared to be a paranoiac and is at any rate considered to be one by me—described his sensations during his bowel movements from the beginning of the movement to its conclusion, and attributed every single peristaltic motion coming to his awareness to the activity of special demons allegedly located in the intestines and entrusted with the performance of each separate motion.

We may now summarize and describe schematically the phenomena that in some cases appear to be produced by the influencing machine and that in other cases occur without it.

1. We note, first, simple sensations of inner change, in the beginning devoid of, and later accompanied by, a sense of estrangement, without awareness of an originator. The sensations are of changes in the psychical and physical functions within various parts of one's own body. In many cases this stage of the illness probably occurs at a very early age, before puberty. Since at this age no exact reports can be obtained on inner conditions, and since, in addition, pathological changes are not infrequently compensated by infantile peculiarities of character, such as naughtiness, aggressiveness, concealed fantasies, masturbation, seclusiveness, dullness and so forth, this stage either remains unrecognized or else is misnamed. It is only at puberty, when special adjustments to the environment are required of the individual, who is compelled to relinquish all crude expressions of his abnormality, that the illness comes to the surface; it is at this time, too, that further development of symptoms is stimulated.

2. Feelings of inner change in the form of abnormal sensations, with awareness of an originator,—in this instance the patient himself (case Josef H.).
3. Feelings of inner change accompanied by awareness of an originator, who, although existing within the patient, is nevertheless not the patient himself (case Staudenmayer).
4. Feelings of inner change accompanied by hallucinatory projection of the inner occurrence to the external world, without awareness of an originator; at first, feelings of estrangement are not present, but later on they appear (seeing pictures).
5. Feelings of inner change accompanied by awareness of an external originator as a result of identification (case Emma A.).
6. Feelings of inner change accompanied by projection of the inner occurrence to the outer world and belief in an originator produced by the paranoid mechanism (causing pictures to appear, influencing by suggestion, hypnotism, electricity, producing or draining off thoughts and feelings, effecting bodily motions, weakening potency, producing erection, seminal emissions, and so forth).
7. Feelings of inner change attributed to the workings of the influencing machine manipulated by enemies. At first, the enemies are usually unknown to the patient and only vaguely discerned by him; later on he is able to make them out, knows who they are, and enlarges their circle after the pattern of the paranoid conspiracy. Similarly, the patient is at first completely unable to explain the construction of the influencing apparatus, but familiarizes himself with it gradually.

Having solved the relation between ideas of reference and the influencing apparatus, we may proceed to an examination of the latter without reference to its effects.

It is not necessary to discuss the magic lantern which produces pictures or images, because its structure harmonizes perfectly with the function attributed to it, and because it does not reveal any error of judgment beyond the fact of its nonexistence. This rational superstructure is absolutely impenetrable. We must, at the start, use structures less solidly built, the walls of which reveal gaps through which it is possible to look inside.

(a) The ordinary influencing machine has a very obscure construction; large parts of it are completely unimaginable. In cases where the patient believes he understands the construction of the apparatus well, it is obvious that this feeling is, at best, analogous to that of a dreamer who has a feeling of understanding, but has not the understanding itself. This characteristic may be discovered whenever an accurate description of the apparatus is demanded of the patient.

(b) The apparatus is, as far as I know, always a machine; and a very complicated one.

The psychoanalyst cannot for a moment doubt that this machine must be a symbol—a view recently emphasized by Freud in one of his lectures, in which he stated that the complicated machines appearing in dreams always represent the genitalia. Having studied machine dreams analytically over a long period of time, I can fully confirm Freud's statement; I may add, moreover, that the machines always stand for the dreamer's own genitalia and that the dreams are of a masturbatory character. I can state further that these dreams are dreams of escape, of the type described in my paper on alcoholic delirium.[2] In this paper it is shown that whenever an urge to masturbate, or rather a readiness to ejaculate semen, leads to a dream fantasy which is favorable to discharge, another fantasy is hastily substituted, by means of which a new state of inhibition is induced momentarily, and the ejaculation of semen is made difficult if not impossible. The dream reacts to the repudiated wish for discharge with a successive alteration of symbols.

The machine dream possesses an analogous mechanism, except that the introduction of single components of the machine is not accompanied by the simultaneous disappearance of the other components for which they are substituted, the new components being simply added to the old ones. This is how the hopelessly complex machine originates. In order to strengthen the inhibition, the symbol has been made complex, instead of being displaced by another one; but the result is the same. Each complexity draws the attention of the dreamer to himself, rouses his intellectual interest, reciprocally weakens his libidinal interest, and effects in this manner inhibition of instinct.

In machine dreams the dreamer awakens, more often than not, with his hand on his genitalia, after having dreamed of manipulating the machine. It may, therefore, be assumed that the influencing apparatus is a representation of the patient's genitalia projected to the outer world, analogous in origin to the machine in dreams. The frequent complaint of the schizophrenic that the apparatus causes erection, drains off semen, and weakens potency only confirms this view. At any rate, the analogy of the symptom to a dream production, as well as the accessibility of the symptom to psychoanalytic dream interpretation is a step beyond the rationalizations and the demand for causal connections that underlie the usual clinical interpretation of the influencing machine in schizophrenia. I can now present my example, which will not only strengthen our hypothesis, but will enlarge it materially.

The patient is Miss Natalija A., thirty-one years old, formerly a student of philosophy. She has been completely deaf for a great number of years, due to an ulcer of the ear, and can make herself understood only by means of writing. She declares that for six and a half years she has been under the influence of an electrical machine made in Berlin, though this machine's use is prohibited by the police. It has the form of a human body, indeed, the patient's own form, though not in all details. Her mother, likewise the patient's male and female friends, are also under the influence of this machine or of similar machines. Of the latter she gives no explanation, describing only the apparatus to which she herself is subjected. She is certain that for men there is a masculine machine representing the masculine form and for women a female one. The trunk (torso) has the shape of a lid, resembling the lid of a coffin and is lined with silk or velvet. Regarding the limbs two significant explanations are given. At the first interview she described them as entirely natural parts of the body. A few weeks later these limbs were not placed on the coffin lid in their natural form, but were merely drawn on it in two dimensions, in the position they would occupy in the natural state of the body. She cannot see the head—she says that she is not sure about it and she does not know whether the machine bears her own head. She has practically nothing to report about the head. The patient does not know definitely how this machine is to be handled, neither does she know how it is connected with her; but she vaguely thinks that it is by means of telepathy. The outstanding fact about the machine is that it is being manipulated by someone in a certain manner, and everything that occurs to it happens also to her. When someone strikes this machine, she feels the blow in the corresponding part of her own body. The ulcer (lupus) now present on her nose was first produced on the nose of the machine, and some time later the patient herself became afflicted with it. The inner parts of the machine consist of electric batteries, which are supposed to represent the internal organs of the human body. Those who handle the machine produce a slimy substance in her nose, disgusting smells, dreams, thoughts, feelings, and disturb her while she is thinking, reading or writing. At an earlier stage, sexual sensations were produced in her through manipulation of the genitalia of the machine; but now the machine no longer possesses any genitalia, though why or how they disappeared she cannot tell. Ever since the machine lost its genitalia, the patient has ceased to experience sexual sensations.

She became familiar with the apparatus, about which she had previously heard, through all kinds of occurrences, especially through conversation among people, that is, through auditory hallucinations. The man who utilizes the apparatus to persecute her, her rejected suitor, a college professor, is prompted by jealousy. Very soon after she had refused his courtship she felt that he was trying by means of suggestion to bring about a friendship between his sister-in-law, her mother, and herself, his obvious purpose being to use this influence to make her accept him. When, however, suggestion failed, he subjected her to the influence of the machine; not only she herself but also her mother, her physicians, her friends, all those who had her welfare at heart, came under the influence of this diabolical apparatus, with the result that the physicians submitted a mistaken diagnosis to her, the apparatus deluding them into diagnosing other ailments than those with which she was afflicted. She could no longer get along with her friends and relatives, arousing everyone's animosity, and feeling compelled to run away. It was impossible to obtain any further details from the patient. On her third visit she became inaccessible and only stated that the analyst, too, was under the influence of the apparatus, that he had become hostile to her, and that they could no longer understand each other.

This case provides a definite reason for believing that the influencing machine represents a stage in the development of a symptom which can also appear without this stage, as a delusion of reference. The patient clearly stated that her persecutor had recourse to the apparatus only when his attempt to influence her by suggestion failed. The fact that she seems to have previously heard about the machine is also enlightening. This vague recognition obviously awakened in the patient old familiar sensations that she had experienced before she was subjected to the apparatus; this is analogous to the well-known fact that persons in a state of infatuation have the feeling of having always known the beloved one—in reality they are merely rediscovering one of their old libidinal imagos. We shall hear later in how remote a past she had first experienced sensations similar to those caused by the influencing apparatus.

The peculiar construction of the machine substantiates our assumptions to a great extent, especially with regard to the significance of the machine as a projected symbol of the genitalia. We may add that the apparatus represents not only the patient's genitalia but obviously, her whole person. It represents the projection of the patient's body on to the outer world. At least, the following results are unquestionably obtained from the patient's report: the apparatus is distinguished above all by its human form, easily recognized despite many non-human characteristics. In form it resembles the patient itself, and she senses all manipulations performed on the apparatus in the corresponding part of her own body and in the same manner. All effects and changes undergone by the apparatus take place simultaneously in the patient's body, and *vice versa.* Thus, the apparatus loses its genitalia following the patient's loss of her genital sensations; it had possessed genitalia for as long a period as her genital sensations had lasted.

Applying the technique of dream interpretation to this case, it may be said that the patient's inability to provide any detailed description of the head of the apparatus, and especially her inability to decide whether it was her own head or not, proves conclusively that it is her own head. We know from analytic observations that the person not recognized in a dream is actually the dreamer himself. In my analysis of the *Dream of the Clinic,*[3] it was clear that the dreamer meant herself when she dreamt of a person whose head she could not see.

A further detail in the description of the apparatus—namely, that the lid is lined with silk or velvet—may substantiate this opinion. Women very frequently describe in such terms the feelings evoked by caressing their own skin. That the intestines appear in the form of batteries is only of slight significance here, although it will assume a profounder meaning later on. This superficial interpretation may be associated with the information given directly or indirectly to school children to the effect that the viscera resemble a very complicated machine. In our case the tendency seems to be towards a verbal interpretation of this infantile conception. This conclusion regarding its ontogeny is arrived at with the help of the description given by the patient of her influencing apparatus.

At the very beginning the patient reported that the limbs of the apparatus appeared in their natural form and position. Several weeks later, she declared that the limbs were drawn on the lid. This is obviously a manifestation of the progressive distortion undergone by the apparatus, which, consequently, eventually loses all human characteristics and becomes a typical, unintelligible, influencing machine. First the genitalia, then the limbs are eliminated in this process. The patient, to be sure, is unable to report how the genitalia are removed. She states, however, that the limbs are removed in the following manner: they lose their three-dimensional human form and flatten to a two-dimensional plane. It would not have been surprising if after a lapse of several weeks, the patient had declared that the apparatus did not possess any limbs at all. Nor would it have been astonishing had she stated that the apparatus had never had any limbs. A failure to recall the developmental stages of the apparatus has obviously the same significance as that of forgetting the origin of dream pictures. It is not too bold a conclusion to draw that the coffin lid of the machine is a product of such successive distortions and that originally it had represented a human being—namely, the patient herself.

Psychoanalytic experience brings to light the causative factors in such distortion. Underlying every distortion of a psychic phenomenon there is a defense mechanism which has as its aim the protection of the conscious ego against the appearance or reappearance of undisguised fantasies. The patient obviously seeks not to recognize herself in the influencing machine and therefore in self-protection she divests it of all human features; in a word, the less human the appearance of the delusion, the less does she recognize herself in it. The origin of this rejection will be examined later.

When the influencing machine of Miss Natalija A. first came to my attention, it was in a special stage of development; I was fortunate, moreover, in observing the machine in the process of development as concerned the limbs, and also in obtaining specific information from the patient herself regarding the genitalia. I assume that this process will end with the production of the typical influencing apparatus known to clinical observation, but I cannot affirm that this apparatus will pass through all the stages of development to the very end. It is very possible that it will stop at a middle point, without proceeding further.

III

In the meantime, we may consider a second hypothesis that may have suggested itself to the reader. It must be taken into consideration that, notwithstanding all that has been said above, the influencing machine of Miss Natalija A. may be merely an inexplicable exception to the general rule. The complex, unintelligible machine as fantastically described and interpreted by other patients would perhaps first have to be studied and defined before an explanation of Miss N.'s influencing machine could be undertaken. For want of other material at hand to substantiate our hypothesis, except the machine dream, we shall start with the assumption that the influencing apparatus is a projection of the patient's genitalia. In presenting this second hypothesis together with, or in lieu of, the first, I realize how much indulgence is exacted of the reader, and I should not be surprised if I were reproached with levity or legerdemain. I myself was unpleasantly surprised to discover that this second hypothesis was probably as valid as the first, and that in consequence both became improbable or worthless, since their content differs and each leads to quite a different theory. Fortunately, another theory suggests itself which brings into immediate harmony both interpretations of the influencing apparatus. This problem will be touched upon again towards the end of this paper.

Attention may be called now to a symptom in schizophrenia, which I have named "loss of ego boundaries." This symptom is the complaint that "everyone" knows the patient's thoughts, that his thoughts are not enclosed in his own head, but are spread throughout the world and occur simultaneously in the heads of all persons. The patient seems no longer to realize that he is a separate psychical entity, an ego with individual boundaries. A sixteen-year-old patient in the Wagner-Jauregg Clinic indulged in gay laughter whenever she was asked for her thoughts. Catamnesis revealed that for a long while when being questioned, she had believed I had been jesting; she knew that I must be familiar with her thoughts, since they occurred at the same time in my own head.

We are familiar with this infantile stage of thinking, in which a strong belief exists that others know of the child's thoughts. Until the child has been successful in its first lie, the parents are supposed to know everything, even its most secret thoughts. Later on, in the event that the child has been caught lying, this conception may be formed again, now caused by the feeling of guilt. The striving for the right to have secrets from which the parents are excluded is one of the most powerful factors in the formation of the ego, especially in establishing and carrying out one's own will. The developmental stage observed in the above-mentioned case falls into this period, in which the child does not yet sense this right to privacy and does not yet doubt that the parents and educators know everything.[4]

The symptom with the content that "thoughts are given to them," the patients deduce subsequently from their belief that others know their thoughts. This must be attributed to the infantile impressions originating in an earlier period in life, when the child knows nothing through its own efforts but obtains all its knowledge from others: how to make use of its limbs, its language, its thoughts. At that period all is "given to" the child, all joy and all sorrow, and it is difficult to evaluate what share the child itself has in its accomplishments.[5] The sudden discovery that it is able to accomplish a task without the help of others is greeted by the child with a great deal of surprise and excitement. It is probable, therefore, that this symptom represents a regression to this particular stage of infancy. But this special period of infancy presents a problem: How far back does it go? What causes the formation of the ego and, as a reaction to the outer world, the ego boundaries, and what arouses the realization of individuality, of self, as a distinct psychical unit?

Theoretically we cannot assume that the ego begins to take form earlier than the time of object finding. The latter comes with gratification and renunciation of instinctual drives, whereas an awareness of the outer world, independent of the infant's drives and desires, is established only gradually. It is hardly possible that the sex instincts should have a greater influence upon the development of this awareness than the drive to be nourished. To be sure, the sex instincts will soon take on a special significance which must not be underestimated. But for the time being, it should be stated that there is a stage when no objects of the outer world exist, and therefore there is no realization that one has an ego. At that period there nevertheless exist desires and drives, and a specific urge to obtain mastery over whatever stimulates the sex organs is observable. The developmental stage that precedes the stage of object finding has been recognized as that of *identification.* This became evident from the analysis of neurotics, in whom the inability to obtain possession of objects of gratification, or to reach goals of pleasure, was seen to be due to their identification with the objects. The neurotic himself simply stands for what attracts him in the outer world; he has not found his way to the outer world and, therefore, is unable to develop an adequate ego in his stunted, exclusively libidinal relationships. This peculiar organization of libido has been termed narcissistic. The libido in such cases has been directed towards the neurotic's own personality; it is attached to his own ego and not to the objects of the outer world. Observations and theoretical considerations, especially those of Freud, have led to the assumption that this libido organization characterizes the beginning of psychical development, the "objectless" period, and that, at any rate, this libido organization must be considered a correlate, if not a cause, of the "objectlessness." This organization of libido corresponds also to the stage of intellectual development in which the person considers all the sensory stimuli he receives as endogenous and immanent. At this stage of development the psyche does not yet perceive that intervals of time and space exist between the object from which the stimulus emanates and the sensory response.

The next stage of development is then that of an outward projection of the stimulus and the attributing of this stimulus to a distant object, hence a stage of distancing and objectivation of the intellect, and along with this a transfer of libido to the discovered, or rather, self-created, outer world. As a safeguard to this psychical achievement, and as a kind of critical authority for objectivation, there is evolved at the same time the faculty of distinguishing between objectivity and subjectivity, an awareness of reality, which enables the individual to recognize his inner experiences as distinct from the outer stimuli—in other words, to regard inner experiences as internal and not to confuse them with the objects of sensory response.

This correlative developmental process, however, is apt to meet with inhibitions. There are inhibitions from the intellectual side, or as we say, from the ego—the chief weapon of which is the intellect—and there are inhibitions that arise from the transference of libido in various stages of development, and with various results depending upon the relation of the ego to the libido. These points of inhibition are called, after Freud, fixation-points. In most cases the factor that causes ego disturbances seems to lie in lesions of the libido. Thus, it is clear from Freud's interpretation that paranoia is a reaction to repressed homosexuality. The prohibition against finding an object for the homosexual drive, which results in an inhibition of the transference of homosexual libido organization, should be recognized as originating from within and remaining within. This projection is a defensive measure of the ego against the renounced homosexual libido that emerges with onrushing force out of repression. Libidinal inhibition leads to intellectual inhibition, which may be manifested in impaired judgment, or in insanity. An internal psychical process due to displacement and projection is mistaken for an external one, which leads to more or less marked "affective weakness of judgment," with the accompanying reactions of the psyche quantitatively and qualitatively determined by the morbid process.

We may say that in the case of an impaired libido organization, the ego finds itself facing the task of mastering an insane outer world, and hence behaves insanely.[6]

In the neuropsychoses that usually appear in later life, with a history of previous relative psychic health, it is not difficult to observe that the impairment of the ego is caused by an impairment of the libido. However, in cases of psychosis that develop gradually and insidiously, beginning with earliest infancy, we may assume not so much a successive impairment of libido and ego as a correlative inhibition, primarily, of the entire development of the individual. The one group of instinctual drives does not develop normally, and this is paralleled by an arrest of the functions of the other group of drives and by a simultaneous development of secondary relations, which are to regarded as attempts at self-cure and at adaptation to the functional disturbance by means of compensations and overcompensations. Furthermore, there occur regressions on the part of functions which have developed normally but which, whenever there is a marked discordance between the diseased and the normal portions of the psyche, abandon their normal level and retreat, for the purpose of adaptation, to the lower level of the impaired functions. During this retreat, there may arise various temporary or permanent symptom formations of different clinical types; and from these develop all mixed psychotic formations. The existence of these partial processes and their great variety with regard to levels of regression at a given moment requires careful consideration. In considering inhibitions of instinctual drives we must constantly keep in mind that all inhibited drives are capable of being transformed into, or being discharged as, anxiety. To quote Freud, "It may be said that, in a certain theoretical sense, symptoms are formed only in order to forestall an otherwise inevitable development of anxiety."

IV

We have learned from Freud that the projection of the homosexual libido in paranoia is to be regarded as a defensive measure of the ego against an inopportune and socially reprehensible sexual urge pressing from the unconscious. Is it possible to regard the projection of the patient's own body in the case of Miss Natalija as an analogous situation? Naturally, the projection would have to subserve the defense of that libido which belongs to the patient's own body, and which has become either too extensive or too inopportune in its demands for the patient to be able to tolerate it as her own. It is also necessary to assume that this projection pertains only to the libido of the body and not to the libido of the psychic ego, as well, that, moreover, the libido of the psychic ego[7] has facilitated the defense against the bodily libido because it was, so to speak, ashamed of it. That a projection mechanism has been chosen for the purpose of defense—a mechanism belonging to the primary functioning of the ego in the process of object finding—gives us reason to believe that we are here dealing with a libido position which is coëval with the beginnings of intellectual object finding and which is achieved either by regression or by the persistence of a vestigial phenomenon (*Resterscheinung*—Freud), which has been for years and up to the onset of the illness effectively compensated or concealed. In regressions, however, there is always an effort to reach the formerly uninhibited libido positions. In paranoia, regression reaches a stage when homosexual object choice has not yet come under the prohibition of the ego and there is free homosexual libido which is only later subjected to repression at the behest of the cultural demands of the ego.

The libido directed towards a person's own self, which the ego tries to get rid of by projecting its own body, naturally, is characteristic of a period when it was still free from conflict with the demands of other love-objects. This period must coincide with the developmental stage of the psyche in which object finding still occurs within the individual's own body, and when the latter is still regarded as part of the outer world.

I am intentionally differentiating between object choice and object finding. By the former, I mean only libidinal cathexis; by the latter, the intellectual awareness of this cathexis. An object is *found* by the intellect, and *chosen* by the libido. These processes may occur either simultaneously or in sequence, but for my purpose they are to be regarded as distinct.

The projection of one's body may, then, be traced back to the developmental stage in which one's own body is the goal of the object finding. This must be the time when the infant is discovering his body, part by part, as the outer world, and is still groping for his hands and feet as though they were foreign objects. At this time, everything that "happens" to him emanates from his own body; his psyche is the object of stimuli arising in his own body but acting upon it as if produced by outer objects. These disjecta membra are later on pieced together and systematized into a unified whole under the supervision of a psychic unity that receives all sensations of pleasure and pain from these separate parts. This process takes place by means of identification with one's own body. The ego, thus discovered, is cathected with the available libido; in accordance with the psychic nature of the ego, narcissism develops; and, in accordance with the function of individual organs as sources of pleasure, autoeroticism results.

But if the psychoanalytic theories previously employed are correct, this object finding within one's own organs, which can be regarded as parts of the outer world only by projection, must be preceded by a stage of identification with a narcissistic libido position,[8] and it is necessary to assume two successive stages of identification and projection.

The projection which participated in the object finding within one's own organs would, then, be the second phase of the preceding stage, although the part that depends upon the postulated identification has still to be discovered.

I am, then, assuming the existence of these two successive phases of identification and projection in object finding and object choice within one's own body.

I do not run counter to psychoanalytic conceptions in contending that the individual comes into the world as an organic unity in which libido and ego are not yet separated, and all available libido is related to that organic unity, which does not deserve the name "ego" (i.e., a psychical self-protective organization) any more than does the cell. In this situation the individual is equally a sexual and an individual being, simultaneously performing ego and reproductive functions, like the cell that takes nourishment up to the time when it divides. This stage of the newly born child is biological up to the time of conception, but must be regarded as psychological from the time when—at an indeterminable stage of fœtal life—cerebral development takes place. From the point of view of libido, we may say that the newly born child is a sexual being. I am in accord with Freud's assumption that the individual's first renunciation is the renunciation of the protection of the mother's body imposed upon the libido and accompanied by that expression of anxiety, the birth-cry. However, once this first trauma is over and no discontent arises to bring the infant into a clash with himself and with the environment, he is in complete possession of his own libido and knows nothing of the outer world, not even that part of the world which he will soon discover within himself. It is this stage of identity that precedes the first projection for the purpose of object finding within one's own body. This stage did not come about because of that psychic activity which may be called identification, but is present from the beginning. Nevertheless the result is the same as in actively established identity—absolute self-satisfaction, no outer world, no objects. Let us designate this stage as the innate narcissistic one. In this situation the libido is directed outward, first cathects the subject's own body by the indirect way of projection, and returns by way of self-discovery to the ego. In the meantime, the ego has undergone a decided alteration under the influence of these first psychic stirrings, which one may call experience, and is now again cathected by libido. Let us call this stage, acquired narcissism. The latter finds a considerable quantity of innate narcissism already present and is superimposed on it. The condition of innate narcissism normally remains attached for all time to the organs and their functions, and is in constant conflict with the various further stages of ego development which, with the assistance of anxiety and judgment, take place under the ægis of all the faculties that have been gradually acquired in the meantime. The struggle is carried on, at first, chiefly in the sphere of excretory functions and of the autoerotic sources of pleasure, since these are the spheres that give rise to the greatest difficulties in the individual's relation to the environment. Nevertheless, we must definitely understand that throughout life the ego develops with constant shiftings in the narcissistic libido position, that man in his struggle for existence is constantly compelled to find and recognize himself anew, and that the acquisition of narcissism is immanent in culture and is conceivable only on the basis of intact inborn narcissism that serves as a source of nourishment and regeneration. This constant struggle centering about the self occurs in various degrees in relation to various instinctual drives; it concerns homo- and hetero-sexuality and every libido component in different degrees at different times, and provokes various reactions, compensations, superstructures and eliminations. These secondary psychical formations then enter again into combination and produce insoluble dynamic, qualitative, relative and modal relations, resulting in a great variety of character types and symptoms. The development both of the ego and of the libido—so far as concerns either alone or in their relation to each other—may become arrested and may set up goals of regression at as many points as there are primary, secondary, tertiary (etc.) factors of relationship and development. The entire problem is further complicated by the elements of time and space and so made insoluble. Let us suppose that the projection of one's own body is a pathological repetition of that psychical stage when the individual was endeavoring to discover his body by means of projection. It would not be too much to say that just as the projection in normal primary development has been successful because the innate narcissistic libido position had to be renounced under the attack of outer stimuli, so also pathological projection takes place because there has developed an accumulation of narcissistic libido analogous to the primary narcissism, though here anachronistic, regressive or fixated, but resembling it in character in so far as it isolates the individual from the outer world. Hence, projection of one's own body may be regarded as a defense against a libido position corresponding to the end of fœtal existence and the beginning of extrauterine development. Freud, indeed, has not hesitated to declare, in his *Introductory Lectures*, that psychological problems are to be traced back to intrauterine existence.

These considerations may be used as a starting point for the explanation of various schizophrenic symptoms. Is it not possible that catalepsy, *flexibilitas cerea*, corresponds to the stage when man senses his own organs as foreign, as not belonging to himself, and as being dominated by an outside force? A similar instance is the symptom of having one's limbs moved by someone. This symptom reproduces especially well the situation in which one's own body becomes strange and, so to speak, part of an outer world dominated by outer forces. May we not say that catatonic stupor, which represents a complete rejection of the outer world, is a return to the uterus? May not these severest catatonic symptoms be the ultimate refuge of a psyche that has given up even the most primitive ego functions and has retreated *in toto* to the fœtal and nursing stages, because it cannot use in the present state of its libido even the simplest ego functions that maintain the relation to the outer world? The catatonic symptom, the negativistic stare of the schizophrenic, is nothing else than a renunciation of the outer world expressed in "organ language." Does not also the "nursing reflex" in the terminal stages of general paralysis indicate such a regression to infancy?[9]

The psychic correlate of *flexibilitas cerea* and of that stage in which man regards himself as a part of the outer world, lacks consciousness of his own volition and of his own ego boundaries, is the feeling that everyone knows and is in possession of the thoughts of the patient. In the period here duplicated pathologically there are indeed no thoughts, but even thoughts are subjected, as already stated above, to the same process of being regarded at first as coming from the outer world before they are accounted among the functions of the ego. Thoughts must first be assimilated into the consciousness of ego-unity before they can be an automatic ego-function; and this cannot occur before the intellect has advanced to the stage of memory perceptions. Freud has taught that this, too, is a later process, and that it is preceded by the stage of hallucinations of memory pictures, that is, a stage when the perceptions actually appear in the outer world and are not regarded as internal occurrences. Moreover, this stage of hallucinatory perceptions, in itself representing a kind of objectivation, object finding and object choice, also belongs to the first period of life. The regression, of course, does not occur equally in all psychical faculties and relationships. The capacity for thinking with memory perceptions is still intact, but the libido is already degraded to the nursing stage and sets up a relation with the thinking faculty as it exists. The consciousness of personality has been lost, and this loss is shown in the patient's inability to locate his intact psychical inventory. The patient who declares that his thoughts and feelings are in all people's minds merely declares, in words and concepts derived from the memory-reserve of a later developmental stage, that his libido finds itself at the stage when it is still identical with the outer world, still has no ego-boundaries set up against the outer world, and his libido is now compelled therefore to renounce the normal intellectual object relations in so far as these depend upon the degraded libido position.

These feelings and this mode of expression depend upon the

intactness of the psyche's ability to operate with memory perceptions. This faculty, too, may undergo regression.[10] In this case the patient hallucinates. The libido has retreated behind the stage of identification, the intellect no longer shows how to establish a relation to the outer world, even by means of identification. The psyche is approaching closer and closer to the mother's womb.

Furthermore, may not perhaps "picture-seeing in planes" represent a stage of the development of the visual sense still earlier than the hallucinatory stage?

V

I have stated that narcissistic self-discovery and self-choice repeat themselves with every new acquisition of the ego, to this effect, that, under the guidance of conscience and judgment, each new acquisition is either rejected, or cathected with libido and attributed to the ego. Let us call this narcissism, psychic narcissism, and let us contrast it with the organic narcissism that guarantees in the unconscious the unity and functioning of the organism. There is nothing new in calling attention to the great dependence of physical health, and even of life itself, upon what is called love of life, or in the reminder that one can actually die of a "broken heart," and that, as Ostwald mentions in his book on *Great Men*, university professors emeritus often die soon after they have been absolved of their duties, even when they have previously been in the best of health. They die, not of old age, but because they lose the love of life when they can no longer perform the duties they have loved. Freud tells of a famous musician who succumbed to his illness because of the discontinuance of his creative work.

We must assume that the libido flows through the entire body, perhaps like a substance (Freud's view), and that the integration of the organism is effected by a libido tonus, the oscillations of which correspond to the oscillations of psychic narcissism and object libido.[11] Upon this tonus depends the resistance to illness and death. Love of live has saved many a man who was given up by physicians as incurable.

Whenever there occurs an influx of organic narcissism to a given organ as a site of predilection,[12] there may also occur a consciousness of organ relations and organic functions which in normal life are relegated to an unconscious and vegetative role. Analogously, objects cathected by psychic narcissism and object love come to consciousness wherever the cathexis has reached a sufficient degree of strength. This influx of libido directs attention to the organ and provides the consciousness of a transformation of the organ or its functions, i.e., the feeling of estrangement. This is the mechanism described by Freud as hypochondria. This influx of libido is followed by the turning away of the ego from the organ pathologically overcharged with libido, or from its functions; that is, by estrangement.[13] This is to be considered a defensive measure against the anxiety associated with hypochondria. The feeling of strangeness is a defense against libidinal cathexis, no matter whether it concerns objects of the outer world, one's own body, or its parts. Of course, the estrangement does not cause the giving up of the unconscious libido position. The estrangement is not a destructive force but merely a denial of the pathological cathexis; it is an instance of the ostrich tactics of the ego, which may be very easily reduced *ad absurdum*, and which must ultimately be supplanted by other or more effective measures of defense.

When, in paranoia, the feeling of estrangement no longer affords protection, the libidinal drive towards the homosexual object is projected on to the latter and appears, by a reversal of direction, as aggression towards the loving one (the patient himself) in the form of a sense of persecution. Strangers become enemies. The enmity is a new and more energetic attempt at protection against the rejected unconscious libido.

The narcissism organ libido in schizophrenia may undergo a similar transformation. The estranged organ—in our case, the entire body—appears as an outer enemy, as a machine used to afflict the patient.

We are, then, compelled to distinguish three principal stages in the history of the "influencing machine":

1. The sense of internal alteration produced by the influx of libido into a given organ (hypochondria).
2. The feeling of estrangement produced by rejection, whereby the pathologically altered organs or their functions are so to

speak denied and eliminated as something alien to the wholly or partially sound organs and functions accepted by the ego.

3. The sense of persecution (*paranoia somatica*) arising from projection of the pathological alteration on to the outer world, (a) by attribution of the alteration to a foreign hostile power, (b) by the construction of the influencing machine as a summation of some or all of the pathologically altered organs (the whole body) projected outward. It is to be noted that among these organs the genitals take precedence in the projection.

The assumption of an influx of libido into specific organs in the physiological sense of the word should receive proper consideration. On the basis of this assumption transient swellings of organs often observed in schizophrenia without inflammation and without an actual œdema may be interpreted as equivalents of erection, produced like erections of the penis and clitoris by an overflow of secretion resulting from libidinal charging of organs.[14]

VI

It is not at all surprising that the hostile apparatus is handled by persons who to an objective observer cannot but appear as love objects—suitors, lovers, physicians. All these persons are associated with sensuousness, deal with the body, and demand a transfer of libido to themselves. This is what actually occurs in normal situations. But the narcissistic libido, whenever too strongly fixated, cannot but regard this demand made by love objects as inimical, and looks upon the object as an enemy. It is to be noted, however, that another group of love objects—mother, the patient's present physician, close friends of the family—are not counted among the patient's persecutors but among the persecuted, compelled to share his fate in being subjected to the influencing machine. In contrast to paranoia, the persecuted and not the persecutors are organized into a passive conspiracy, and this conspiracy is of passive nature. Of this phenomenon the following explanation may be offered:

It is noteworthy that the persecutors are all persons who live at some distance from the patient, whereas the persecuted belong to the closest circle of acquaintanceship and—including the physicians who are imagos of the father and hence also family members—represent a kind of constantly present family. Now, the family members are those love objects who because of their presence from the beginning of the patient's life are subjected to the narcissistic object choice by identification. To these persons our patient still applies this form of object choice in so far as she subjects them to her own fate, identifying herself with them. Normally, the demand for transfer of libido with respect to members of the family is not felt either as requiring the overcoming of any great distance or any substantial sacrifice of narcissism. In establishing an identification with these persons the patient follows a well-trodden path, which does not appear sufficiently inimical to the patient to force her to revolt against the cathexis of these objects and to regard them as hostile. It is different with lovers and suitors. These threaten a narcissistic position with their substantial demands for object libido and are, therefore, repulsed as enemies. The fact that these persons are spatially distant evokes a feeling of distance on the part of the libido. The transfer of libido *par distance* is felt as an extraordinarily strong demand for the acknowledgement of an object position, as a demand for self-denial. This also holds for normal conditions. Spatial distance separating the beloved threatens the object libido; it even leads people ultimately to withdraw themselves and give up the object. To have to love at a distance is a difficult task, only unwillingly performed. Our patient, however, cannot simply give up her love objects in a normal way, because she has not cathected them normally. To those demanding much from her she can only react with the paranoid mechanism; to those demanding less, only with identification. I do not know why the persons who work the influencing machine are in my observations exclusively male. This may be due to faulty observation or to chance. Further investigations must clarify this point. However, that heterosexual objects can appear as persecutors in contradiction to Freud's theory of the exclusively homosexual genesis of paranoia, may be explained by the fact that the influencing machine corresponds to a regressive psychic stage in which the important distinction is not between the sexes but between narcissistic and object libido, and every object demanding a transfer of libido is regarded as hostile irrespective of its sex.

VII

After this long digression—which, I hope, will not be regarded as superfluous—we may return to the question of how even the ordinary, clinically familiar, influencing machine in its typical form can be a projection of the patient's body, as was true in the case of Miss Natalija. The answer should not be difficult to discover. If we do not want to assume that the machine has been established by successive substitutions of the parts of the patient's idea of his own body picture ("*wie Fuchs aus alopex*"),[15] and if we make use, instead of the genitality of the machine, as previously established, to explain the typical influencing machine, we may avail ourselves of the following considerations:

The regression of libido to the early infantile stage determines the re-transformation of the meanwhile genitally centralized libido into the pregenital stage, in which the entire body is a libidinal zone—in which the entire body is a genital. Such fantasies are also found in cases of narcissistically strongly cathected, sexually extremely infantile, neurosis. I have myself observed such cases. The fantasy originates in the intrauterine (mother's body) complex and usually has the content of the man's desire to creep completely into the genital from which he came, refusing to content himself with any lesser satisfaction. The entire individual is in this case a penis. Further, the road of identification with the father (the penis of the father) is overdetermined in the symptom formation of male patients. The symptom is also to be conceived as regression to a stage of diffuse narcissistic organ libido and is in most cases associated with genital impotence. The genital, too, is renounced.[16] The same situation is revealed by the lack of genitalia in the influencing machine of Miss N. The intrauterine fantasy and the identification[17] with mother probably find expression in the dome-like lid of the trunk which perhaps represented the patient's mother during pregnancy. The enclosed batteries are perhaps the child, which is the patient herself. The fact that the child is equated with the batteries, that is, with a machine, lends further support to the supposition that the person feels himself to be a genital, and this all the more because the machine's lack of genitalia stands for the pregenital—in a certain sense, nongenital stage.

The construction of the influencing apparatus in the form of a machine therefore represents a projection of the entire body, now wholly a genital.

The fact that the machine in dreams is nothing but a representation of the genital raised to primacy in no way contradicts the possibility that it is in schizophrenia a symbol of the entire body conceived as a penis, and hence a representative of the pregenital epoch. The patient has indeed not lost the ideational content of his past life. The picture of the genital as a representation of sexuality has been retained in the psychical apparatus. It is therefore used as a means of representation, a mode of expression, a language in which phenomena existing prior to this means of expression are communicated. Here the genital is merely a symbol of a sexuality older than the symbolism and than any means of social expression. The picture, then, is in the language of the later genital period nothing but: "I am sexuality." But the context is, "I am wholly a genital." This test has of course to be translated into the language suited to the actual libido conditions.

It is possible that the ordinary influencing apparatus in the form of the machine owes its existence simply to the fact that its early stages were not formed gradually, because the pathological process seized too precipitately upon remote phases of existence. It is also possible that the early stages were not noticed by observers and not reported by the patient, or not recognized and evaluated as early stages. Thus the connection between the influencing apparatus of Miss N. and the ordinary influencing machine has been lost to science.

But the contradiction between the two concepts—on the one hand, that the machine form of the influencing apparatus originated through successive distortions of the influencing apparatus that represents the projection of the body, and, on the other hand, that the machine form of the influencing apparatus represents, like the machine in a dream, a projection of the genitalia, is now abolished. The evolution by distortion of the human apparatus into a machine is a projection that corresponds to the development of the pathological process which converts the ego into a diffuse sexual being, or—expressed in the language of the genital period—into a genital, a machine independent of the aims of the ego and subordinated to a foreign will.[18] It is no longer subordinated to the will of the ego, but dominates it. Here, too, we are reminded of the astonishment of boys when they become aware for the first time of erection. And the fact that the erection is shortly conceived as an exceptional and mysterious feat, supports the assumption that erection is felt to be a thing independent of the ego, a part of the outer world not completely mastered.

Notes

1. At the Belgrade Neuropsychiatric Division.
2. Tausk, Victor: On the Psychology of the Alcoholic Occupation Delirium.
3. Tausk, Victor: Short Contributions to the Interpretation of Dreams: The Use of Clothes and Colors in Building Up the Dream Picture. Miss N. dreams: I am seated on an upper bench in the surgical amphitheatre. Below a woman is being operated on. She lies with her head towards me, but I cannot see the head, as it seems to be concealed by the lower benches. I see the woman only from her chest down. I see both thighs and a heap of white towels and linens. I see nothing else clearly.

   Analysis of the dream reveals that the dreamer sees herself as the woman operated on. A few days before the night of the dream, the dreamer called on a young physician who made advances to her. On this occasion she was reclining on a couch. The physician raised her skirts and while he operated "below," she perceived the heap of white underclothes overhead. Just as much as she saw of herself in this situation, she sees of the woman in the dream, and the woman's head remains invisible to her in the same way as she could not see her own head in the actual situation. According to Freud, the "woman without a head" in a dream represents the mother. The basic reason for this interpretation will not be discussed here, but will be treated in another section of this paper.
4. This would fall into the period before the first successful lie, which occurs very early in infancy. Lies fabricated in the first year of life are nothing unusual; they can be observed especially in children who resist the regular elimination of bodily wastes which, by means of grimaces, gestures and inarticulated words, they mislead the training person into believing that they have had satisfactory evacuation. The educator who allows herself to be deceived by the child must ultimately look to divine guidance in order to keep the child within the truth, when the latter, to gain forbidden pleasure, begins to enjoy the practice of lying. Very soon the time arrives when recourse to the highest authority of omniscience becomes necessary. The introduction of the omniscient God in the educational system becomes, indeed, a necessity, since, de facto, children learn to lie from parents

and upbringers, who by misrepresentations and unkept promises make the child obey and teach him to disguise his true purposes. In order to safeguard the success of education, teachers cannot but transfer the power of omniscience to God—an authority which they themselves have abandoned. The incomprehensible nature of this deity precludes the possibility of practicing deception on him. Nevertheless, many children do not submit even to this authority, continually test their God with regard to his omniscience, and not infrequently actually succeed in unmasking him as a phantom of the dethroned parental, specifically paternal, power.

5. In the discussion of this paper at the Vienna Psychoanalytic Society, Freud emphasized that the infant's conception that others knew its thoughts has its source in the process of learning to speak. Having obtained its language from others, the infant has also received thoughts from them; and the child's feeling that others know his thoughts as well as that others have "made" him the language and, along with it, his thoughts, has therefore, some basis in reality.
6. The cases in which inhibition endangers the intellect primarily are to be attributed to dementia.
7. The projection of the libido position of the psychic ego produces the symptoms of simple paranoia, the mechanism of which was discovered by Freud. In what follows we shall omit from consideration the fact that ego-libido is necessarily homosexual in its strivings, that is, attracted by the sex which the ego itself represents. We shall describe briefly only one mechanism, which appears to be out of harmony with object-libido and which is exemplified by the symptomatology of our patient, Miss Natalija.

The patient reports: After she had rejected her suitor, she felt that he suggested that her mother and she strike up a friendship with his sister-in-law, so that the patient might be more amenable to a later proposal on his part. What appears here as suggestion on the suitor's part is nothing more than the projection of the patient's own unconscious inclination to accept the proposal of marriage. She had rejected the proposal not without inner conflict and had vacillated between accepting and rejecting her suitor. She gave realization in action to the rejection, while she projected her inclination to accept the proposal on to the object of her conflicting desires and made it appear as the sensory effect of an influence on the part of the object, or in other words as her symptom.

The patient was ambivalent towards her suitor, and projected one side of the conflict, the positive libidinal one, while manifesting in action the negative side, the rejection, because this procedure was in conformity with her ego. The choice, which in this instance has projection as its outcome, may in other cases be the reverse one. Here I am merely calling attention to the mechanism of partial projection of ambivalent tendencies.

A special contribution to the subject of the projection mechanism, which also made me aware of this principle, was made by Dr. Helene Deutsch in her discussion of this paper at the Vienna Psychoanalytic Society. A schizophrenic patient had the feeling that her friends always laid down their work when she herself began to work and that they sat down whenever she stood up; in brief, that others were always performing the opposite of what she herself was doing. The patient merely felt this; she could not possibly see it, since she was blind. Dr. Deutsch regarded the symptom as a projection of one of two tendencies present in every one of her patient's actions—namely, the tendency to do and the tendency not to do. This interpretation was confirmed by cases presented by other discussers. On this occasion Freud proposed the formulation that it is ambivalence that makes the projection mechanism possible. Once expressed, this thesis appears self-evident. It has a corollary in another contention of Freud's, to the effect that ambivalence produces repression. This has as its natural consequence the formulation mentioned, above, since only what is repressed is projected, in so far as boundaries between the unconscious and the conscious still obtain. The entire problem furnishes special justification for Bleuler's term "schizophrenia," and at the same time corroborates Pötzl's views discussed in note 13.

The present paper shows how, albeit unconsciously, I had been demonstrating Freud's formulation.

8. Freud has already indicated in his paper on the Schreber biography, that the libido in schizophrenia is located at a stage even earlier than autoeroticism. I arrive at the same conclusion by a different route, and I take the liberty of presenting this fact as proof of the correctness of Freud's contentions.

9. Many patients are actually aware of this regression to infancy and to the embryonic stage—the latter, though, only as a threat of further illness. A patient said to me: "I feel that I am constantly becoming younger and smaller. Now I am four years old. Shortly, I shall get into diapers and then back into mother."

Dr. Helene Deutsch, during the discussion of this paper, reported the case of a thirty-one year old female schizophrenic who wet and soiled her bed and stated as her justification that "they were making a baby of her."

On the same occasion Freud, referring especially to the influencing machine of Miss Natalija, and to the interchangeability of sexuality and death, called attention to the significance of the mode of burial of Egyptian mummies. To place the mummy in a case resembling the human body suggests the idea of the return to "mother earth," the return to the mother's body in death. Freud's reference shows how as a compensation for the bitterness of death, men take for granted the bliss of existence in the uterus. The fantasy of return to the uterus is, then, an atavistic one, a preformed fantasy, and as such it may be added to the "primal fantasies" postulated by Freud. This fantasy appears symptomatically in schizophrenia as the pathological reality of the regressing, disintegrating psyche. The mummy returns to the mother's body by physical, and the schizophrenic by psychical death. ("*Mutterleibsphantasie*"—an expression, as far as I know, first used by Gustav Grüner.)

10. For further discussion of this subject, see Freud: *Metapsychologische Ergänzung zur Traumlehre.* Int. Ztschr. f. Psa. VI, 1916/1917. (Translated in *Coll. Papers* 4, 137–52.) This work appeared while the present paper was in proofs. I am pleased to be able to refer to the many points of agreement between my contentions and Freud's in his paper, of which I had no knowledge at the time.
11. Melancholia is the illness, the mechanism of which consists in the disintegration of psychic narcissism, in the renunciation of love for the psychic ego. Melancholia, in pure culture, is the paradigm of the dependence of the organic upon the psychic narcissism. The separation of libido from the psychic ego, i.e., the rejection and condemnation of the *raison d'être* of the psychic person, brings with it the rejection of the physical person, the tendency to physical self-destruction. There occurs a consecutive separation of the libido from those organs which guarantee the functioning and the value of the physical individuality, a separation by means of which the organs' function is impaired or given up. Hence appetite is lost, constipation occurs, menstruation ceases, and potency is lost—all as a result of unconscious mechanisms. This failure of function is to be traced to the destruction of the respective organic libido positions which are essentially vegetative, i.e., unconscious; it is thus to be strictly differentiated from the conscious, deliberate suicidal tendency expressed in refusal of nourishment or in activities inimical to life.

    Melancholia is the persecution psychosis without projection; its structure is due to a specific mechanism of identification. (Further discussion on this point in my paper Diagnostic Considerations Concerning the Symptomatology of the So-Called War Psychoses. While this paper was in proof, Freud's article *Trauer und Melancholie* [translated in *Coll. Papers* IV, 152–173] appeared, to which I refer in this connection.)
12. This involves the Freudian principle of the erotogenicity of organs, that is, of the erotogenic zones.
13. Dr. Otto Pötzl suggested on a certain occasion (I do not remember whether it was in connection with a thesis of his own or as an addendum to theories of others) that the catatonic state is an expression of the patient's inability to apportion his motor impulses disintegrated by the split of his volition into agonistic and antagonistic elements, so that a purposeful action may again be performed. (In Meyrinck's story, *Der Fluch der Kröte* ["The Curse of the Toad"],

the milliped is unable to move a limb the moment he focusses his attention upon the activity of any one of his thousand legs.)

Pötzl's conception is in harmony with the psychoanalytic theory that the regressive narcissistic libido undergoes a pathological division with the cathexis of the individual functions of the psyche and the organs, so that the agonistic and antagonistic portions of the purposefully directed antithetical pair of forces are brought into the reach of awareness by the disturbance of the equilibrium between their respective libido quantities and are deprived of automatic functioning. This would be a special case of hypochondria and estrangement related to the antithetical pairs of forces with their respective specific consequences.

Pötzl's view does not contradict the assumption that the outer world may be eliminated as a result of regressive narcissistic libido, and it actually allows the application of the theory of hypochondria to further special points in the psycho-physical make-up of men. Pötzl's concept even suggests the hypothesis that there was in the life of man a period—a not definitely determinable one, it is true, and perhaps only potential—in which the activity of the antagonistic pair of forces was still automatic and had to be discovered and learned by the person himself as if from an alien outer world. This period may well be present in ontogenesis only as an "engram" of phylogenetic stages which comprised the origin of the now complex motor organs from the simplest, single-tracked active formations. Regression in schizophrenia would then be traceable to those "engrams" of the oldest era of the race, and the theory would demand that these phylogenetic traces of function retain their capacity for being reactivated. We must not shrink from this hypothesis. It provides us with another idea to use in investigating problems in schizophrenia, perhaps this remarkable disease consists in just this—that the phylogenetic vestiges of function retain in many individuals an extraordinary capacity for being reactivated. Psychoanalysis would have to make room for this conception, since psychoanalysis has already in many instances uncovered the roots of symptoms in the history of the species. From this it may perhaps be possible, via ontogenesis, to proceed to an explanation of the mysterious "electrical currents" complained of by patients. This paræthesia may once have been a sensation that accompanied the first nerve and muscle functions. It is perhaps a reminiscence of the sensation of the newly born being who enters the strange air of the external world out of the comfortable covering of the mother's womb, or for whom the latter is replaced by its first garments. The bed he first lay in, is perhaps that one which comes to the patient's consciousness when he feels himself, while lying in bed, electrified by invisible wires.

14. These psychological assumptions are strongly supported from the organological standpoint by a report made some years ago by Fauser

at Stuttgart on the presence of sexual secretion in the blood of dementia præcox patients, as demonstrated by Abderhalden's dialytic method. New and important findings in this connection are to be expected from Steinach's experiments. When the present paper was completed, there appeared in the Münchner mediz, Wochenschrift, No. 6, 1981, under the title *Umstimmungen der Homosexualität durch Austausch der Pubertätsdrüsen* ("Transformations of Homosexuality by Exchange of Puberty Glands"), a very interesting and significant article by Steinach and Lichtenstern, which realized these expectations. After the completion of this paper there also appeared in the Internationale Zeitschrift f. ärztl. Psa. Volume IV, 1917, an article by S. Ferenczi, *Von Krankheits- und Pathoneurosen* ("Disease- or Patho-Neuroses," in *Further Contributions to the Theory and Technique of Psychoanalysis*, p. 78–89. London, 1926) in which the assumption of the libidinal cathexis of individual organs in the sense above described appears to be applied with notable success.

15. "Like fox from alopex"—a student parody on etymological derivations consisting of the stringing together of rhyming and nearly rhyming words. —TRANSLATOR.
16. This renunciation of the genitalia is felt by the male schizophrenic as a loss of virility, which is "drained off" from him, or else as a direct transformation into a woman, corresponding to the infantile notion of boys that there is only one kind of genital, namely their own, and that those of women are the result of castration and really represent a loss of the genital. The castration complex is often combined with the infantile identification of semen with urine resulting from urethral eroticism. I have observed an attack of castration anxiety while catheterizing a schizophrenic who refused to empty his bladder. He maintained that I was practicing coitus with him by means of the catheter and that I had emptied him of all his semen. Thus his retention of urine appears as a refusal to yield semen, representing his virility. The patient's playing with excrement is explicable by the narcissistically rooted conception that fæces and urine are parts of the body. Coprophagia is not inhibited by the thought that the excreta are nothing else than the body from which they come.
17. The proof of this identification derived from symbolic language has already been given in the dream of "the woman without a head," note 3.
18. Indeed, the machines produced by man's ingenuity and created in the image of man are unconscious projections of man's bodily structure. Man's ingenuity seems to be unable to free itself from its relation to the unconscious. [See Hanns Sachs' *The Delay of the Machine Age*, *The Psychoanalytic Quarterly*, Vol. 2, 1933.]

10

Ibsen the Druggist

One afternoon I met in the studio of a friend—a studio filled with works of art—the poet and writer, B. On the previous evening we had arranged to meet in order to continue a conversation on dramatic art which we had begun in a café. I had succeeded in directing the discussion into psychoanalytic channels while B. was walking up and down the room. Suddenly he came to a stop before a lifesize bust of Ibsen. His face took on an expression of intense concentration, his brow contracted into wrinkles. I did not know what to make of B.'s reaction and waited for a word from him which would release my tension and his. After a moment of anxious reflection B. asked, pointing to the bust:

> "Who is that man? He seems so familiar to me."
> I could not help laughing heartily.
> "This gentleman is the druggist," I said.

Immediately his face expressed relief, but his eyes had an unhappy look as he replied, echoing my answer, "Ibsen."

B., then, had stopped before Ibsen's portrait-bust and had asked who "the gentleman" was. Anyone familiar with B. will find this incident incredible. B. is exceptionally well versed in the history and biography of the arts, and had made a special study of Ibsen. The resemblance of the statue to Ibsen was beyond any doubt.

Psychoanalytic Quarterly 3 (1934). Posthumous article first published in German in *Almanach der Psychoanalyse*. Vienna: *Int. Psa. Verlag*, 1934. Translated by Dorian Feigenbaum.

Moreover, B. had often looked at the bust on the same pedestal in the very same room and had often commented on it.

We have before us a severe disturbance of memory. It reminds one of the recently married young woman who a few weeks after the wedding saw a "gentleman" across the street who seemed "very familiar" to her—the gentleman being no other than her husband.[1]

My little experiment demonstrated that I had correctly gauged the process which obstructed B.'s recognition of Ibsen. My knowledge of the history of this disturbance enabled me to release the inhibition by a shortcircuit analysis, so to speak. By calling the obstructed content by its name I made possible the immediate entry of the latter into consciousness and laid the ghost.

The history is as follows:

As already stated, I had spent the previous evening with B. in discussing dramatic art and in determining what gifts a dramatist must possess. I had held, rightly or wrongly, that a good playwright must have a good head for the natural sciences. B. opposed my view and cited Ibsen as a great dramatist who had not concerned himself at all with natural science.

"Ibsen," I replied, " is a poor example. Ibsen had even been professionally interested in the natural sciences—he was a druggist."

While saying this I remembered that B. must certainly have known this and, as a matter of fact, B. himself replied an instant later that he had "actually" known that Ibsen was a pharmacist and that he was surprised he had not thought of it and had used such an inappropriate example.

It suddenly dawned upon me that I "actually" knew that there existed a close connection between B. and the idea "druggist" which may have been responsible for his forgetting that Ibsen was a druggist. But our discussion left this subject aside, and it was not touched upon again. I did not elaborate my suspicions, but contented myself with the statement that this time it was not he but I who had forgotten what he "actually" knew very well. Next day, however, when B. failed to recognize Ibsen, the sought-for insight into the connection came to me instantaneously.

Yesterday B. had forgotten that Ibsen had been a pharmacist. Today he failed to recognize Ibsen's portrait—apparently because

Ibsen had been a pharmacist, a fact that he could not have forgotten today since I had called it to his attention yesterday, and because the painful surprise with which he had noted his error yesterday evening must certainly have put him on his guard against another lapse of memory so soon after the first one. It should be remembered, besides, that my very presence must have forced the association between Ibsen and pharmacy into his consciousness and made forgetting impossible. B., therefore, is inevitably forced to make the association "Ibsen"—"druggist" when he sees Ibsen's bust. To escape from the idea "druggist" he had no choice but to eliminate from memory the other idea "Ibsen" which is closely adherent to it. Indeed, he has every reason for this abolition of memory. The history, which I should have really recalled yesterday (since it was "actually" known to me) and which I had so strangely forgotten that I must account for my own lapse of memory, is as follows:

B. had had a love affair with the wife of a pharmacist. The husband had discovered the affair and had threatened B. with assault unless he terminated the liaison. It was an unsavory business. The deceived husband merely threatened because he was too cowardly to act. B., however, used the threat, which he could not but regard as harmless, as an excuse for terminating the affair, of which he had already tired. In leaving the field to the cowardly husband he was therefore no less cowardly than the latter, and knowing this, he feels ashamed. Since he is unable to find a decent solution for this humiliating conflict, he is intent upon forgetting it altogether. First it is the idea "druggist," the obliteration of which indicates the beginning of the process of repression. It is very clear that this idea is most decidedly in league with the repressive process. As long as there exists no memory of a druggist, there cannot be any memory of a love affair with the wife of a druggist. Therefore B. forgets that Ibsen was a druggist. After I had called attention to his lapse, there was established a definite association between "Ibsen" and "druggist." So the next step was to forget that an Ibsen had ever existed. For the idea "Ibsen" might evoke the idea "druggist," and the latter the memory of the unpleasant love affair.

When, upon divining this connection, I threw the thought "druggist" at him, I brought his attempt at repression to naught.

It is certainly to be expected that repressions involving such socially significant ideas as "druggist" and "Ibsen"—the latter having in this instance a further importance owing to the vocation of the subject—should not, in an otherwise normal individual, be too rigorously effected. Indeed, it would mean the deprivation of one's whole intellectual existence, should one thus easily efface ideas which are so much a part of one's daily life and activity. We must, therefore, assume that the conflict of B. was insufficiently prevented from entering consciousness since in his surroundings he could not possibly avoid an awareness of the ideas "Ibsen" and "druggist." In such a case many paths are open to the return of the repressed. The intensity with which the unresolved conflict was forcing itself into consciousness can be seen, moreover, in the fact that during the previous evening's conversation it was precisely the name of Ibsen that occurred to him when he wished to cite an unscientifically minded dramatist. The druggist appeared disguised as Ibsen and demanded a moral reckoning. In order to annihilate this mask throughout the future, B. banishes Ibsen into repression. But the next day Ibsen appears as a "strange man" and presents the same bill for settlement.

Why did B. have to halt precisely before Ibsen's bust, since there was nothing unusual about it to attract his attention? Now, actually there was something unusual about the bust. It had *become strange* to him, and therefore could not but attract his attention in this studio, in which every object had long been familiar to him. The repressed Ibsen returned in this form—as a messenger from the repressed pharmacist. An aspect of the paranoid mechanism is clearly revealed here. Persons from whom the paranoiac has withdrawn his libido reappear to him as *strangers*.[2]

Notes

1. Freud: *Zur Psychopathologie des Alltagslebens*, p. 245. (Trans. by A. A. Brill, *Psychopathology of Everyday Life*, p. 236.)
2. B.'s relation to Ibsen, that of a creative individual to the master who represents his ideals, is patterned after the father complex and is cathected with great quantities of libido. A severe symptom like that presented by B. can only be produced by an intense cathexis. The intense countercathexis in the form of hatred against the druggist,

associatively displaced on to Ibsen, must naturally also be taken into account. In the life of rivals struggling with their masters, the hatred which constitutes the countercathexis is derived from the son-father relation. Hence the conflict between master and disciple striving for independence resembles very closely the severest type of conflict between father and son.

11

Short Contributions to the Interpretation of Dreams: The Use of Clothes and Colors in Building Up the Dream Picture

Clothes and colors often stand for names or personal characteristics, as can be seen in the following selected dream fragments.

I

A. dreamt that his former governess was wearing a black shiny dress (*Lüsterkleid*) fitting closely over her buttocks. This made her look slender.

Interpretation. The governess was actually fat, but the patient liked only slender women. Dresses fitting closely over the buttocks excited him. He had always suspected that women who wore such dresses did so because they wanted to show they were lustful (*lüstern*). He also thought that women who wore them in his presence had designs on him. Thus he implied in his dream that it was to please him that she wore her dress closely fitting over her buttocks and looked slender, which he liked. She was *lüstern*, a characteristic expressed in the dream by the fact that she wore *Lüster*.

Internationale Zeitschrift für ärztliche Psychoanalyse. 2 (1914). Translated by Eric Mosbacher.

II

B. dreamt of a big black (*schwarz*) rat and a small white one. The small rat had a pink (*rosa*) snout, pink ears and paws.

Interpretation. In the dream B. was comparing two women whom he regarded as similar in certain respects. One of them, Frau Schwarz, was taller than the other, a girl known as Roserl. The big black rat stood for Frau Schwarz, the small white one with pink snout, ears and paws stood for little Roserl. Its whiteness meant that Roserl was still a virgin (white is the color of innocence). The fact that the women were visualized as rats was explained by certain homosexual, anal, and castration trends in the dreamer.

III

C. dreamt of a girl flooded in white light and wearing a white blouse, on the country road of X.

Interpretation. The dreamer had had his first sexual intimacies with a Fräulein Weiss ("white") on that country road and she remained in his mind as an ideal of sensuousness and tenderness. She had since married another man, but at the time of the dream he was filled with longing for her. (The flooding in light stood for "ideal," and Fräulein Weiss [Miss White] was in a white blouse, flooded in white light.)

IV

Frau D. dreamt she saw old Blasel* lying on a couch in full armour (*Rüstung*). He rose, leapt over the table and chairs, drew his sword, looked at himself in the mirror and brandished his sword as if fighting an imaginary enemy.

Interpretation. The patient was suffering from a chronic disease of the bladder (*Blase*). She lay on a couch during analysis and when she looked at herself in the mirror, she secretly considered herself very vigorous (rüstig) in spite of her age and her illness. She identified herself with old Blasel, whose vigor and physical agility she greatly admired; he was over eighty, and she wanted

*A Vienna comedian.

to be as vigorous as he was at his age. She used his name in order to represent herself as a sufferer from chronic disease of the bladder. She looked at herself in the mirror and discovered that in spite of being old Blasel, i.e., a sufferer from chronic disease of the bladder, she was still fully armed, i.e., in full possession of her physical vigor and was fighting imaginary enemies,i.e., that the terrors of old age were merely imaginary.

It should be pointed out that someone looking at himself in a mirror in a dream probably always stands for the dreamer, for in a mirror one sees one's own image.

II

Sudden change of scene in dream.

A typical feature of dreams is abrupt change of scene. The new scene which is suddenly introduced represents a reminiscence the contents of which are compared and identified with those of the dream before the change of scene. The whole new scene serves to represent a single idea or a single verbal expression, and in the translation of the dream should be regarded grammatically as a subordinate clause. Here is one example out of many.

Dream fragment

Fräulein N. dreamt: "I was sitting in the top row in the operating theater. Down below a woman was being operated on. She lay with her head towards me, but I could not see her head, as if the view were obstructed by the lower benches. I could see her only from the breast downwards, and over her thighs there was a pile of white cloths and underwear. I could see nothing else distinctly. There was a sudden change of scene, I was no longer in the theater, but in the entrance way under the big gate of the general hospital. The ground was covered with tiles."

Interpretation. The women being operated on was the dreamer herself. A few days earlier she had visited a young doctor who had attempted a sexual assault on her. She had been lying on a couch. The doctor had lifted her skirts, and while he was manipulating her "down below" she saw a heap of white underwear over her thighs; in other words she saw just as much of herself as she saw of the woman in the dream, and she could no more see the woman's head than she could see her own head. The scene was located in the operating theater only in order to provide a plausible pictorial environment for the act of "operating," i.e., in vulgar terminology manipulating. The scene suddenly changed and the action continued under a particular archway at the entrance to the general hospital. At this spot the patient had recently had a minor narrow escape. In avoiding a cart loaded with straw which nearly filled the whole archway she had stumbled and nearly fallen. It was this idea of "nearly falling" that was represented by the new scene. She had "nearly fallen" under the archway just as she had "nearly fallen" to the doctor, and would have done if she had not summoned up all her strength and resisted the temptation. To put it in a nutshell, the translation of the dream reads: "I am in the same danger with the doctor as I was under the archway of the hospital, namely that of falling."

Attention should be called to a dream technique which has not yet been published. I have repeatedly had occasion to interpret scenes in dreams situated at a lower spatial level as representing the genitals. The occasion for this is provided by the custom of referring to the genitals as "lower down" in order to avoid mentioning the parts of the body by name. In dream, "lower down" means "lower down" the body, i.e., the genitals. This technique is particularly clear in our example. "Lower down a woman is being operated on" means "the doctor has been manipulating me lower down," a translation which, taken in conjunction with the meaning of the other elements in her dream gained by our interpretation, turned out exactly to reflect the reality.

12

Contributions to the Psychopathology of Everyday Life

I
A Filial Slip of the Tongue

A young reserve officer who consulted me because of various nervous complaints but chiefly because of great "mental restlessness" among other things told me this story:

> After my father's death my mother carried on his business, which is a big one. At the time I was a law student, and facing the first state examination. Though my mother is a sensible and energetic woman, of whose forcefulness and authority we children had become very well aware, I could not shake off my misgivings about her ability to manage such a big business. A man was needed for a job of that size. She could not possibly fully take my father's place.
>
> I began worrying about the future of the business, which my father had built up into one of very high repute. This affected me so much that I was inhibited in my work, and eventually gave up my law books altogether, because I subsided into a vague state of restlessness that made it impossible for me to concentrate on them. I was unable to sit for the state examination to which I had been so close, and since then, that is, for the past four years, I have made no progress in my studies. I spent my time in taverns and places of entertainment. This led me to big rows with my mother, who tried to make me change my ways by reducing my allowance. The result of this disciplinary

Internationale Zeitschrift für ärztliche Psychoanalyse. 4 (1916). Translated by Eric Mosbacher.

> measure was that my nervousness grew considerably worse and my ability to work (in so far as I could do any at all) diminished.
>
> But I am by no means happy doing nothing. I know that hard work would do me good. But I cannot make up my mind to do anything. I can find no job that offers me satisfaction.

"Not even in your father's business?" I asked.

"In that case I should have to put up with my mother as my boss," the patient replied, "because she will not give up running it. I could not adapt myself to such a situation."

"Then you have no alternative to desiring your mother's death, so that you could take your father's place, to which you obviously feel yourself entitled."

"My mother's death? What are you suggesting, doctor? My mother is the dearest person under the earth to me—I mean, under the sun."

Let me add that the patient was honest enough to take his slip of the tongue seriously.

II
The Wrong Streetcar

I was on leave from active service in Vienna. An old patient of mine heard I was there and asked me to call on him, as he was ill in bed. I did so, and spent two hours with him. When I left, he enquired what he owed me.

"I am here on leave and not professionally," I replied. "Please consider my visit as an act of friendship."

The patient objected, evidently feeling that he had no right to accept my professional services on those terms. But he finally gave in, the pleasure of saving money causing him to express the respectful opinion that as a psychoanalyst I could be relied on to do the right thing.

A little later I begin to have doubts about the genuineness of my grand gesture and, still full of doubts—which scarcely permit any doubtfulness of interpretation—I boarded a No. X streetcar. After a short distance I had to change to a No. Y. While waiting at the stop I forgot about the fee and started thinking about the patient's symptoms, and the streetcar I was waiting for arrived and I got in. But I had to get out again at the next stop. I had inadvertently got into a No. X car and was going back in the direction from which I had come, towards the patient whose fee I had refused. My unconscious wanted to go and collect the fee.

III
The Faith of Our Fathers

"As my fiancée was a Christian," Herr A. related, and was unwilling to adopt the Jewish faith, I was converted from Judaism to Christianity to enable us to marry. I did not change my religion without some internal resistance, but I felt it was justified by the purpose behind it, the more so because it involved abandoning no more than an outward adherence to Judaism, not a religious conviction (which I never had). Nevertheless, afterwards I always continued to acknowledge the fact of my being a Jew, and few of my acquaintances know I have been baptised. I have two sons by this marriage, who were given Christian baptism. When the boys were sufficiently old, they were told of their Jewish background, so as to prevent them from being influenced by anti-Semitism at their school and from turning against their father for such a superfluous reason. Some years ago I and my children, who were then at their primary school, were spending a summer holiday with a teacher's family at D. One day, while we were sitting at tea with our otherwise friendly hosts, the lady of the house, who had no suspicion of her summer guests' Jewish ancestry, made some sharp outbursts against the Jews. I ought to have boldly explained the situation in order to set my sons an example of having the courage of one's convictions, but I was afraid of the unedifying exchanges that usually follow an avowal of this sort. Besides, I was alarmed at the possibility of having to leave the good lodgings we had found, and of thus spoiling my own and my children's short holiday, should our hosts' behaviour towards us take an unfriendly turn because of the fact that we were Jews. As, however, I had reason to expect that my sons, in their candid and ingenuous way, would betray the momentous truth if they heard any more of the conversation, I tried to get them to leave the company by sending them into the garden. I said: "Go into the garden, *Juden* [Jews]," quickly correcting it to "*Jungen* [youngsters]." In this way I enabled the "courage of my convictions" to be expressed in a parapraxis. The others did not in fact draw any conclusions from my slip of the tongue, since they attached no significance to it; but I was obliged to learn the lesson that the "faith of our fathers" cannot be disavowed with impunity if one is a son and has sons of one's own.

Index